2016 Fantasy Football Draft Guide

TheFantasyGreek.com

Your Second Opinion For Your Fantasy Football Instinct

TheFantasyGreek.com

ISBN: 069275329X
ISBN-13: 9780692753293

Football is an honest game. It's true to life. It's a game about sharing.
Football is a team game. So is life.

--- Joe Namath

CONTENTS

Credits and Advertising

1	Welcome to 2016	8
2	2016 Draft Highlights: Wide Receivers Are King, But Don't Ignore the Best Running Backs	9
3	Approaching Fantasy Football Drafts & Seasons	10
4	Top 10 Story Lines of 2016	14
5	Mock Draft This!	17
6	Mock Draft Rosters, Analysis, & Strategies	22
7	Top 200: PPR/4-point Pass TD Leagues	34
8	Top 200: Non-PPR/4-point Pass TD Leagues	39
9	Top 200: PPR/6-point Pass TD Leagues	44
10	Top 200: Non-PPR/6-point Pass TD Leagues	49
11	QFG Rankings: Top 50 (PPR)	54
12	QFG Rankings: Top 50 (Non-PPR)	56
13	Quarterback Fantasy Football Handcuffs	58
14	Quarterback-Defense Pairings	62
15	Quarterback Rankings (4-point TD Leagues)	63
16	Quarterbacks Rankings (6-point TD Leagues)	64
17	Quarterback Profiles	65
18	Running Back Rankings (PPR)	73
19	Running Back Rankings (Non-PPR)	75
20	Running Back Profiles	77
21	Wide Receiver Rankings (PPR)	93
22	Wide Receiver Rankings (Non-PPR)	95
23	Wide Receiver Profiles	97
24	Tight End Rankings (PPR)	118
25	Tight End Rankings (Non-PPR)	119

26	Tight End Profiles	120
27	Defense / Special Teams Rankings & Profiles	129
28	Kicker Rankings & Profiles	133
29	Top IDP Ranks	137
30	Top 10 Comeback Players	140
31	Top 10 Undervalued Players	142
32	Top 10 Sleepers	144
33	Top 10 Deep Sleepers	146
34	Top 10 Second Year Receivers	148
35	Top 10 Third Year Receivers	150
36	Top 10 Rookies	152
37	Top 10 Overrated Players	154
38	Top 10 Injury Risks	156
39	FREE TFG Access	158
40	Draft Grids	160
41	Ourlads Scouting Services	167

TheFantasyGreek.com

CREDITS

Jim Saranteas, Managing Editor / Senior Fantasy Writer

Kristen Saranteas, Editor

<u>Writers:</u> **Todd Ambuel (TA)**
Sammy Bassett (SB)
Rick Briggs (RB)
Chad Bellin (CB)
Gavin Crowell (GC)
Ilir Emini (IE)
Rick Fleeger (RF)
Evan Gardiner (EG)
Fred Goodman (FG)
Alexander George (AG)
Derek Guilford (DG)
David Kromelow (DK)
Andrew Miley
Jordan Quertermous (JQ)
Jim Saranteas (JS)
Jim Weidner (JW)
Rachel Wold

Cover Photo Credit: Todd Kirkland/Icon Sportswire

Cover Photo Caption: December 14, 2014: Pittsburgh Steelers running back Le'Veon Bell (26) rushes in for a touchdown in the Pittsburgh Steelers 27-20 victory over the Atlanta Falcons at the Georgia Dome in Atlanta, Georgia.

ADVERTISING

For advertising information, please contact support@thefantasygreek.com. In the subject line write, "Advertising Info for 2017 TFG Draft Guide."

Welcome to the 2016 Fantasy Football Draft Guide of TheFantasyGreek.com!

"Your Second Opinion for Your Fantasy Football Instinct"

This is TFG's best most comprehensive Draft Guide yet! We've listened to our readers and expanded some of our coverage into a more meaningful format. Previously recognized as an Amazon Top Seller and Amazon Top New Release in the fantasy sports space, the Draft Guide is chock full of what you the reader want: information and advice.

While you'll still find our special **Top 200 Draft Boards** for *four scoring formats*, top player rankings, and specialized 'Top 10' lists, we've added our first ever rankings for **Individual Defensive Players Ranks**, or **IDP Ranks**. Many of you can't get enough of the traditional fantasy football leagues and want to take it a step further by incorporating defensive players to your league rosters. Fair enough. The rankings provide a meaningful way to incorporate defensive players with little fuss. And, on the Top 200 Draft Boards, we've added defenses and kickers, so you don't have to think when to draft them.

We're also introducing **Quality Fantasy Game (QFG) Rankings**. To know which players to target, we show you who. Each player exceeded a threshold number of fantasy points over enough games to score high on the metric in 2015. If they are on the list, they're expected to do well in 2016 too. Get as many of these players on your team as you can.

Rather than just write about draft strategies (we're still doing that), TheFantasyGreek.com rolls out its first ever **TFG Mock Draft!** Twelve analysts gathered together to go head-to-head and pick their teams weeks before most would even think about it. Experience the draft here and learn about the approaches and strategies utilized by picks one through twelve in standard sized leagues. Want to learn about the **Zero Running Back Draft Approach**? Don't read about it, watch it at work here.

We've also expanded the **Player Profiles** found in the magazine from 250-plus to 300-plus. With the injuries last season, fringe players are getting more opportunities than ever.

The Draft Guide also contains lists of top **comeback players, undervalued players, sleepers, deep sleepers, rookies, overvalued players, undervalued players,** and **injury risks**. With wide receivers making impacts earlier in their careers, we provide Top 10 **second-year** and **third-year receivers** lists too.

As usual, don't be without our **QB Handcuff List** and **QB-Defense Pairing List** on draft day. With your **Top 200 Draft Board** and **Top 50 QFR Rakings**, this should be everything you need to work your way through your draft. If there is anything else The Fantasy Greek can provide, please let me know.

If The Fantasy Greek.com helps you become a fantasy football aficionado this season, TheFantasyGreek.com has done its job. If The Fantasy Greek.com helps you have fun playing fantasy football, win, *and* gets you to appreciate the sport, and not just your favorite team, then The Fantasy Greek has done a great job.

Cheers and . . . "May The Fantasy Gods Smile Upon You!"

Jim Saranteas

President
Strabos Communications, Inc.

2016 Draft Highlights: Wide Receivers Are King, But Don't Ignore the Best Running Backs

By Jim Saranteas
Managing Editor, TheFantasyGreek.com

The first draft pick in all fantasy formats should be the Steelers **Antonio Brown** who is projected to crush his fantasy numbers from last season as the Steelers primary producer. In points-per-reception (PPR) leagues, the top three picks should be wide receivers given, in part, the number of receptions the top three are projected to have.

If you want to get an idea of how much the production of running backs has decreased, as compared to how much the production of wide receivers has increased, go to TheFantasyGreek.com's home page menu bar, and click 'Fantasy Draft Board.' There, read the article entitled, "Fantasy Football: Wide Receivers Trumping Running Backs in the Date ... Sort of," from May 10, 2016, for the details. The bottom line is, there are nine more 1,000 yards receivers in 2016 (17 total) than there were in 2010, while the number of 1,000 yard rushers dwindled by ten, declining from 17 in 2010 to seven in 2016.

What's more, the risk of a top running back going down seems higher than ever. Last season, several top running backs went down to injury for part or all of the season including, among others, **Jamaal Charles, Le'Veon Bell,** and **LeSean McCoy.** If you drafted anyone of the three, you likely struggled all season, and didn't win a fantasy championship, despite the performance of the other players on your team.

Still, the running backs at the very top remain an object of fantasy stardom. The running backs at the very top, if healthy, can you lead your team to fantasy glory as **Adrian Peterson** did for many last season.

What's true of the top running backs, however, is after the top eight are drafted, questions abound on the remaining running backs on the board. These questions might have to do with health. These questions might have to do with offensive scheme. These questions might have to do with production. What's true is the risk gets higher with the running backs selected after the top eight and as you go deeper into the draft. You are better off drafting a wide receiver if you miss out on the top three running backs.

It's become popular to avoid selecting running backs early in fantasy drafts the past few seasons. In this year's twelve team mock draft, picks one, two, three, and seven all selected wide receivers with their first three draft picks and finished with some good teams.

The bottom line is if you miss out on the very top of the running back class, don't fear going wide receiver heavy. Wide receivers are as productive, especially in PPR leagues, and get hurt less. They're even better flex plays than running backs.

APPROACHING FANTASY FOOTBALL
DRAFTS & SEASONS

By Jim Saranteas
Managing Editor, TheFantasyGreek.com

Every year, The Fantasy Greek shares tips on how to approach fantasy football drafts. Hopefully, based on your experience level, there are at least one or two things you never considered before that could prove helpful when your draft rolls around.

Know Your Scoring System: Are You In A PPR League or Non-PPR League?

This is important. For the uninitiated, "PPR" stands for points-per-reception. This means every time one of your players just catches the ball, they score you a point, or half-point, as may be the case. The distinction regarding a PPR league is critical.

Brandon Marshall caught 109 catches last season for the Jets. His rank in PPR leagues was higher than in non-PPR leagues despite the other stats he posted because of the high number of receptions he hauled in. The reverse is true for a player like the Buccaneers **Mike Evans**. By comparison, Evans hauled in 74 receptions in 2015. In PPR leagues, he naturally loses value against other wide receivers who post similar receiving numbers but more receptions.

Compare the Top 200s in this Guide, PPR versus non-PPR, and you'll see how player values fluctuate because of the league scoring system. If you compare the Top 50 QFG Rankings, the variation of the rankings due to the scoring system becomes even more apparent.

Know Your Scoring System: Does your quarterback get 4 points for a passing TD or 6 points for a TD?

Most leagues award four points for a passing touchdown. However, some still award six points for a passing touchdown. Much like the difference between PPR leagues and non-PPR leagues, whether your quarterback receives four points for a passing TD versus six points for a passing TD is important in much the same way.

A great example is **Tyrod Taylor** of the Bills. Taylor is ranked higher in non-PPR leagues than PPR leagues. The reason is he can score touchdowns with his legs, which are worth 6 points. Switching to 6 point passing TDs, Taylor loses this advantage to those quarterbacks who throw more TDs but don't have as many rushing TDs as he does.

Regardless, use the right Top 200 Draft Board from this Guide.

Know your Team's Roster Size and Positions Started: Wide Receivers Are Important

Generally, leagues are ten-team leagues or twelve-team leagues. However, fourteen-team and sixteen-team leagues exist.

Ten-team leagues are a little easier to draft in because for every passing round, there are more players to choose from in each round than a twelve-team league. In a ten-team league, by the end of Round 4, there are eight more players available than there would have been in a twelve-team league. For any beginners out there, try a ten-team league to get your feet wet in your first year or two of fantasy football.

Regardless of how many teams are in your league, you will have roster spots to fill. Some of the more typical roster-formats are:

QB, RB, RB, WR, WR, TE, K, DST
QB, RB, RB, WR, WR, WR, TE, K, DST
QB, RB, RB, RB/WR, WR, WR, TE, K, DST
QB, RB, RB, WR, WR/TE, WR/TE, K, DST

Most leagues then allow fantasy footballers to carry from six to seven bench players during the season.

Regardless of whether your flexing a running back/wide receiver (RB/WR) or a wide receiver/tight end (WR/TE), filling the wide receiver position with some quality players is important. Statistically, the trend is wide receivers are more productive than most running backs and most tight ends, especially in PPR leagues.

Treat Your Tight Ends like Wide Receivers

Not too long ago, the tight end position was an afterthought if you didn't draft one of the top two or three. In the past few seasons, however, many tight ends have played like their team's best or second best receiver, like **Rob Gronkowski** and **Greg Olsen**. Treat the tight end position like you are drafting a wide receiver. If the next best receiver on your fantasy football draft board is a tight end, you can draft a tight end if you need one.

Draft Defenses Late, Draft Kickers Later

When you compare the top-twelve kickers from year to year, you will note there is turnover among the top twelve in the fantasy football rankings every season. There might be one to three go-to guys every season. But, kickers' weekly performances are difficult to predict.

On kickers then, just get a good one on a team which will give the kicker an opportunity to score a lot of extra points (on a high scoring offense like the Patriots or Cardinals) or a lot of field goals (on a low scoring, but field position orientated offense like the Vikings or Broncos).

Sacrifice no quality position player for a kicker. There are always good kickers available in the last two rounds of fantasy football drafts.

There always good defenses available in the last two rounds of fantasy drafts too. But the good ones are good.

The problem is even the good ones can falter occasionally in what's become a big play, high flying pass-oriented league. When you compare the top-twelve defenses from year to year, you will note that there is not as much turnover as compared to kickers, but there are always defenses that disappoint and a few defenses that surprise.

Avoid the temptation to draft a top-tiered defense earlier than the ninth round of fantasy drafts. And then, don't think you have to draft one after the top three are off the board until later in the draft. You are better off stocking up on playmakers or potential playmakers.

Unless you must draft two defenses, you can add a defense off waivers for bye weeks, to play a match-up, or because there' a surprise defense outplaying its preseason projection.

Have a CURRENT List of Rankings by Position for Your Scoring Format

The Fantasy Greek has provided you **four** Top 200s in this Draft Guide which vary by scoring system. Stay *current* by visiting TheFantasyGreek.com to get *free updates* -- **free** with the purchase of the Draft Guide.

If you are at a live draft or just like to be hands on with your drafts, physically cross out names of players as they are drafted from your Top 200 Draft Board list. You can also have a bracket showing each pick, for each round. TFG provides you one at the end of this Draft Guide. This is a great way to spot a player who has yet to be drafted and get good value for the selection. Put another way, by crossing names off your list, if the player who should have been drafted in Round 4, is still undrafted in Round 6 when it's your time to draft, you'll know it.

It's also a great way to see what player groupings have been exhausted and which ones haven't been exhausted. If all the top RBs are gone, then you know the next level of running backs picked (RB2s or flex-players) will be drafted next.

Do Some MOCK Drafts In Advance of Your LIVE Fantasy Football Draft

If you have a live draft, whether on-line or in person, doing mock drafts are helpful to see what kind of team you draft.

If you do not know your pick in advance, do as many mock drafts as time allows, picking from the front (picks 1-4), middle (5-8), and end (9-12) of the draft order.

At a minimum, do one or two mock drafts to familiarize yourself with your league's draft system features. Most sites have a queue where you can drag players from a list down to a queue box to make it easier to see if the player is still available. You can put players in the queue who you may consider drafting with a future pick. If the player you dragged into the queue box is gone (there is sometimes a special audible sound indicating a queued player has been drafted), they have been drafted. If the player you dragged into the queue box is still there, they are still available. Nothing could be worse than thinking a player you would like to draft has already been drafted when the player is still available. The lesson: get used to your site's functions and features.

Besides getting used to your site's functions and features, get a feel for what 90 seconds to draft feels like (a typical draft time) because on draft day, it seems to go faster than you would think.

If There Is a Player You Don't Trust or Don't Like for Other Reasons, Then Don't Draft Them . . . Unless

Let's say you disagree with the rankings of certain players. There is nothing wrong with taking a player off the draft board you do not feel will play well, you do not care for, or, don't want to take a risk on, such as players coming off injury or holding out for a contract.

Or, let's say, you are a fan of one team and don't want to draft your rival's players in fantasy football. Well, The Fantasy Greek supposes you don't have to draft them, but why not? Believe it or not, the team you root for can win its game despite your fantasy football player on the opposing team playing well.

Your Back-Up QB Can Be a Bye-Week Filler

There is always some trepidation among fantasy players that if their No. 1 QB goes down to injury, without a very good back-up, their season is lost. But, remember this: outside of the wide receiver position, quarterbacks likely sustain the least number of season-ending injuries. If injury strikes, move on with your back-up QB (if you have one), or by picking up a QB or QBs off waivers (playing the match-ups).

Fantasy championships have been won by playing the match-ups through multiple QBs. So, with the QB position being one of the least vulnerable to injury, it would be a waste to draft **Aaron Rodgers** and then **Ben Roethlisberger,** just to watch Roethlisberger sit on your bench for the entire season except for Rodgers' bye week. Why would you ever bench a top quarterback like Aaron Rodgers?

By drafting a high caliber QB like Roethlisberger as your back-up means you will pass up on a good player to fill a position you will need to fill and play every week either at RB, WR, or TE. Besides, there is a lot of depth at the quarterback position this season and a few QB2s could play like a QB1 more often than not.

Keep Track of the Players You Drafted and Their Bye Weeks

Many a seasoned player has drafted a team where many of their drafted players have the same bye weeks, creating a must-drop or must-trade situation. Many owners can maneuver the situation. But, if you feel you may not maneuver this well, don't create the problem in the first place.

Injuries Happen, and Players Sometimes Tank, So Do Your Best

Drafting is about walking out of your draft with a good team on paper. We don't know who will be injured and we don't always know which players will play below our expectations. The point of drafting is to give yourself a chance on Day 1 and to have a core group of players to build from. From then on, they just have to play the games!

Good luck!

Top 10 Storylines of 2016

By Rachel Wold
    fantasyfootballchick.com

Every season begins with a fresh look at the major storylines. Why? Because the shape, the tone, and the tenor of the football season have consequences wholly applicable to your fantasy football season.

1.   Can the Denver Broncos thrive without Peyton Manning?

All good things eventually come to an end and this happened when the legendary **Peyton Manning** retired not long after the Broncos were crowned the 2016 Super Bowl Champions. To add misery to the situation for the Broncos, presumptive 2016 starter, backup **Brock Osweiler** left in free agency to the Texans after they offered him a lucrative contract.

Beginning from scratch, the Broncos look to be headed towards a quarterback competition comprising of none other than turnover-prone **Mark Sanchez**, second year man **Trevor Siemian**, and rookie **Paxton Lynch**. Fortunately the Broncos' defense remains stout, although it lost two key defenders in free agency. Playmakers **Demaryius Thomas, Emmanuel Sanders** and **C.J. Anderson** will definitely help whoever is under center in 2016. However, there is little fantasy appeal beyond Anderson in this offense.

2. If Tom Brady's suspension holds, can the New England Patriots win the AFC East?

Yes. The Patriots are competing in a division stocked with some of the NFL's most suspect teams. Offseason injuries are already plaguing the Bills, while the Jets are potentially looking at life without **Ryan Fitzpatrick**. If that's the case, **Geno Smith** (or any other quarterback on the Jets roster) will be hard-pressed to lead this team to a repeat of last year's 10 wins. The Dolphins are making strides, though they haven't won over eight games since 2008.

If **Tom Brady** sits out four games, he will miss only one away game, which is against the Cardinals in Week 1. Then, the Patriots host the Dolphins, Texans and Bills. When Tom Brady returns, the Patriots hit the road to face the Browns in Week 5. If the Patriots are 5-0, 4-1, or even 3-2 in Week 6, the rest of the division is doomed.

Don't let the prospect of **Jimmy Garoppolo** starting at quarterback the first four games of the season for the Patriots scare you from drafting **Robert Gronkowski**. Gronkowski is still fantasy's No. 1 tight end.

3. Could the AFC South be starting a new trend?

The AFC South belonged to a dominant **Andrew Luck**-led Indianapolis Colts from 2012 to 2014. But this changed in 2015 when the Texans upstaged the Colts and won the division after the Colts lost a banged up Luck for half the season. Luck returns in 2016 and this means the Colts will likely rebound. The Texans remain a force and made some terrific offseason additions bound to pay off.

Besides the Colts and Texans, the Jaguars and Titans also made some amazing offseason enhancements. A better defense in Jacksonville will lead to more field time for **Blake Bortles** and the offense. And, the Titans' additions of **DeMarco Murray** and rookie **Derrick Henry** should do wonders to help **Marcus Mariota**'s overall efficiency. With both the Jaguars and Titans poised for more wins, the AFC South stage is set for some excitement as one of these teams tries to win the division. There will be several fantasy football starlets who play in this division.

4. Will the Rams contend with Jared Goff as their Quarterback?

It will take a mountain of work for **Jared Goff** and the Rams to conquer a division housing the Seahawks and Cardinals. But the Rams believe he will eventually lead the team to more success than the franchise has seen in over a decade. Plus, the move back to the West Coast keeps Goff comfortable at home in California.

The rookie will begin his NFL career after a successful 2015 college season where he completed 64.5 percent of his passes for 4,714 yards, 43 touchdowns, and 13 interceptions. The emergence of running back **Todd Gurley** will aid in keeping the Rams' offense balanced this season. After Gurley, however, there is no fantasy player on the Rams that is a sure thing.

5. How will Matthew Stafford and the Lions fare without Calvin Johnson?

After compiling a franchise-record 11,619 receiving yards and 83 touchdowns, the Lions' former first-round pick from 2007, **Calvin Johnson** hung up his cleats for good. But rather than fear the worst for the Lions and their fantasy players, the Lions should be in good hands. **Matthew Stafford** will now be forced to spread his targets around. **Golden Tate** and the newly-signed **Marvin Jones** should benefit most.

Tate was phenomenal picking up the slack left when Johnson dealt with injuries in 2014. That season, Tate hauled in 99 catches for 1,331 yards compared to Johnson's 71 receptions for 1,077 yards. The Lions also went 11-5 and appeared in one postseason game. The show must go on, and nothing will stop Stafford, the Lions' all-time passing leader from slinging the football an average of 40 times per game.

6. Is Robert Griffin III the answer for the Browns?

Probably not. After burning through 12 starting quarterbacks since 2003, we cannot assume the Browns will ever have the perfect solution at the quarterback position, though, **Robert Griffin III** represents a refreshing change after the disastrous two-year Johnny Manziel era.

Entering 2016, new head coach Hugh Jackson seems sold on RGIII, who is returning to the field after spending his final season with the Redskins on the bench. Although most factors would indicate that RGIII is the frontrunner to win the starting job from veterans **Josh McCown** and **Austin Davis**, and third-round rookie **Cody Kessler**, Griffin must reportedly compete for the starting job this training camp. With less drama, fans can only hope the Browns win more games than the three they managed in 2015. The Browns will also have two or three fantasy players worth the investment in 2016.

7. Will Brock Osweiler boom or bust with the Texans?

That is the $72 million dollar question heading into the season. All eyes will be on **Brock Osweiler** as training camp gets underway to gauge how well he will handle his first season paid as an "elite" quarterback. The Texans went all-in when they wooed Osweiler, a player with only 7 career starts, away from the Broncos.

With the Texans, Osweiler has a terrific supporting cast at his disposal. Stud wideout **DeAndre Hopkins** should continue his dominance as an elite wide receiver. The Texans drafted an intriguing pair of rookie receivers in **Will Fuller** and **Braxton Miller**. Fuller should be in line to make an immediate impact (at least in reality as opposed to fantasy) with Miller's impact likely longer term. Plus, running back **Lamar Miller**, a player who has flashed in a limited role with the Dolphins, is now the Texans' workhorse running back and a major asset in Osweiler's new offense.

Like any quarterback new to a team, Brock Osweiler should have ups and downs, depressing his fantasy at least this season.

8. Will Head Coach Chip Kelly find success with the 49ers?

After an unsuccessful tenure with the Philadelphia Eagles, Chip Kelly will try his hand at coaching the 49ers, a team in the dumps. Obviously, the goal is to better last season's win-record of five games.

Adding to Kelly's uphill battle will be a summer quarterback competition between **Blaine Gabbert** and former starter **Colin Kaepernick**. As it stands, Gabbert is the front-runner while Kaepernick continues to rehab from injury. When the quarterback "competition" sorts itself out, hopefully, the other issues the 49ers are facing will fall into place. The return of **Carlos Hyde** and some rookie enhancements made on the offensive line and defense should help.

Though Chip Kelly's job won't be easy considering the fierce competition the team faces within NFC West, Kelly has orchestrated a proven offense which may not have had the right pieces in place last season. Two or three 49ers players could be fantasy finds in 2016.

9. Can the Cowboys rebound and potentially dominate the NFC East?

The Cowboys can view the 2016 season as a do-over of a putrid 2015 season. Quarterback **Tony Romo** should be healthy after sustaining back-to-back clavicle breaks. An out-of-sorts **Dez Bryant** will also hit the field far removed from his bothersome foot injury. Plus, the reward to the Cowboys for winning a lowly four games last season landed them the top running back prospect in the 2016 draft in **Ezekiel Elliott**. Romo, Bryant and Elliott will offer the Cowboys a one-two-three punch sorely missing since the 2014 departure of **DeMarco Murray**.

If the defense can absorb some early suspensions, the Cowboys could turn up the heat in an NFC East which saw the Redskins win the division with nine wins last season. Considering the Eagles managed just seven wins and the Giants scraped by with six, the Cowboys could rise to the top of a division handily up for grabs annually. Don't expect Tony Romo to top 4,000 yards passing, however.

10. Does the rest of the NFC South stand a chance against the Panthers?

Quite the opposite of a division up for grabs is the case of the NFC South, where the Panthers finished 15-1 last season. **Cam Newton** and his teammates scored the most offensive points on average per game in the league, while leaving their divisional competition far behind. Interestingly enough, the 8-8 Falcons with their 21.2 points scored per game, were the only team to defeat the Panthers in 2015.

The Saints won seven games in 2015 despite having the No. 2 offense in the league. While **Drew Brees** and the offense were busy scoring, the Saints wretched defense was ceding an average of 29.8 points per game.

The Buccaneers brought up the rear with six wins. Overall, **Jameis Winston** was impressive in his rookie season as were the Buccaneers as an entire unit.

Unfortunately for the Falcons, Saints and Bucs, there isn't much to suggest the Panthers will suddenly take a cliff dive and make things easier for them to win games. There are plenty of enticing fantasy options from each of these four teams this season.

MOCK DRAFT THIS!

By Jim Saranteas
   Managing Editor, TheFantasyGreek.com

Over a mid-June weekend, twelve fantasy scribes and football personalities gathered for TheFantasyGreek.com's inaugural fantasy Mock Draft. The results were outstanding!

The participants included, in order of draft pick:

Dave Cherney, FakePigskin.com
Josh Cosner, Dynasty Football Factory
Jim Saranteas, TheFantasyGreek.com
David Kromelow, Sports Krunch with DKrom
Derek Guilford, TheFantasyGreek.com
Rick Briggs, Fireside Sports
Herb Lawrence, Mighty 1090 Producer
Dan Clasgens, SiriusXM Fantasy Sports Radio
Sammy Bissett, TheFantasyGreek.com
Rick Fleeger, Asylum Fantasy Sports
Sam Ingro, The Orange and Brown Report Draft Writer
John Bush, FantasySportsProfessors.FantasySportsProfessors.com.

As you'll note, the first round was heavy with wide receivers which should come as no surprise in a PPR league. The first quarterback wasn't selected until Round 3. This is a sign of the times and the depth at the position.

The biggest news may well be who *wasn't selected* compared to who was. Notable quarterback snubs included **Matt Stafford, Ryan Fitzpatrick,** and **Jay Cutler**. Notable running back snubs, not even as back-ups, included the Cowboys **Darren McFadden** *and* **Alfred Morris**. At wide receiver, people passed on **Devin Funchess, Mike Wallace,** and **Philip Dorsett**, and at tight end, people passed on **Jason Witten** and **Zach Miller**. As for defenses, this season's sleeper defense, the **Jaguars**, is still available.

Team rosters follow. This was a twelve team, 0.5 PPR league with 4-points for passing TDs.

Enjoy the Mock Draft! Rosters with manager comments to follow.

The Draft Picks

	ROUND 1		ROUND 2	
	Player	**Team**	**Player**	**Team**
1	WR Antonio Brown, Steelers	Dave Cherney	RB Devonta Freeman, Falcons	John Bush
2	WR Odell Beckham, Giants	Josh Cosner	RB Ezekiel Elliott, Cowboys	Sam Ingro
3	WR Julio Jones, Falcons	Jim Saranteas	RB Jamaal Charles, Chiefs	Rick Fleeger
4	WR DeAndre Hopkins, Texans	David Kromelow	WR A.J. Green, Bengals	Sammy Bissett
5	RB Le'Veon Bell, Steelers	Derek Guilford	RB Lamar Miller, Texans	Dan Clasgens
6	WR Brandon Marshall, Jets	Rick Briggs	WR Alshon Jeffery, Bears	Herb Lawrence
7	TE Rob Gronkowski, Patriots	Herb Lawrence	WR Jordy Nelson, Packers	Rick Briggs
8	WR Dez Bryant, Cowboys	Dan Clasgens	RB Eddie Lacy, Packers	Derek Guilford
9	RB David Johnson, Cardinals	Sammy Bissett	RB Doug Martin, Buccaneers	David Kromelow
10	RB Adrian Peterson, Vikings	Rick Fleeger	WR Keenan Allen, Chargers	Jim Saranteas
11	RB Todd Gurley, Rams	Sam Ingro	WR Amari Cooper, Raiders	Josh Cosner
12	WR Allen Robinson, Jaguars	John Bush	WR Demaryius Thomas, Broncos	Dave Cherney

	ROUND 3		ROUND 4	
	Player	**Team**	**Player**	**Team**
1	WR Sammy Watkins, Bills	Dave Cherney	TE Jordan Reed, Redskins	John Bush
2	WR Doug Baldwin, Seahawks	Josh Cosner	QB Cam Newton, Panthers	Sam Ingro
3	WR Mike Evans, Buccaneers	Jim Saranteas	WR Allen Hurns, Jaguars	Rick Fleeger
4	WR T.Y. Hilton, Colts	David Kromelow	RB Matt Forte, Jets	Sammy Bissett
5	QB Aaron Rodgers, Packers	Derek Guilford	RB LeSean McCoy, Bills	Dan Clasgens
6	RB C.J. Anderson, Broncos	Rick Briggs	RB Carlos Hyde, 49ers	Herb Lawrence
7	WR Kelvin Benjamin, Panthers	Herb Lawrence	RB Thomas Rawls, Seahawks	Rick Briggs
8	WR Brandin Cooks, Saints	Dan Clasgens	WR Jeremy Maclin, Chiefs	Derek Guilford
9	WR Julian Edelman, Patriots	Sammy Bissett	QB Russell Wilson, Seahawks	David Kromelow
10	WR Jarvis Landry, Dolphins	Rick Fleeger	TE Greg Olsen, Panthers	Jim Saranteas
11	WR Randall Cobb, Packers	Sam Ingro	RB Dion Lewis, Patriots	Josh Cosner
12	RB Mark Ingram, Saints	John Bush	QB Andrew Luck, Colts	Dave Cherney

	ROUND 5		ROUND 6	
	Player	Team	Player	Team
1	RB Jonathan Stewart, Panthers	Dave Cherney	RB Latavius Murray, Raiders	John Bush
2	RB Chris Ivory, Jaguars	Josh Cosner	WR Marvin Jones, Lions	Sam Ingro
3	QB Drew Brees, Saints	Jim Saranteas	WR Michael Floyd, Cardinals	Rick Fleeger
4	RB Giovani Bernard, Bengals	David Kromelow	TE Travis Kelce, Chiefs	Sammy Bissett
5	TE Tyler Eifert, Bengals	Derek Guilford	RB DeMarco Murray, Titans	Dan Clasgens
6	WR Larry Fitzgerald, Cardinals	Rick Briggs	RB Ryan Mathews, Eagles	Herb Lawrence
7	WR Eric Decker, Jets	Herb Lawrence	RB Jeremy Hill, Bengals	Rick Briggs
8	WR Golden Tate, Lions	Dan Clasgens	WR Emmanuel Sanders, Broncos	Derek Guilford
9	WR John Brown, Cardinals	Sammy Bissett	WR Tyler Lockett, Seahawks	David Kromelow
10	QB Ben Roethlisberger, Steelers	Rick Fleeger	RB Jeremy Langford, Bears	Jim Saranteas
11	WR Jordan Matthews, Eagles	Sam Ingro	TE Delanie Walker, Titans	Josh Cosner
12	WR DeVante Parker, Dolphins	John Bush	RB Jay Ajayi, Dolphins	Dave Cherney

	ROUND 7		ROUND 8	
	Player	Team	Player	Team
1	TE Zach Ertz, Eagles	Dave Cherney	WR Kevin White, Bears	John Bush
2	QB Tom Brady, Patriots	Josh Cosner	WR Corey Coleman, Browns	Sam Ingro
3	RB Danny Woodhead, Chargers	Jim Saranteas	WR Markus Wheaton, Steelers	Rick Fleeger
4	TE Ladarius Green, Steelers	David Kromelow	QB Eli Manning, Giants	Sammy Bissett
5	WR DeSean Jackson, Redskins	Derek Guilford	QB Tony Romo, Cowboys	Dan Clasgens
6	QB Blake Bortles, Jaguars	Rick Briggs	WR Dorial Green-Beckham, Titans	Herb Lawrence
7	QB Carson Palmer, Cardinals	Herb Lawrence	TE Coby Fleener, Saints	Rick Briggs
8	WR Michael Crabtree, Raiders	Dan Clasgens	WR Josh Gordon, Browns	Derek Guilford
9	RB Matt Jones, Redskins	Sammy Bissett	WR Sterling Shepard, Giants	David Kromelow
10	TE Gary Barnidge, Browns	Rick Fleeger	RB Ameer Abdullah, Lions	Jim Saranteas
11	WR Josh Doctson, Redskins	Sam Ingro	QB Derek Carr, Raiders	Josh Cosner
12	WR Donte Moncrief, Colts	John Bush	Broncos DST	Dave Cherney

	ROUND 9		ROUND 10	
	Player	**Team**	**Player**	**Team**
1	K Stephen Gostkowski, Patriots	Dave Cherney	WR Tavon Austin, Rams	John Bush
2	RB Melvin Gordon, Chargers	Josh Cosner	RB T.J. Yeldon, Jaguars	Sam Ingro
3	WR Steve Smith Sr., Ravens	Jim Saranteas	RB Justin Forsett, Ravens	Rick Fleeger
4	WR Laquon Treadwell, Vikings	David Kromelow	WR Mohamed Sanu, Falcons	Sammy Bissett
5	RB Frank Gore, Colts	Derek Guilford	RB Karlos Williams, Bills	Dan Clasgens
6	WR Willie Snead, Saints	Rick Briggs	TE Jimmy Graham, Seahawks	Herb Lawrence
7	QB Philip Rivers, Chargers	Herb Lawrence	RB Rashad Jennings, Giants	Rick Briggs
8	RB Duke Johnson Jr., Browns	Dan Clasgens	RB Isaiah Crowell, Browns	Derek Guilford
9	WR Travis Benjamin, Chargers	Sammy Bissett	TE Martellus Bennett, Patriots	David Kromelow
10	WR Stefon Diggs, Vikings	Rick Fleeger	WR Torrey Smith, 49ers	Jim Saranteas
11	TE Julius Thomas, Jaguars	Sam Ingro	Seahawks DST	Josh Cosner
12	RB Tevin Coleman, Falcons	John Bush	QB Andy Dalton, Bengals	Dave Cherney

	ROUND 11		ROUND 12	
	Player	**Team**	**Player**	**Team**
1	WR Vincent Jackson, Buccaneers	Dave Cherney	QB Marcus Mariota, Titans	John Bush
2	TE Dwayne Allen, Colts	Josh Cosner	RB C.J. Prosise, Seahawks	Sam Ingro
3	RB LeGarrette Blount, Patriots	Jim Saranteas	Cardinals DST	Rick Fleeger
4	RB Kenneth Dixon, Ravens	David Kromelow	Texans DST	Sammy Bissett
5	QB Kirk Cousins, Redskins	Derek Guilford	QB Jameis Winston, Buccaneers	Dan Clasgens
6	WR Kendall Wright, Titans	Rick Briggs	K Graham Gano, Panthers	Herb Lawrence
7	Panthers DST	Herb Lawrence	WR Breshad Perriman, Ravens	Rick Briggs
8	TE Austin Seferian-Jenkins, Buccaneers	Dan Clasgens	RB Derrick Henry, Titans	Derek Guilford
9	RB Charles Sims, Buccaneers	Sammy Bissett	RB Devontae Booker, Broncos	David Kromelow
10	WR Sammie Coates, Steelers	Rick Fleeger	RB Wendell Smallwood, Eagles	Jim Saranteas
11	WR Michael Thomas, Saints	Sam Ingro	WR Jeff Janis, Packers	Josh Cosner
12	RB Theo Riddick, Lions	John Bush	TE Antonio Gates, Chargers	Dave Cherney

	ROUND 13		ROUND 14	
	Player	**Team**	**Player**	**Team**
1	RB Paul Perkins, Giants	Dave Cherney	Chiefs DST	John Bush
2	WR Ted Ginn Jr., Panthers	Josh Cosner	QB Matt Ryan, Falcons	Sam Ingro
3	RB Javorius Allen, Ravens	Jim Saranteas	RB Arian Foster, FA	Rick Fleeger
4	RB DeAngelo Williams, Steelers	David Kromelow	WR Will Fuller, Texans	Sammy Bissett
5	Rams DST	Derek Guilford	Bengals DST	Dan Clasgens
6	TE Eric Ebron, Lions	Rick Briggs	WR Anquan Boldin, FA	Herb Lawrence
7	RB Jordan Howard, Bears	Herb Lawrence	QB Tyrod Taylor, Bills	Rick Briggs
8	WR Nelson Agholor, Eagles	Dan Clasgens	TE Jordan Cameron, Dolphins	Derek Guilford
9	TE Jared Cook, Packers	Sammy Bissett	Vikings DST	David Kromelow
10	WR Pierre Garcon, Redskins	Rick Fleeger	K Justin Tucker, Ravens	Jim Saranteas
11	Patriots DST	Sam Ingro	RB Darren Sproles, Eagles	Josh Cosner
12	Kamar Aiken, Ravens	John Bush	WR Terrance Williams, Cowboys	Dave Cherney

	ROUND 15		
	Player	**Team**	
1	RB Chris Johnson, Cardinals	Dave Cherney	
2	WR Rishard Matthews, Titans	Josh Cosner	
3	Steelers DST	Jim Saranteas	
4	K Steven Hauschka, Seahawks	David Kromelow	
5	K Dan Bailey, Cowboys	Derek Guilford	
6	QB Ryan Tannehill, Dolphins	Rick Briggs	
7	Bills DST	Herb Lawrence	
8	K Adam Vinatieri, Colts	Dan Clasgens	
9	K Chandler Catanzaro, Cardinals	Sammy Bissett	
10	K Cairo Santos, Chiefs	Rick Fleeger	
11	K Brandon McManus, Broncos	Sam Ingro	
12	K Mason Crosby, Packers	John Bush	

MOCK DRAFT ROSTERS, ANALYSIS, STRATEGIES

By Jim Saranteas
Managing Editor, TheFantasyGreek.com

Over a mid-June weekend, twelve fantasy scribes and football personalities gathered for TheFantasyGreek.com's inaugural fantasy Mock Draft. These are the teams selected in this twelve team, 0.5 PPR league with 4-points for passing TDs.

If you're considering employing a Zero Running Back Approach or a Zero Wide Receiver Approach, these were strategies employed by a few teams below.

Post draft, fantasy team owners were asked to answer five questions:

1. What was your plan going into the draft?

2. Did you adjust that plan and how?

3. What was your favorite pick and why?

4. What was your least favorite pick and why?

5. Overall, how do you feel you did?

Here are their answers.

Team – 1: Dave Cherney, FakePigskin.com, @RoadWarrior_D

1. (1)   Antonio Brown (Steelers, WR)
2. (24) Dem. Thomas (Broncos, WR)
3. (25) Sammy Watkins (Bills, WR)
4. (48) Andrew Luck (Colts, QB)
5. (49) Jon. Stewart (Panthers, RB)
6. (72) Jay Ajayi (Dolphins, RB)
7. (73) Zach Ertz (Eagles, TE)
8. (96) Broncos DST
9. (97) S. Gostkowski (Patriots, K)
10. (120)   Andy Dalton (Bengals, QB)
11. (121)   V. Jackson (Buccaneers, WR)
12. (144)   Antonio Gates (Chargers, TE)
13. (145)   Paul Perkins (Giants, RB)
14. (168)   Ter. Williams (Cowboys, WR)
15. (169)   Chris Johnson (Cardinals, RB)

1. What was your plan going into the draft?

Lock up my wide receivers early and often. This league is a 'start' three minimum wide receivers, so it was imperative to stock up, especially having the 1st, 24th and 25th picks. Then, my plan was to go for value picks for the remaining starter slots.

2. Did you adjust that plan and how?

Yes. Seeing how the draft was unfolding, I went for a quarterback, defense and kicker unusually early. There were enough risk / reward running backs still on the board so I wanted to lock up those positions before filling the back end of the roster.

3. What was your favorite pick and why?

Jay Ajayi at 6.12. While I'm in the minority on the value of Ajayi, I was thrilled to get him as my RB2 having waited so long. He can be a three-down running back in what should be a high powered offense. His great receiving skills are an added bonus and I don't fear the speculation on his supposed knee problems at least this year. I view **Kenyan Drake** as only a change-of-pace back.

4. What was your least favorite pick and why?

Andrew Luck at 4.12. Being on the 'turn' in this draft carried advantages but also serious drawbacks. Waiting 23 picks after the second of consecutive picks can always be dicey. I probably should have waited until the seventh round to address the quarterback position, but then I could have been left with fool's gold. Luck has tremendous upside after the sub-par 2015 season he had. Still, I'm never comfortable taking a quarterback this early in the draft.

5. Overall, how do you feel you did?

I'd give myself an average grade. This team, if healthy, should compete. However, the overall makeup with several players who could bust will likely make this a high maintenance squad. Being successfully active on the waiver-wire will be the key to this team's playoff chances.

Team – 2: Josh Cosner, Dynasty Football Factory, @EyeOfTheOracle

1. (2)   Odell Beckham Jr. (Giants, WR)
2. (23) Amari Cooper (Raiders, WR)
3. (26) Doug Baldwin (Seahawks, WR)
4. (47) Dion Lewis (Patriots, RB)
5. (50) Chris Ivory (Jaguars, RB)
6. (71) Delanie Walker (Titans, TE)
7. (74) Tom Brady (Patriots, QB)
8. (95) Derek Panthers (Raiders, QB)
9. (98) Melvin Gordon (Chargers, RB)
10. (119)   Seahawks DST
11. (122)   Dwayne Allen (Colts, TE)
12. (143)   Jeff Janis (Packers, WR)
13. (146)   Ted Ginn Jr. (Panthers, WR)
14. (167)   Darren Sproles (Eagles, RB)
15. (170)   Rishard Matthews (Titans, WR)

1. What was your plan going into the draft?

With the age of the workhorse RB dying out, I knew I would be able to land either **Antonio Brown** or **Odell Beckham Jr.** with the second overall pick. Once I had my star producer, I wanted to stock up at the WR position in the 2nd and 3rd rounds knowing I could grab two capable running backs such as **Dion Lewis** in the 4th and 5th rounds. There was no need to overextend myself for a RB early in this format. After that, I took the best value player on the board to add solid depth behind my starting roster.

2. Did you adjust that plan and how?

When you have such an early pick in the draft, you typically have a good idea of what you will get in the 1st round and what you can acquire later on. Knowing I could land two capable running backs in a 0.5 PPR format in the 4th and 5th rounds gave me greater maneuverability in the early rounds so I got to execute my plan and stay on the path I had laid out early on.

3. What was your favorite pick and why?

My favorite pick of this draft is **Dion Lewis** for several reasons. Lewis was having a fantastic season in 2016 before it was cut short by injury. If he can stay healthy, he is primed to have a great year. Knowing I could grab him in the 4th round allowed me to take three heavy hitters at the WR position and lay out a scary foundation for my team.

4. What was your least favorite pick and why?

I simply don't trust **Le'Veon Bell** coming off of another injury. For me, **David Johnson** is a great RB but it's a small sample size for such a high pick.

5.   Overall, how do you feel you did?

I feel I had a fantastic draft. **Odell Beckham** is always solid, but the additions of **Amari Cooper** and **Doug Baldwin**, who are primed for fantastic seasons as the #1 receivers in their offenses, had me overjoyed. Panning ahead at certain positions left me with the flexibility to add a player or two I could afford to stash away, such as **Tom Brady**, who after serving a suspension, should come out and play with the fury of a man possessed. I have a solid core group.

Team – 3: Jim Saranteas, TheFantasyGreek.com, @JimSaranteas

1.   (3)   Julio Jones (Falcons, WR)
2.   (22)   Keenan Allen (Chargers, WR)
3.   (27)   Mike Evans (Buccaneers, WR)
4.   (46)   Greg Olsen (Panthers, TE)
5.   (51)   Drew Brees (Saints, QB)
6.   (70)   Jeremy Langford (Bears, RB)
7.   (75)   D. Woodhead (Chargers, RB)
8.   (94)   Ameer Abdullah (Lions, RB)
9.   (99)   Steve Smith Sr. (Ravens, WR)
10.   (118)   Torrey Smith (49ers, WR)
11.   (123)   LeGar. Blount (Patriots, RB)
12.   (142)   Wen. Smallwood (Eagles, RB)
13.   (147)   Javorius Allen (Ravens, RB)
14.   (166)   Justin Tucker (Ravens, K)
15.   (171)   Steelers DST

1.   What was your plan going into the draft?

With the No. 3 pick, my plan was to draft either **Odell Beckham, Jr.** or **Julio Jones**, assuming Antonio Brown, this year's No. 1 overall pick in PPR leagues, was gone. Had I drawn the fourth round pick or later, I would have considered drafting one of three running backs I gave a first round grade to in PPR leagues. Otherwise, I waited to see how running backs would be selected.

2.   Did you adjust that plan and how?

Because the best running backs were all selected by my second pick, I employed a Zero-Running Back Approach to my draft. Using this approach, I selected three wide receivers, one tight end, and one quarterback before selecting my first running back in Round 6. As you can see from my roster, all three of my wide receivers are top fifteen talents, my tight end **Greg Olsen**, top five, and my quarterback, **Drew Brees**, top five. This approach to your fantasy drafts works well when you miss out on the top running backs and everyone else is chasing lesser valued players to fill positions.

Once I got to Round 6, it was about drafting running backs and back-ups. I adjusted again in Round 12 where I selected running backs with high upside because they play behind injury prone starters.

3. What was your favorite pick and why?

I couldn't believe I could select **Drew Brees** in Round 5 but my favorite pick was **Jeremy Langford** in Round 6. Langford has the makings of a true workhorse running back but there's offseason speculation Head Coach John Fox will use a running-back-by-committee approach. I just don't see it given the resumes of the Bears running backs. Regardless of what happens, Langford should be the team's No. 1 and should top 1,000 yards easily this season. That's great value for a running back in Round 6 of a PPR league.

4. What was your least favorite pick and why?

Probably **LeGarrette Blount**. Blount isn't as involved in the passing game and this is a PPR league. And, you never know who the Patriots will employ in their rushing attack in any week. Still, Blount was hard to pass up in Round 11.

5. Overall, how do you feel you did?

I did fine. I selected a great group of core players in Rounds 1 through 8; players who should post fantasy relevant performances in 60% or more of their games this season. My bench players are a little more speculative but their upside is undeniable.

Team – 4: David Kromelow, Sports Krunch with DKrom, @dkrom59

1. (4) DeAndre Hopkins (Texans, WR)
2. (21) Doug Martin (Buccaneers, RB)
3. (28) T.Y. Hilton (Colts, WR)
4. (45) Russell Wilson (Seahawks, QB)
5. (52) Giovani Bernard (Bengals, RB)
6. (69) Tyler Lockett (Seahawks, WR)
7. (76) Ladarius Green (Steelers, TE)
8. (93) Sterling Shepard (Giants, WR)
9. (100)   Laquon Treadwell (Vikings, WR)
10. (117)   Martellus Bennett (Patriots, TE)
11. (124)   Kenneth Dixon (Ravens, RB)
12. (141)   Devontae Booker (Broncos, RB)
13. (148)   DeAngelo Williams (Steelers, RB)
14. (165)   Vikings DST
15. (172)   Steven Hauschka (Seahawks, K)

1. What was your plan going into the draft?

My initial plan heading into the draft was to load up at the WR position early since this was a 0.5 PPR format. I also thought about employing the "Zero Running Back Strategy."

2. Did you adjust that plan and how?

I adjusted the plan SLIGHTLY in the second round when the first tier of receivers went flying off the board. I wound up taking the best player available which was **Doug Martin**. After that, I continued to load up on WR's and/or pass-catching running backs

3. What was your favorite pick and why?

My favorite pick in my draft class was **Martellus Bennett** in Round 10. Bennett has the potential to put up Aaron Hernandez-type stats (if not better) alongside **Rob Gronkowski**. Could be a HUGE steal.

4. What was your least favorite pick and why?

My least favorite pick in my draft was **Laquon Treadwell** in Round 9. I am personally high on Treadwell long-term, but **Michael Thomas** was still on the board, and I think he has the highest fantasy ceiling of the two this season given the circumstances he is in.

5.   Overall, how do you feel you did?

Overall, I think I had a solid draft. I selected high-volume WRs (**DeAndre Hopkins, TY Hilton**), three potentially solid middle-round value picks (**Bennett, Tyler Lockett, Sterling Shepard**), and loaded up on RBs who will likely have an impact at some point this season in the later rounds (**Kenneth Dixon, Devontae Booker, DeAngelo Williams**).

Team – 5: Derek Guilford, TheFantasyGreek.com, @derekguilford

1.   (5)   Le'Veon Bell (Steelers, RB)
2.   (20) Eddie Lacy (Packers, RB)
3.   (29) Aaron Rodgers (Packers, QB)
4.   (44) Jeremy Maclin (Chiefs, WR)
5.   (53) Tyler Eifert (Bengals, TE)
6.   (68) Emm. Sanders (Broncos, WR)
7.   (77) D. Jackson (Redskins, WR)
8.   (92) Josh Gordon (Browns, WR)
9.   (101)   Frank Gore (Colts, RB)
10.   (116)   Isaiah Crowell (Browns, RB)
11.   (125)   Kirk Cousins (Redskins, QB)
12.   (140)   Derrick Henry (Titans, RB)
13.   (149)   Rams DST
14.   (164)   Jor. Cameron (Dolphins, TE)
15.   (173)   Dan Bailey (Cowboys, K)

1.   What was your plan going into the draft?

My plan going into the draft was to grab two starting RBs within the first three picks. With the lack of depth in the clear cut number one running back starter department, it was paramount to target a couple studs I could plug in and play as an RB1 and RB2, then not have to worry about their production. With it being a PPR league, my game plan was to acquire RBs with PPR upside. Then, the plan was to grab a QB and a couple WRs who fell in the draft, with a rookie running back and WR or two to fill in the gaps.

2.   Did you adjust that plan and how?

I got **Le'Veon Bell** and **Eddie Lacy,** filling both starting running back spots. I adjusted when **Aaron Rodgers** was available in the mid-third round. **Emmanuel Sanders** was available in the 4th, then I chose to go TE with **Tyler Eifert** in Round 5. Minor adjustments were on the fly, but that's what fantasy football drafts are all about

3.   What was your favorite pick and why?

Le'Veon Bell with the fifth overall. The consensus #1 overall pick last season, Bell is coming off a torn MCL but is supposed to be healthy in time for the preseason. He has the potential to put up enormous numbers in a PPR format.

4.   Overall, how do you feel you did?

I feel I did well. Drafting among eleven other fantasy savants will always be challenging. But, grabbing Bell and Lacy in the first two rounds after being ranked the top two players last season, and primed for huge 2016 seasons, is the core of this squad. Rodgers (3rd), Sanders (4th), and **Jeremy Maclin** (6th) offer plus value given when they were selected. Eifert may be a reach in round 5 with **Travis Kelce** still on the board. Opting to select suspended WR **Josh Gordon** in Round 8 over **Stefon Diggs** may prove costly. You'll never win a fantasy league if you don't take a chance or two.

Team – 6: Rick Briggs, Fireside Sports, @fireside_sports

1. (6)   Brandon Marshall (Jets, WR)
2. (19) Jordy Nelson (Packers, WR)
3. (30) C.J. Anderson (Broncos, RB)
4. (43) Thomas Rawls (Seahawks, RB)
5. (54) Larry Fitzgerald (Cardinals, WR)
6. (67) Jeremy Hill (Bengals, RB)
7. (78) Blake Bortles (Jaguars, QB)
8. (91) Coby Fleener (Saints, TE)
9. (102)   Willie Snead (Saints, WR)
10. (115)   Rashad Jennings (Giants, RB)
11. (126)   Kendall Wright (Titans, WR)
12. (139)   Breshad Perriman (Ravens, WR)
13. (150)   Jets DST
14. (163)   Tyrod Taylor (Bills, QB)
15. (174)   John Browns (Giants, K)

1. What was your plan going into the draft?

My plan was to build a solid foundation early and add depth as I went along.

2. Did you adjust that plan and how?

I adjusted with different players, obviously. Every plan is just a framework, but when 11 other guys are implementing their plans, you must change and adjust.

3. What was your favorite pick and why?

My favorite pick was **Larry Fitzgerald** at 5.7. I am amazed one of the most gifted WRs coming off a 105 catch season is being cast aside as if he is washed up.

4. What was your least favorite pick and why?

My least favorite pick is **CJ Anderson** in the third. After going WR/WR, I felt I should nail down a running back. I think it was way too premature and I would have been better served going with **Kelvin Benjamin**, or another top wide receiver.

5. Overall, how do you feel you did?

I could have done better. If **Blake Bortles** and **Coby Fleener** come through as I hope, I will be competitive.

Team – 7: Herb Lawrence, Mighty 1090, @Ecnerwal23

1. (7)   Rob Gronkowski (Patriots, TE)
2. (18) Alshon Jeffery (Bears, WR)
3. (31) Kel. Benjamin (Panthers, WR)
4. (42) Carlos Hyde (49ers, RB)
5. (55) Eric Decker (Jets, WR)
6. (66) Ryan Mathews (Eagles, RB)
7. (79) Car. Palmer (Cardinals, QB)
8. (90) D. Green-Beckham (Titans, W)
9. (103)   Philipp Rivers (Chargers, QB)

10. (114)   J. Graham (Seahawks, TE)
11. (127)   Panthers DST
12. (138)   Graham Gano (Panthers, K)
13. (151)   Jordan Howard (Bears, RB)
14. (162)   Anquan Boldin (49ers, WR)
15. (175)   Bills DST

1. What was your plan going into the draft?

My plan was to grab as many good pass catchers as I could. With the 7th pick in the draft, I knew I would not get the top guys. So, I planned on selecting **Robert Gronkowski** who puts up WR1 numbers at TE or a top RB1. I wanted to grab WR1s throughout the draft.

2. Did you adjust that plan and how?

I didn't deviate from my plan even though two my targets were taken right before my respective picks.

3. What was your favorite pick and why?

Kelvin Benjamin. I selected a player everyone overlooked with great value in Round 3. Benjamin's monster rookie season impressed me and with **Cam Newton** coming off an MVP season, I'm excited to see what these two can do.

4. What was your least favorite pick and why?

Carson Palmer. I was thinking about drafting **Derek Carr** with the pick after I selected Palmer but I panicked. It's not that I don't like Carson Palmer. I just saw more value in Carr after reviewing the draft.

5. Overall, how do you feel you did?

I would give myself a B-. Great receivers who catch a lot of balls and touchdowns, solid QB, but I have questions about my running backs. Can't wait to see how this team fares during the season.

Team – 8: Dan Clasgens, SiriusXM Fantasy Sports Radio, @DanClasgens

1. (8)   Dez Bryant (Cowboys, WR)
2. (17)   Lamar Miller (Texans, RB)
3. (32)   Brandin Cooks (Saints, WR)
4. (41)   LeSean McCoy (Bills, RB)
5. (56)   Golden Tate (Lions, WR)
6. (65)   DeMarco Murray (Titans, RB)
7. (80)   Michael Crabtree (Raiders, WR)
8. (89)   Tony Romo (Cowboys, QB)
9. (104)   Duke Johnson Jr. (Browns, RB)
10. (113)   Karlos Williams (Bills, RB)
11. (128)   A. Seferian-Jenkins (Bucs, TE)
12. (137)   Jameis Winston (Bucs, QB)
13. (152)   Nelson Agholor (Eagles, WR)
14. (161)   Bengals DST
15. (176)   Adam Vinatieri (Colts, K)

1. What was your plan going into the draft?

Even though it's 0.5 PPR instead of a full-point PPR format, I still wanted to have an elite WR1. With the No. 8 pick I was hoping to grab one of my top five players at the position. Despite being plagued by injuries in 2015, I still consider **Dez Bryant** a Top 5 WR heading into this season. The trend lately is to select wide receivers in the early rounds. The trend has become mainstream lately, so I am finding in early drafts there is great value to be had in Rounds 2 through 3 as fantasy football managers reach for wide receivers early. In some formats it makes sense, but in this format I wanted to take a balanced approach. Waiting on selecting a quarterback was always part of the plan.

2. Did you adjust that plan and how?

You always need to be willing to adjust. I found in this draft though, I didn't have to go far off my intended plan. I was open to grabbing a top three tight end, but none fell. So, I had a backup plan which included late-round targets.

3. What was your favorite pick and why?

LeSean McCoy (4.5, 41 overall): McCoy is healthier entering 2016 than he was in his first year with the Bills. Rex Ryan will pound the football. McCoy showed flashes last season what he could do when he was the focal point of the team's run-first approach. Grabbing him in the fourth round as my RB2 is a steal. There is injury concern, but at this price, the risk is minimal.

4. What was your least favorite pick and why?

Tony Romo (Round 8) was a pick I wasn't very excited to make. At 36 years of age, Romo is on the "back nine" of his career. He has failed to play in all 16 games in each of the last three seasons, including a year ago when collar bone issues limited him to four games. I was waiting on quarterbacks, but in each of the previous two rounds, the QB I was targeting went of the board just before my pick. With Dez Bryant my first-round pick, I doubled my exposure to Romo's injury woes. However, I loved my late QB2 selection of **Jameis Winston**, whom I feel is primed for a breakout sophomore campaign.

5. Overall, how do you feel you did?

My plan was executed and executed well. There are questions marks, mainly at quarterback and tight end, but that was by design. My wide receivers are deep and as complete of a unit as any team in the league, and the duo of Miller-McCoy can prove very dangerous. Leagues aren't won on draft day, but I am confident this squad is built to compete and manage through byes and injuries.

Team – 9: Sammy Bissett, TheFantasyGreek.com, @SammyBissett

1. (9)   David Johnson (Cardinals, RB)
2. (16) A.J. Green (Bengals, WR)
3. (33) Julian Edelman (Patriots, WR)
4. (40) Matt Forte (Jets, RB)
5. (57) John Brown (Cardinals, WR)
6. (64) Travis Kelce (Chiefs, TE)
7. (81) Matt Jones (Redskins, RB)
8. (88) Eli Manning (Giants, QB)
9. (105)   T. Benjamin (Chargers, WR)
10. (112)   Mohamed Sanu (Falcons, WR)
11. (129)   Charles Sims (Bucs, RB)
12. (136)   Texans DST
13. (153)   Jared Cook (Packers, TE)
14. (160)   Will Fuller (Texans, WR)
15. (177)   C. Catanzaro (Cardinals, K)

1.   What was your plan going into the draft?

Having a deep team is a priority for me. I like to find a Top 5 RB early and then load up on WRs, particularly in a three WR league. I wanted to find three or four legitimate WRs with the upside of a low-end WR1, but with the floor of a low-end WR2. This is why I selected three WRs with my first five picks. They're all PPR studs, even if their touchdown numbers aren't high. I also specifically targeted dual-threat running backs knowing they are likely to see 3-6 more touches a game which means I'm earning an extra 1.5-3 points each week on receptions alone. I figured a premium TE and a reliable QB would be available in the middle rounds, and I was right. Selecting **Travis Kelce** in Round 6 may have landed me a Top 5 tight end. I was very happy with QB **Eli Manning** in Round 8 seeing he finished sixth in fantasy last season and the Giants are expected to throw plenty this year.

2. Did you adjust that plan and how?

I wasn't thrilled selecting ninth as you rarely get an elite RB or WR there. So, I decided to target 3 or 4 players at those positions likely to challenge the Top 10 instead. I was fortunate to land **David Johnson** and **AJ Green** at 9 and 12. I stayed to my strategy with what I thought was a low-risk, high-floor approach in the middle rounds. I made it a point to get a likely Top 5 DST, QB and TE.

3. What was your favorite pick and why?

Matt Jones in the 7th was a satisfying steal. The Redskins let **Alfred Morris** walk because they must see Jones as a great option as a dual-threat player. He should be a Top 10 or 15 player in PPR formats despite being drafted toward the middle rounds. Yet, I could pick him in Round 7. He's my RB3 for now, but he could be my RB2.

4. What was your least favorite pick and why?

I wasn't thrilled with selecting **Matt Forte** in the fourth round, but I saw the writing on the wall with how the draft was going, and played it safe. Forte is a safer alternative to injury-prone players like **LeSean McCoy** and **Carlos Hyde** or questionable players like Thomas Rawls whose broken ankle may not have healed nearly six months later. Matt Forte should flirt with the Top 10 like he does every season, but I made the pick out of stress I wouldn't find a quality RB2 later.

5. Overall, how do you feel you did?

I'm confident I have a top team with how consistent each position group is. The only uncertain situations are on my bench. Will **Travis Benjamin** maintain his upward trajectory with **Phillip Rivers** as his quarterback to become my WR3? Can **Jared Cook** getting healthy/being **Aaron Rodgers** #1 TE like the Packers want him to be? Does **Charles Sims** or **Matt Jones** hit their likely end of season Top 20 projections at RB? The answers to at least two of those questions are likely 'yes' in my book. I coupled it with guys who are high volume backups or lottery tickets in **Will Fuller** or **Mohamed Sanu**. Neither will start for me, but they are in great situations as #2 WRs. I likely won't finish #1 or #2 in points every week, however I will likely finish in the Top 3-5 range each week regardless and I have capable backups at every position. Depth is the main ingredient to winning Fantasy Football championships.

Team – 10: Rick Fleeger, Asylum Football, @asylumfootball

1. (10) Adrian Peterson (Vikings, RB)
2. (15) Jamaal Charles (Chiefs, RB)
3. (34) Jarvis Landry (Dolphins, WR)
4. (39) Allen Hurns (Jaguars, WR)
5. (58) B. Roethlisberger (Steelers, QB)
6. (63) Michael Floyd (Cardinals, WR)
7. (82) Gary Barnidge (Browns, TE)
8. (87) Markus Wheaton (Steelers, WR)
9. (106)   Stefon Diggs (Vikings, WR)
10. (111)   Justin Forsett (Ravens, RB)
11. (130)   Sammie Coates (Steelers, WR)
12. (135)   Cardinals DST
13. (154)   Pierre Garcon (Redskins, WR)
14. (159)   Arian Foster (Texans, RB)
15. (178)   Cairo Santos (Chiefs, K)

1. What was your plan going into the draft?

I had a Zero RB strategy leading up to the draft. Circumstances changed that plan right away.

2. Did you adjust that plan and how?

After seven WRs (if you include Gronkowski) went in the first nine picks, I abandoned my plan right away. I didn't want to reach for a WR so I went old school and load up with **Adrian Peterson** and **Jamaal Charles** with the first two picks.

3. What was your favorite pick and why?

Jarvis Landry in the third round (34th Overall). Four teams ahead of me drafted three wide receivers with their first three picks while many others took two. I was thrilled to land a wide receiver I have slotted as a number one in the third round after solidifying my running back position. This was a huge bonus.

4. What was your least favorite pick and why?

Markus Wheaton in the eighth round (87th Overall). After drafting **Ben Roethlisberger**, my goal was to land both Wheaton and **Sammie Coates** in this draft. I don't think it's clear who Roethlisberger's second target will be and I wanted to make sure I was covered as either could be a legitimate fantasy threat in the Steelers high powered offense. However, I think I got caught up in my plan and reached at least a round too early for Wheaton.

5. Overall, how do you feel you did?

This is a solid, but unspectacular team. I would still prefer three top wide receivers, but I like the depth and that I am solid and deep at every position.

Team – 11: Sam Ingro, Draft Writer for The Orange and Brown Report, @SamIngro

1. (11) Todd Gurley (Rams, RB)
2. (14) Ezekiel Elliott (Cowboys, RB)
3. (35) Randall Cobb (Packers, WR)
4. (38) Cam Newton (Panthers, QB)
5. (59) Jor. Matthews (Eagles, WR)
6. (62) Marvin Jones (Lions, WR)
7. (83) Josh Doctson (Redskins, WR)
8. (86) Corey Coleman (Browns, WR)
9. (107)   Julius Thomas (Jaguars, TE)
10. (110)   T.J. Yeldon (Jaguars, RB)
11. (131)   Michael Thomas (Saints, WR)
12. (134)   C.J. Prosise (Seahawks, RB)
13. (155)   Patriots DST
14. (158)   Matt Ryan (Falcons, QB)
15. (179)   B. McManus (Broncos, K)

1. What was your plan going into the draft?

My plan going into the mock draft was to lock down the running back position. While many have put the emphasis on drafting wide receivers early, the number of bell cow running backs in the league dwindles by the year due to the committee approach.

2. Did you adjust that plan and how?

I stayed true to my plan, although the speed that the top wide receivers went off the board put my board in a tight spot. The lack of proven receiver talent in the middle rounds led to two reaches in the middle rounds to fill out my season opener depth chart.

3. What was your favorite pick and why?

Corey Coleman in round 8 was likely my favorite pick due to the value and potential, though I'm very pleased with **Todd Gurley** being there at No. 11 in the first round. Coleman has Top 15 wide receiver potential, and I think with the strength of RGIII's arm, there is a high likelihood of big plays for him this season.

4. What was your least favorite pick and why?

My least favorite pick is **Randall Cobb** in Round 3. I'm not high on his production potential this year after his down 2015 numbers. The Cobb pick was forced due to the amount of quality receivers available there, and I did not want to get left out in the cold as far as rounding out my depth chart properly. Cobb could bounce back, but it was definitely a big leap of faith for me.

5. Overall, how do you feel you did?

I feel my team has perhaps the most upside of any team in the draft due to the impact rookies stockpiled on my bench. While my roster may come out of the gate slow, I believe by mid-season, I will see rookies like Coleman, **Michael Thomas, Josh Doctson** and **Ezekiel Elliot** pay large dividends for my team.

Team – 12: Dr. John Bush, FantasySportsProfessors.FantasySportsProfessors.com, @Prof_Fantasy1

1.   (12) Allen Robinson (Jaguars, WR)
2.   (13) Devonta Freeman (Falcons, RB)
3.   (36) Mark Ingram (Saints, RB)
4.   (37) Jordan Reed (Redskins, TE)
5.   (60) DeVante Parker (Dolphins, WR)
6.   (61) Latavius Murray (Raiders, RB)
7.   (84) Donte Moncrief (Colts, WR)
8.   (85) Kevin White (Bears, WR)
9.   (108)   Tevin Coleman (Falcons, RB)
10. (109)   Tavon Austin (Rams, WR)
11. (132)   Theo Riddick (Lions, RB)
12. (133)   Marcus Mariota (Titans, QB)
13. (156)   Kamar Aiken (Ravens, WR)
14. (157)   Chiefs DST
15. (180)   Mason Crosby (Packers, K)

1. What was your plan going into the draft?

My plan is to draft upside value players. I use my own projections based upon my statistical analysis. I generate my own player risk rankings. Overall, my data shows that on average, the level of player risk increases as you draft. Therefore, my tolerance for player risk broadens into the draft. This means *acceptable* player risk will increase each round. My plan was also to draft quarterbacks late and use a "barbell" tight-end approach to take one of the top 1 to 3 TEs early, or wait and draft an upside TE late. I planned to select lower risk WRs in this PPR environment. I wanted to grab one high upside RB in the first 3 picks and then switch to stockpiling WRs.

2. Did you adjust that plan and how?

My draft position was tougher than I expected and I had to reach a little for my first two picks of **Allen Robinson** and **Devonta Freeman**. I then executed my early TE option of **Jordan Reed** because I felt Reed had enough risk relevant to his upside *and* draft position to select him instead of using my preferred late TE drafting strategy.

The biggest change when selecting a WR2. I was not happy with the options on the board for me. In Round 4, only two WRs (**Allen Hurns** and **Jeremy Maclin**) were picked and I thought they were over-priced. I was not pleased and was looking for any of the four WRs selected before me in Round 3: **Kelvin Benjamin, Brandin Cooks, Julian Edelman,** or **Jarvis Landry**. So, I switched my plan and selected **Mark Ingram** instead. This selection made me feel like I was playing catch-up for the whole draft.

3. What was your favorite pick and why?

My favorite picks were my next two picks, **DeVante Parker** and **Latavius Murray**. I had pre-draft ranked both at this point in the draft as bargain targets. However, I wanted Parker as my WR3 instead of my WR2. I was very surprised **Latavius Murray** dropped to the sixth round. My data suggests he was a steal at this "price" and the first value steal of the in the draft.

4. What was your least favorite pick and why?

Mark Ingram was my least favorite pick as I was forced out of my comfort zone. I think he has potential but was hopeful for another strong wide receiver instead.

5. Overall, how do you feel you did?

At the conclusion of the draft, my analysis was I ranked seventh in the league given my core group of starters. I had a nice slate of low risk, high upside bench players.

TOP 200
(PPR / 4-point Pass TD Leagues)

	Pos	Player	Team	Value	Bye
1.	WR	Antonio Brown	Steelers	444.5	8
2.	WR	Julio Jones (IRSK)	Falcons	363.0	11
3.	WR	Odell Beckham Jr. (3)	Giants	349.0	8
4.	RB	DeVonta Freeman	Falcons	323.2	11
5.	WR	Allen Robinson (3)	Jaguars	317.0	5
6.	WR	Brandon Marshall	Jets	315.5	11
7.	RB	Le'Veon Bell	Steelers	311.5	8
8.	WR	Jordy Nelson	Packers	311.4	4
9.	RB	David Johnson	Cardinals	302.6	9
10.	RB	Jamaal Charles	Chiefs	300.5	5
11.	WR	Dez Bryant	Cowboys	297.0	7
12.	TE	Rob Gronkowski (IRSK)	Patriots	294.3	9
---	----	-----------------------------	--------------------	-------	----
13.	WR	DeAndre Hopkins	Texans	295.8	9
14.	WR	Golden Tate	Lions	288.0	10
15.	WR	Keenan Allen	Chargers	285.0	11
16.	WR	TY Hilton	Colts	284.7	10
17.	WR	Alshon Jeffrey	Bears	284.0	9
18.	WR	Mike Evans (3)	Buccaneers	282.0	6
19.	WR	AJ Green	Bengals	273.1	9
20.	RB	Todd Gurley	Rams	268.6	8
21.	RB	Lamar Miller (NO)	Texans	263.6	9
22.	RB	Ezekiel Elliott (R)	Cowboys	257.1	7
23.	RB	Mark Ingram	Saints	256.0	5
24.	RB	Adrian Peterson (IRSK)	Vikings	252.4	6
---	----	-----------------------------	--------------------	-------	----
25.	WR	Brandin Cooks (3)	Saints	271.5	5
26.	WR	Randall Cobb	Packers	270.0	4
27.	WR	Sammy Watkins (3) (INJ)	Bills	267.8	10
28.	WR	Jeremy Maclin	Chiefs	264.6	5
29.	WR	Jarvis Landry	Dolphins	264.0	8
30.	WR	Amari Cooper (2)	Raiders	259.5	10
31.	WR	Kelvin Benjamin (3)	Panthers	256.0	7
32.	TE	Jordan Reed (IRSK)	Redskins	231.6	9
33.	RB	LeSean McCoy	Bills	250.5	10
34.	RB	Matt Forte (NO)	Jets	245.6	11
35.	RB	Jeremy Langford	Bears	243.0	9
36.	QB	Cam Newton	Panthers	409.0	7
---	----	-----------------------------	--------------------	-------	----
37.	WR	Eric Decker	Jets	253.8	11
38.	WR	Allen Hurns (3)	Jaguars	248.0	5
39.	WR	Larry Fitzgerald	Cardinals	246.9	9
40.	RB	Eddie Lacy	Packers	242.5	4

41.	QB	Aaron Rodgers	Packers	387.0	4
42.	RB	Doug Martin	Buccaneers	236.6	6
43.	RB	Thomas Rawls (INJ) (UPS)	Seahawks	236.0	5
44.	RB	Dion Lewis (DNS)	Patriots	235.4	9
45.	TE	Gary Barnidge (NO)	Browns	228.4	13
46.	RB	C.J. Anderson	Broncos	228.5	11
47.	RB	Carlos Hyde (NO) (UPS)	49ers	224.1	8
48.	RB	Danny Woodhead (NO)	Chargers	223.0	11
---	----	--------------------------	-------------------	-------	---
49.	WR	Marvin Jones (NO)	Lions	246.1	10
50.	QB	Drew Brees	Saints	376.5	5
51.	WR	Jordan Mathews (3) (NO)	Eagles	239.2	4
52.	WR	John Brown (3)	Cardinals	237.7	9
53.	WR	Steve Smith	Ravens	236.0	8
54.	TE	Greg Olsen	Panthers	218.2	7
55.	RB	DeMarco Murray (IRSK)	Titans	222.0	13
56.	RB	Latavius Murray	Raiders	220.0	10
57.	QB	Tom Brady (SUS4)	Patriots	375.0 (281.3)	9
58.	RB	Jay Ajayi (NO) (UPS) (IRSK)	Dolphins	213.2	8
59.	RB	Duke Johnson (NO)	Browns	211.0	13
60.	RB	Ryan Mathews (NO) (IRSK) (UPS)	Eagles	206.5	4
---	----	--------------------------	-------------------	-------	---
61.	WR	Julian Edelman	Patriots	227.4	9
62.	WR	Donte Moncrief (3)	Colts	227.2	10
63.	WR	Michael Crabtree	Raiders	223.5	10
64.	WR	Torrey Smith (NO) (DNS)	49ers	221.0	8
65.	TE	Tyler Eiffert (INJ)	Bengals	207.6	9
66.	QB	Russell Wilson	Seahawks	360.5	5
67.	QB	Andrew Luck	Colts	359.0	10
68.	RB	Melvin Gordon (NO)	Chargers	205.0	11
69.	RB	Ameer Abdullah (UPS)	Lions	203.8	10
70.	RB	Jonathan Stewart (IRSK)	Panthers	200.8	7
71.	TE	Coby Fleener (NO)	Saints	201.7	5
72.	RB	Matt Jones (UPS)	Redskins	197.0	9
---	----	--------------------------	-------------------	-------	---
73.	WR	Tavon Austin	Rams	216.5	8
74.	WR	DeVante Parker (2)	Dolphins	215.4	8
75.	WR	Willie Snead (2)	Saints	212.2	5
76.	QB	Blake Bortles	Jaguars	345.5	5
77.	WR	Mike Wallace (NO)	Ravens	206.2	8
78.	TE	Antonio Gates (NO)	Chargers	199.7	11
79.	RB	Isaiah Crowell (NO)	Browns	196.1	13
80.	RB	Jeremy Hill	Bengals	192.7	9
81.	RB	Frank Gore	Colts	189.5	10
82.	TE	Jimmy Graham	Seahawks	194.2	5
83.	RB	Javorius "Buck" Allen	Ravens	184.5	8
84.	QB	Ben Roethlisberger	Steelers	341.0	8
---	----	--------------------------	-------------------	-------	---
85.	WR	Doug Baldwin	Seahawks	205.5	5
86.	WR	Markus Wheaton	Steelers	196.0	8

87.	WR	Michael Floyd	Cardinals	195.0	9
88.	TE	Travis Kelce (3)	Chiefs	185.4	5
89.	RB	Justin Forsett (DNS)	Ravens	183.9	8
90.	RB	LeGarrette Blount	Patriots	181.6	9
91.	QB	Kirk Cousins	Redskins	338.5	9
92.	QB	Eli Manning	Giants	338.0	8
93.	RB	Theo Riddick	Lions	180.0	10
94.	RB	Chris Ivory	Jaguars	175.0	5
95.	RB	T.J. Yeldon	Jaguars	167.3	5
96.	RB	Rashad Jennings	Giants	161.6	8
---	----	----------------------------	--------------------	-------	---
97.	WR	Vincent Jackson	Buccaneers	195.0	6
98.	WR	Corey Coleman (R) (UPS)	Browns	189.3	13
99.	WR	DeSean Jackson	Redskins	186.2	9
100.	WR	Kevin White (2) (UPS)	Bears	186.0	9
101.	TE	Zach Ertz	Eagles	185.4	4
102.	DST	Cardinals DST	Cardinals	DST	9
103.	TE	Delanie Walker	Titans	184.8	13
104.	WR	Travis Benjamin	Chargers	184.0	11
105.	WR	Tyler Lockett (2) (UPS)	Seahawks	184.0	5
106.	TE	Julius Thomas	Jaguars	182.0	5
107.	QB	Carson Palmer	Cardinals	338.0	9
108.	RB	Charles Sims	Buccaneers	158.4	6
---	----	----------------------------	--------------------	-------	---
109.	QB	Derek Carr	Raiders	334.0	10
110.	QB	Tyrod Taylor	Bills	334.0	10
111.	WR	Demaryius Thomas	Broncos	180.0	11
112.	WR	Bruce Ellington (3) (UPS)	49ers	178.2	8
113.	WR	Brandon LaFell (NO)	Bengals	172.2	9
114.	RB	DeVontae Booker (R) (UPS)	Broncos	154.0	11
115.	RB	Karlos Williams	Bills	153.0	10
116.	DST	Broncos DST	Broncos	DST	11
117.	DST	Texans DST	Texans	DST	9
118.	WR	Laquon Treadwell (R)	Vikings	171.6	6
119.	WR	Terrance Williams	Cowboys	163.5	7
120.	RB	Bilal Powell	Jets	141.9	11
---	----	----------------------------	--------------------	-------	---
121.	TE	Jason Witten	Cowboys	177.0	7
122.	TE	Zach Miller (UPS)	Bears	176.8	9
123.	DST	Seahawks DST	Seahawks	DST	5
124.	WR	Kendall Wright	Titans	161.6	13
125.	WR	Pierre Garcon	Redskins	159.8	9
126.	WR	Marlon Moore (NO)	Browns	159.6	13
127.	RB	Gio Bernard	Bengals	141.5	9
128.	RB	Paul Perkins (R)	Giants	141.0	8
129.	RB	Wendell Smallwood (R) (UPS)	Eagles	138.0	4
130.	RB	Shane Vereen	Giants	128.5	8
131.	QB	Andy Dalton	Bengals	331.0	9
132.	QB	Philip Rivers (NO)	Chargers	329.0	11
---	----	----------------------------	--------------------	-------	---

133.	TE	Martellus Bennett (NO)	Patriots	176.0	9
134.	TE	Lardarius Green (NO) (UPS)	Steelers	175.2	8
135.	WR	Rishard Matthews (NO) (UPS)	Titans	159.0	13
136.	WR	Sterling Shepard (R) (UPS)	Giants	156.0	8
137.	WR	Devin Funchess (2)	Panthers	155.8	7
138.	WR	Emmanuel Sanders	Broncos	155.2	11
139.	K	Stephen Gostkowski	Patriots	K	9
140.	DST	Panthers DST	Panthers	DST	7
141.	DST	Bengals DST	Bengals	DST	9
142.	QB	Matt Stafford	Lions	327.5	10
143.	QB	Ryan Fitzpatrick*	Jets	323.0	11
144.	WR	Stefon Diggs (2)	Vikings	149.0	6
---	----	---------------------------	--------------------	-------	---
145.	RB	DeAndre Washington (R)	Raiders	128.0	10
146.	RB	Kenyan Drake (R)	Dolphins	122.5	8
147.	QB	Tony Romo (IRSK)	Cowboys	320.0	7
148.	TE	Will Tye (2)	Giants	173.4	8
149.	TE	Dwayne Allen	Colts	166.0	10
150.	WR	Josh Doctson (R)	Redskins	148.0	9
151.	WR	Will Fuller (R)	Texans	146.5	9
152.	WR	Eddie Royal	Bears	146.0	9
153.	WR	Kenny Britt	Rams	143.0	8
154.	WR	Mohamed Sanu (NO) (UPS)	Falcons	139.0	11
155.	K	Steven Hauschka	Seahawks	K	5
156.	K	Justin Tucker	Ravens	K	8
---	----	---------------------------	--------------------	-------	---
157.	RB	Benny Cunningham	Rams	117.0	8
158.	RB	Derrick Henry (R) (UPS)	Titans	113.0	13
159.	DST	Vikings DST	Vikings	DST	6
160.	DST	Chiefs DST	Chiefs	DST	5
161.	DST	Patriots DST	Patriots	DST	9
162.	DST	Rams DST	Rams	DST	8
163.	DST	Steelers DST	Steelers	DST	8
164.	DST	Jets DST	Jets	DST	11
165.	WR	Robert Woods	Bills	134.0	10
166.	WR	Dorial Green-Beckham (2) (UPS)	Titans	128.0	13
167.	WR	Davante Adams (3) (DNS)	Packers	126.7	4
168.	QB	Jay Cutler	Bears	304.0	9
---	----	---------------------------	--------------------	-------	---
169.	QB	Marcus Mariota	Titans	301.0	13
170.	QB	Matt Ryan	Falcons	300.5	11
171.	QB	Joe Flacco	Ravens	296.0	8
172.	K	Graham Gano	Panthers	K	7
173.	K	Mason Crosby	Packers	K	4
174.	K	Blair Walsh	Vikings	K	6
175.	K	John Brown	Giants	K	8
176.	K	Chris Boswell	Steelers	K	8
177.	K	Dan Bailey	Cowboys	K	7
178.	K	Chandler Catanzaro	Cardinals	K	9
179.	K	Adam Vinatieri	Colts	K	10

180.	K	Brandon McManus	Broncos	K	11
---	----	-----------------------------	--------------------	-------	---
181.	QB	Jameis Winston	Buccaneers	293.0	6
182.	QB	Brock Osweiler (NO)	Texans	283.0	9
183.	WR	Jermaine Kearse	Seahawks	126.4	5
184.	WR	Chris Hogan (NO)	Patriots	124.8	9
185.	WR	Breshad Perriman (2) (INJ)	Ravens	123.5	8
185.	WR	Seth Roberts (2)	Raiders	120.0	10
186.	WR	Tajae Sharpe (R) (UPS)	Titans	118.0	13
187.	WR	Victor Cruz	Giants	118.0	8
188.	WR	Michael Thomas (R) (UPS)	Saints	114.0	5
189.	WR	Phillip Dorsett (2)	Colts	114.0	10
190.	RB	James White	Patriots	110.2	9
191.	RB	James Starks	Packers	105.4	4
192.	RB	CJ Spiller (IRSK)	Saints	105.4	5
---	----	-----------------------------	--------------------	-------	---
193.	TE	Jordan Cameron (NO)	Dolphins	162.0	8
194.	TE	Vance McDonald (UPS)	49ers	161.4	8
195.	WR	Nelson Agholor (2)	Eagles	113.2	4
196.	WR	Kenny Stills	Dolphins	109.5	8
197.	WR	Sammie Coates (2) (UPS)	Steelers	108.4	8
198.	RB	Alfred Blue	Texans	103.8	9
199.	RB	Chris Thompson	Redskins	103.0	9
200.	RB	Tevin Coleman	Falcons	99.0	11

*Assumes the Week 1 Starter
(SUS4) = Assumes Tom Brady is suspended for the first 4-games of the season

Ranks reflect value based on 16 weeks of play. Past performance was considered as were issues relating to each team's offense including the offense run by the team's offensive coordinator, any coaching changes and personnel changes, and which players are listed as starters and back-ups on the most recent depth charts. Historical draft patterns were considered to help assign players by position to each round.

KEY: (NO) = New Offense; (UPS) = Upside; (IRSK) = Injury Risk; (INJ) = Injured; (DNS) = Downside; (R) = Rookie; (2) = 2nd Year WR; (3) = 3rd Year WR

TOP 200

(Non-PPR / 4-point Pass TD Leagues)

	Pos	Player	Team	Value	Bye
1.	WR	Antonio Brown	Steelers	286.5	8
2.	RB	David Johnson	Cardinals	252.6	9
3.	RB	Todd Gurley	Rams	248.6	8
4.	RB	DeVonta Freeman	Falcons	246.2	11
5.	WR	Odell Beckham Jr. (3)	Giants	244.0	8
6.	RB	Le'Veon Bell (IRSK)	Steelers	241.5	8
7.	RB	Jamaal Charles	Chiefs	240.5	5
8.	WR	Julio Jones (IRSK)	Falcons	233.0	11
9.	RB	Lamar Miller (NO)	Texans	223.6	9
10.	WR	Allen Robinson (3)	Jaguars	222.0	5
11.	WR	Jordy Nelson	Packers	216.4	4
12.	TE	Rob Gronkowski (IRSK)	Patriots	204.3	9
---	----	----------------------------	--------------------	-------	----
13.	RB	Adrian Peterson (IRSK)	Vikings	222.4	6
14.	RB	Ezekiel Elliott (R)	Cowboys	222.1	7
15.	WR	Brandon Marshall	Jets	215.5	11
16.	WR	Dez Bryant	Cowboys	207.0	7
17.	RB	Doug Martin	Buccaneers	206.6	6
18.	WR	DeAndre Hopkins	Texans	205.8	9
19.	RB	LeSean McCoy	Bills	205.5	10
20.	RB	Jeremy Langford	Bears	203.0	9
21.	RB	Eddie Lacy	Packers	202.5	4
22.	WR	Keenan Allen	Chargers	195.0	11
23.	WR	Sammy Watkins (3) (INJ)	Bills	194.8	10
24.	WR	TY Hilton	Colts	194.7	10
---	----	----------------------------	--------------------	-------	----
25.	RB	Thomas Rawls (INJ) (UPS)	Seahawks	201.0	5
26.	RB	Carlos Hyde (NO) (UPS)	49ers	199.1	8
27.	RB	Mark Ingram	Saints	196.0	5
28.	RB	Matt Forte (NO)	Jets	195.6	11
29.	WR	Alshon Jeffrey	Bears	194.0	9
30.	RB	C.J. Anderson (UPS)	Broncos	193.5	11
31.	WR	Mike Evans (3)	Buccaneers	192.0	6
32.	WR	AJ Green	Bengals	188.1	9
33.	WR	Golden Tate	Lions	188.0	10
34.	WR	Brandin Cooks (3)	Saints	181.5	5
35.	WR	Randall Cobb	Packers	180.0	4
36.	QB	Cam Newton	Panthers	409.0	7
---	----	----------------------------	--------------------	-------	----
37.	RB	Ryan Mathews (NO) (UPS) (IRSK)	Eagles	186.5	4
38.	RB	Jonathan Stewart (IRSK)	Panthers	181.8	7
39.	RB	Latavius Murray	Raiders	180.0	10
40.	WR	Kelvin Benjamin (3)	Panthers	176.0	7
41.	WR	Amari Cooper (2)	Raiders	174.5	10

42.	QB	Aaron Rodgers	Packers	387.0	4
43.	WR	Jarvis Landry (3)	Dolphins	172.0	8
44.	RB	Melvin Gordon (NO)	Chargers	180.0	11
45.	RB	Ameer Abdullah (UPS)	Lions	178.8	10
46.	WR	Jeremy Maclin	Chiefs	169.6	5
47.	WR	Eric Decker	Jets	168.8	11
48.	TE	Gary Barnidge (NO)	Browns	148.4	13
---	----	-------------------------	-------------------	-------	---
49.	QB	Drew Brees	Saints	376.5	5
50.	QB	Tom Brady (SUS4)	Patriots	375.0 (281.3)	9
51.	RB	Melvin Gordon (NO)	Chargers	180.0	11
52.	RB	Ameer Abdullah (UPS)	Lions	178.8	10
53.	RB	Jay Ajayi (R) (IRSK) (UPS)	Dolphins	178.3	8
54.	RB	Jeremy Hill	Bengals	177.7	9
55.	WR	Allen Hurns (3)	Jaguars	168.0	5
56.	WR	John Brown (3)	Cardinals	162.7	9
57.	WR	Marvin Jones (NO)	Lions	161.1	10
58.	WR	Larry Fitzgerald	Cardinals	156.9	9
59.	TE	Tyler Eiffert (INJ)	Bengals	147.6	9
60.	TE	Jordan Reed (IRSK)	Redskins	146.6	9
---	----	-------------------------	-------------------	-------	---
61.	RB	Isaiah Crowell (NO) (UPS)	Browns	176.1	13
62.	RB	Matt Jones (IRSK) (UPS)	Redskins	172.0	9
63.	RB	DeMarco Murray (NO) (DNS)	Titans	172.0	13
64.	RB	LeGarrette Blount (IRSK)	Patriots	171.6	9
65.	RB	Duke Johnson (NO)	Browns	171.0	13
66.	QB	Russell Wilson	Seahawks	360.5	5
67.	QB	Andrew Luck	Colts	359.0	10
68.	WR	Tavon Austin	Rams	156.5	8
69.	WR	Steve Smith	Ravens	156.0	8
70.	WR	Torrey Smith (NO) (DNS)	49ers	156.0	8
71.	WR	Jordan Mathews (3) (NO) (UPS)	Eagles	154.2	4
72.	TE	Greg Olsen	Panthers	143.2	7
---	----	-------------------------	-------------------	-------	---
73.	QB	Blake Bortles	Jaguars	345.5	5
74.	QB	Ben Roethlisberger	Steelers	341.0	8
75.	TE	Coby Fleener (NO)	Saints	131.7	5
76.	RB	Justin Forsett (IRSK)	Ravens	168.9	8
77.	RB	Dion Lewis	Patriots	163.4	9
78.	RB	Frank Gore (IRSK)	Colts	159.5	10
79.	WR	DeVante Parker (2)	Dolphins	155.4	8
80.	RB	Danny Woodhead (NO)	Chargers	148.0	11
81.	RB	Karlos Williams	Bills	148.0	10
82.	WR	Donte Moncrief (3)	Colts	147.2	10
83.	WR	Tyler Lockett (2) (UPS)	Seahawks	145.0	5
84.	WR	Michael Crabtree	Raiders	143.5	10
---	----	-------------------------	-------------------	-------	---
85.	QB	Kirk Cousins	Redskins	338.5	9
86.	QB	Eli Manning	Giants	338.0	8
87.	QB	Carson Palmer	Cardinals	338.0	9

88.	RB	Chris Ivory (NO)	Jaguars	145.0	5
89.	WR	Michael Floyd	Cardinals	140.0	9
90.	WR	Julian Edelman	Patriots	137.4	9
91.	WR	Willie Snead (2)	Saints	137.2	5
92.	WR	Mike Wallace (NO)	Ravens	136.2	8
93.	WR	Markus Wheaton	Steelers	136.0	8
94.	RB	DeVontae Booker (R) (UPS)	Broncos	134.0	11
95.	TE	Antonio Gates	Chargers	124.7	11
96.	TE	Jimmy Graham	Seahawks	124.2	5
---	----	-----------------------------	--------------------	-------	---
97.	DST	Cardinals DST	Cardinals	DST	9
98.	DST	Broncos DST	Broncos	DST	11
99.	TE	Delanie Walker	Titans	119.8	13
100.	TE	Julius Thomas	Jaguars	117.0	5
101.	TE	Zach Miller (UPS)	Bears	116.8	9
102.	TE	Dwayne Allen	Colts	116.0	10
103.	QB	Tyrod Taylor	Bills	334.0	10
104.	QB	Derek Carr	Raiders	334.0	10
105.	WR	Doug Baldwin	Seahawks	135.5	5
106.	WR	Vincent Jackson	Buccaneers	135.0	6
107.	WR	Travis Benjamin (NO)	Chargers	134.0	11
108.	WR	DeSean Jackson	Redskins	132.2	9
---	----	-----------------------------	--------------------	-------	---
109.	DST	Texans DST	Texans	DST	9
110.	DST	Seahawks DST	Seahawks	DST	5
111.	RB	Rashad Jennings	Giants	131.6	8
112.	WR	Kevin White (2) (UPS)	Bears	126.0	9
113.	WR	Demaryius Thomas	Broncos	120.0	11
114.	WR	Corey Coleman (R) (UPS)	Browns	119.3	13
115.	WR	Bruce Ellington (3) (NO)	49ers	118.2	8
116.	RB	Wendell Smallwood (R) (UPS)	Eagles	118.0	4
117.	RB	Javorius 'Buck' Allen	Ravens	114.5	8
118.	RB	Paul Perkins (R)	Giants	111.0	8
119.	WR	Terrance Williams	Cowboys	113.5	7
120.	WR	Laquon Treadwell (R)	Vikings	111.6	6
---	----	-----------------------------	--------------------	-------	---
121.	WR	Devin Funchess (3)	Panthers	110.8	7
122.	WR	Emmanuel Sanders	Broncos	110.2	11
123.	DST	Panthers DST	Panthers	DST	7
124.	DST	Bengals DST	Bengals	DST	9
125.	RB	Charles Sims	Buccaneers	108.4	6
126.	TE	Zach Ertz	Eagles	115.4	4
127.	TE	Travis Kelce (3)	Chiefs	115.2	5
128.	TE	Will Tye (2)	Giants	113.4	8
129.	QB	Andy Dalton	Bengals	331.0	9
130.	QB	Philip Rivers (NO)	Chargers	329.0	11
131.	QB	Matt Stafford	Lions	327.5	10
132.	WR	Brandon LaFell (NO)	Bengals	107.2	9
---	----	-----------------------------	--------------------	-------	---
133.	WR	Sterling Shepard (R)	Giants	106.0	8

134.	RB	Derrick Henry (R) (UPS)	Titans	103.0	13
135.	K	Stephen Gostkowski	Patriots	K	9
136.	RB	T.J. Yeldon	Jaguars	102.3	5
137.	WR	Will Fuller (R)	Texans	101.5	9
138.	QB	Ryan Fitzpatrick*	Jets	323.0	11
139.	QB	Tony Romo (IRSK)	Cowboys	320.0	7
140.	TE	Lardarius Green (NO) (UPS)	Steelers	109.2	8
141.	TE	Jason Witten	Cowboys	107.0	7
142.	RB	Theo Riddick	Lions	100.0	10
143.	RB	Kenyan Drake (R)	Dolphins	97.5	8
144.	RB	Bilal Powell	Jets	96.9	11
---	----	------------------------------	--------------------	-------	---
145.	DST	Vikings DST	Vikings	DST	6
146.	DST	Chiefs DST	Chiefs	DST	5
147.	RB	Tevin Coleman	Falcons	94.0	11
148.	RB	Gio Bernard (UPS)	Bengals	91.5	9
149.	TE	Martellus Bennett (NO) (UPS)	Patriots	106.0	9
150.	WR	Marlon Moore (NO)	Browns	99.6	13
151.	WR	Rishard Matthews (NO)	Titans	99.0	13
152.	WR	Josh Doctson (R)	Redskins	98.0	9
153.	WR	Kendall Wright	Titans	96.6	13
154.	QB	Jay Cutler	Bears	304.0	9
155.	QB	Marcus Mariota	Titans	301.0	13
156.	TE	Jordan Cameron	Dolphins	102.0	8
---	----	------------------------------	--------------------	-------	---
157.	K	Steven Hauschka	Seahawks	K	5
158.	K	Justin Tucker	Ravens	K	8
159.	K	Graham Gano	Panthers	K	7
160.	RB	Alfred Blue	Texans	88.8	9
161.	DST	Patriots DST	Patriots	DST	9
162.	DST	Rams DST	Rams	DST	8
163.	DST	Steelers DST	Steelers	DST	8
164.	DST	Jets DST	Jets	DST	11
165.	TE	Vance McDonald (UPS)	49ers	101.4	8
166.	RB	DeAndre Washington (R)	Raiders	88.0	10
167.	RB	James Starks	Packers	85.4	4
168.	RB	Shane Vereen	Giants	78.5	8
---	----	------------------------------	--------------------	-------	---
169.	WR	Eddie Royal	Bears	96.0	9
170.	WR	Pierre Garcon	Redskins	94.8	9
171.	WR	Stefon Diggs (2)	Vikings	94.0	6
172.	WR	Kenny Britt	Rams	93.0	8
173.	K	Mason Crosby	Packers	K	4
175.	K	Blair Walsh	Vikings	K	6
176.	K	John Brown	Giants	K	8
177.	K	Chris Boswell	Steelers	K	8
178.	K	Dan Bailey	Cowboys	K	7
179.	K	Chandler Catanzaro	Cardinals	K	9
180.	K	Adam Vinatieri	Colts	K	10
180.	K	Brandon McManus	Broncos	K	11

| --- | ---- | ----------------------------- | -------------------- | ------- | --- |
181.	TE	Eric Ebron (3)	Lions	98.7	10
182.	TE	Jared Cook (UPS)	Packers	97.0	4
183.	TE	Crockett Gillmore (INJ)	Ravens	96.0	8
184.	WR	Dorial Green-Beckham (2) (UPS)	Titans	92.0	13
185.	QB	Matt Ryan	Falcons	300.5	11
186.	QB	Joe Flacco	Ravens	296.0	8
187.	QB	Jameis Winston	Buccaneers	293.0	6
188.	WR	Mohamed Sanu (NO) (UPS)	Falcons	89.0	11
189.	WR	Jermaine Kearse	Seahawks	86.4	5
190.	WR	Davante Adams (3) (DNS)	Packers	81.7	4
191.	WR	Robert Woods	Bills	81.0	10
192.	WR	Seth Roberts (2)	Raiders	80.0	10
193.	WR	Chris Hogan (NO)	Patriots	74.8	9
194.	WR	Phillip Dorsett (2)	Colts	74.0	10
195.	WR	Victor Cruz	Giants	78.0	8
196.	WR	Tajae Sharpe (R)	Titans	78.0	13
197.	RB	Benny Cunningham	Rams	72.0	8
198.	RB	Andre Ellington (IRSK)	Cardinals	70.2	9
199.	RB	James White	Patriots	70.2	9
200.	RB	C.J. Prosise (R) (UPS)	Seahawks	68.0	5

*Assumes the Week 1 Starter
(SUS4) = Assumes Tom Brady is suspended for the first 4-games of the season

Ranks reflect value based on 16 weeks of play. Ranks also reflect that a passing TD is worth 4 points for quarterbacks. Past performance was considered as were issues relating to each team's offense including the offense run by the team's offensive coordinator, any coaching changes and personnel changes, and which players are listed as starters and back-ups on the most recent depth charts. Historical draft patterns were considered to help assign players by position to each round.

KEY: (NO) = New Offense; (UPS) = Upside; (IRSK) = Injury Risk; (INJ) = Injured; (DNS) = Downside; (R) = Rookie; (2) = 2nd Year WR; (3) = 3rd Year WR

TOP 200
(PPR / 6-point Pass TD Leagues)

	Pos	Player	Team	Value	Bye
1.	WR	Antonio Brown	Steelers	444.5	8
2.	WR	Julio Jones (IRSK)	Falcons	363.0	11
3.	WR	Odell Beckham Jr. (3)	Giants	349.0	8
4.	RB	DeVonta Freeman	Falcons	323.2	11
5.	WR	Allen Robinson (3)	Jaguars	317.0	5
6.	WR	Brandon Marshall	Jets	315.5	11
7.	RB	Le'Veon Bell	Steelers	311.5	8
8.	WR	Jordy Nelson	Packers	311.4	4
9.	RB	David Johnson	Cardinals	302.6	9
10.	RB	Jamaal Charles	Chiefs	300.5	5
11.	WR	Dez Bryant	Cowboys	297.0	7
12.	TE	Rob Gronkowski (IRSK)	Patriots	294.3	9
---	----	------------------------------	--------------------	-------	---
13.	WR	DeAndre Hopkins	Texans	295.8	9
14.	WR	Golden Tate	Lions	288.0	10
15.	WR	Keenan Allen	Chargers	285.0	11
16.	WR	TY Hilton	Colts	284.7	10
17.	WR	Alshon Jeffrey	Bears	284.0	9
18.	WR	Mike Evans (3)	Buccaneers	282.0	6
19.	WR	AJ Green	Bengals	273.1	9
20.	RB	Todd Gurley	Rams	268.6	8
21.	RB	Lamar Miller (NO)	Texans	263.6	9
22.	RB	Ezekiel Elliott (R)	Cowboys	257.1	7
23.	RB	Mark Ingram	Saints	256.0	5
24.	RB	Adrian Peterson (IRSK)	Vikings	252.4	6
---	----	------------------------------	--------------------	-------	---
25.	WR	Brandin Cooks (3)	Saints	271.5	5
26.	WR	Randall Cobb	Packers	270.0	4
27.	WR	Sammy Watkins (3) (INJ)	Bills	267.8	10
28.	WR	Jeremy Maclin	Chiefs	264.6	5
29.	WR	Jarvis Landry	Dolphins	264.0	8
30.	WR	Amari Cooper (2)	Raiders	259.5	10
31.	WR	Kelvin Benjamin (3)	Panthers	256.0	7
32.	RB	LeSean McCoy	Bills	250.5	10
33.	RB	Matt Forte (NO)	Jets	245.6	11
34.	RB	Jeremy Langford	Bears	243.0	9
35.	TE	Jordan Reed (IRSK)	Redskins	231.6	9
36.	QB	Cam Newton	Panthers	479.0	7
---	----	------------------------------	--------------------	-------	---
37.	WR	Eric Decker	Jets	253.8	11
38.	WR	Allen Hurns (3)	Jaguars	248.0	5
39.	WR	Larry Fitzgerald	Cardinals	246.9	9
40.	RB	Eddie Lacy	Packers	242.5	4
41.	QB	Aaron Rodgers	Packers	463.0	4

42.	RB	Doug Martin	Buccaneers	236.6	6
43.	RB	Thomas Rawls (INJ) (UPS)	Seahawks	236.0	5
44.	RB	Dion Lewis (DNS)	Patriots	235.4	9
45.	RB	C.J. Anderson	Broncos	228.5	11
46.	TE	Gary Barnidge (NO)	Browns	228.4	13
47.	RB	Carlos Hyde (NO) (UPS)	49ers	224.1	8
48.	RB	Danny Woodhead (NO)	Chargers	223.0	11
49.	WR	Marvin Jones (NO)	Lions	246.1	10
50.	QB	Drew Brees	Saints	444.5	5
51.	WR	Jordan Mathews (3) (NO)	Eagles	239.2	4
52.	WR	John Brown (3)	Cardinals	237.7	9
53.	WR	Steve Smith	Ravens	236.0	8
54.	RB	DeMarco Murray (IRSK)	Titans	222.0	13
55.	RB	Latavius Murray	Raiders	220.0	10
56.	TE	Greg Olsen	Panthers	218.2	7
57.	QB	Tom Brady (SUS4)	Patriots	440 (330)	9
58.	RB	Jay Ajayi (NO) (UPS) (IRSK)	Dolphins	213.2	8
59.	RB	Duke Johnson (NO)	Browns	211.0	13
60.	RB	Ryan Mathews (NO) (IRSK) (UPS)	Eagles	206.5	4
61.	WR	Julian Edelman	Patriots	227.4	9
62.	WR	Donte Moncrief (3)	Colts	227.2	10
63.	WR	Michael Crabtree	Raiders	223.5	10
64.	WR	Torrey Smith (NO) (DNS)	49ers	221.0	8
65.	TE	Tyler Eiffert (INJ)	Bengals	207.6	9
66.	QB	Russell Wilson	Seahawks	428.5	5
67.	QB	Andrew Luck	Colts	427.0	10
68.	RB	Melvin Gordon (NO)	Chargers	205.0	11
69.	RB	Ameer Abdullah (UPS)	Lions	203.8	10
70.	TE	Coby Fleener (NO)	Saints	201.7	5
71.	RB	Jonathan Stewart (IRSK)	Panthers	200.8	7
72.	RB	Matt Jones (UPS)	Redskins	197.0	9
73.	WR	Tavon Austin	Rams	216.5	8
74.	WR	DeVante Parker (2)	Dolphins	215.4	8
75.	WR	Willie Snead (2)	Saints	212.2	5
76.	QB	Blake Bortles	Jaguars	409.5	5
77.	QB	Eli Manning	Giants	408.0	8
78.	WR	Mike Wallace (NO)	Ravens	206.2	8
79.	TE	Antonio Gates (NO)	Chargers	199.7	11
80.	RB	Isaiah Crowell (NO)	Browns	196.1	13
81.	TE	Jimmy Graham	Seahawks	194.2	5
82.	RB	Jeremy Hill	Bengals	192.7	9
83.	RB	Frank Gore	Colts	189.5	10
84.	RB	Javorius "Buck" Allen	Ravens	184.5	8
85.	WR	Doug Baldwin	Seahawks	205.5	5
86.	WR	Markus Wheaton	Steelers	196.0	8
87.	WR	Michael Floyd	Cardinals	195.0	9

88.	TE	Travis Kelce (3)	Chiefs	185.4	9
89.	RB	Justin Forsett (DNS)	Ravens	183.9	8
90.	RB	LeGarrette Blount	Patriots	181.6	9
91.	QB	Kirk Cousins	Redskins	402.5	9
92.	QB	Carson Palmer	Cardinals	402.0	9
93.	QB	Ben Roethlisberger	Steelers	401.0	8
94.	RB	Theo Riddick	Lions	180.0	10
95.	RB	Chris Ivory	Jaguars	175.0	5
96.	RB	T.J. Yeldon	Jaguars	167.3	5
---	----	--------------------------	--------------------	-------	---
97.	WR	Vincent Jackson	Buccaneers	195.0	6
98.	QB	Philip Rivers (NO)	Chargers	393.0	11
99.	WR	Corey Coleman (R) (UPS)	Browns	189.3	13
100.	WR	DeSean Jackson	Redskins	186.2	9
101.	WR	Kevin White (2) (UPS)	Bears	186.0	9
102.	TE	Zach Ertz	Eagles	185.4	5
103.	DST	Cardinals DST	Cardinals	DST	9
104.	TE	Delanie Walker	Titans	184.8	4
105.	WR	Travis Benjamin	Chargers	184.0	11
106.	WR	Tyler Lockett (2) (UPS)	Seahawks	184.0	5
107.	TE	Julius Thomas	Jaguars	182.0	5
108.	RB	Rashad Jennings	Giants	161.6	8
---	----	--------------------------	--------------------	-------	---
109.	WR	Demaryius Thomas	Broncos	180.0	11
110.	QB	Andy Dalton	Bengals	391.0	9
111.	QB	Derek Carr	Raiders	390.0	10
112.	WR	Bruce Ellington (3) (UPS)	49ers	178.2	8
113.	WR	Brandon LaFell (NO)	Bengals	172.2	9
114.	RB	DeVontae Booker (R) (UPS)	Broncos	154.0	11
115.	RB	Karlos Williams	Bills	153.0	10
116.	DST	Broncos DST	Broncos	DST	11
117.	DST	Texans DST	Texans	DST	9
118.	WR	Laquon Treadwell (R)	Vikings	171.6	6
119.	RB	Charles Sims	Buccaneers	158.4	6
120.	WR	Terrance Williams	Cowboys	163.5	7
---	----	--------------------------	--------------------	-------	---
121.	QB	Ryan Fitzpatrick*	Jets	389.0	11
122.	TE	Jason Witten	Cowboys	177.0	7
123.	TE	Zach Miller (UPS)	Bears	176.8	9
124.	DST	Seahawks DST	Seahawks	DST	5
125.	WR	Kendall Wright	Titans	161.6	13
126.	WR	Pierre Garcon	Redskins	159.8	9
127.	RB	Bilal Powell	Jets	141.9	11
128.	WR	Marlon Moore (NO)	Browns	159.6	13
129.	RB	Gio Bernard	Bengals	141.5	9
130.	RB	Paul Perkins (R)	Giants	141.0	8
131.	RB	Wendell Smallwood (R) (UPS)	Eagles	138.0	4
132.	RB	Shane Vereen	Giants	128.5	8
---	----	--------------------------	--------------------	-------	---
133.	TE	Martellus Bennett (NO)	Patriots	176.0	9

134.	TE	Lardarius Green (NO) (UPS)	Steelers	175.2	8
135.	WR	Rishard Matthews (NO) (UPS)	Titans	159.0	13
136.	WR	Sterling Shepard (R) (UPS)	Giants	156.0	8
137.	WR	Devin Funchess (2)	Panthers	155.8	7
138.	WR	Emmanuel Sanders	Broncos	155.2	11
139.	K	Stephen Gostkowski	Patriots	K	9
140.	DST	Panthers DST	Panthers	DST	7
141.	DST	Bengals DST	Bengals	DST	9
142.	QB	Matt Stafford	Lions	387.5	10
143.	QB	Tyrod Taylor	Bills	382.0	10
144.	WR	Stefon Diggs (2)	Vikings	149.0	6
---	----	-----------------------------	--------------------	-------	---
145.	RB	DeAndre Washington (R)	Raiders	128.0	10
146.	RB	Kenyan Drake (R)	Dolphins	122.5	8
147.	QB	Tony Romo (IRSK)	Cowboys	365.0	7
148.	TE	Will Tye (2)	Giants	173.4	8
149.	TE	Dwayne Allen	Colts	166.0	10
150.	WR	Josh Doctson (R)	Redskins	148.0	9
151.	WR	Will Fuller (R)	Texans	146.5	9
152.	WR	Eddie Royal	Bears	146.0	9
153.	WR	Kenny Britt	Rams	143.0	8
154.	WR	Mohamed Sanu (NO) (UPS)	Falcons	139.0	11
155.	K	Steven Hauschka	Seahawks	K	5
156.	K	Justin Tucker	Ravens	K	8
---	----	-----------------------------	--------------------	-------	---
157.	RB	Benny Cunningham	Rams	117.0	8
158.	RB	Derrick Henry (R) (UPS)	Titans	113.0	13
159.	DST	Vikings DST	Vikings	DST	6
160.	DST	Chiefs DST	Chiefs	DST	5
161.	DST	Patriots DST	Patriots	DST	9
162.	DST	Rams DST	Rams	DST	8
163.	DST	Steelers DST	Steelers	DST	8
164.	DST	Jets DST	Jets	DST	11
165.	WR	Robert Woods	Bills	134.0	10
166.	WR	Dorial Green-Beckham (2) (UPS)	Titans	128.0	13
167.	WR	Davante Adams (3) (DNS)	Packers	126.7	4
168.	QB	Marcus Mariota	Titans	361.0	13
---	----	-----------------------------	--------------------	-------	---
169.	QB	Jay Cutler	Bears	358.0	9
170.	QB	Joe Flacco	Ravens	356.0	8
171.	WR	Jermaine Kearse	Seahawks	126.4	5
172.	K	Graham Gano	Panthers	K	7
173.	K	Mason Crosby	Packers	K	4
174.	K	Blair Walsh	Vikings	K	6
175.	K	John Brown	Giants	K	8
176.	K	Chris Boswell	Steelers	K	8
177.	K	Dan Bailey	Cowboys	K	7
178.	K	Chandler Catanzaro	Cardinals	K	9
179.	K	Adam Vinatieri	Colts	K	10
180.	K	Brandon McManus	Broncos	K	11

| --- | ---- | -------------------------- | -------------------- | ------- | --- |
181.	QB	Jameis Winston	Buccaneers	341.0	6
182.	QB	Brock Osweiler (NO)	Texans	331.0	9
183.	QB	Teddy Bridgewater	Vikings	331.0	6
184.	WR	Chris Hogan (NO)	Patriots	124.8	9
185.	WR	Breshad Perriman (2) (INJ)	Ravens	123.5	8
185.	WR	Seth Roberts (2)	Raiders	120.0	10
186.	WR	Tajae Sharpe (R) (UPS)	Titans	118.0	13
187.	WR	Victor Cruz	Giants	118.0	8
188.	WR	Michael Thomas (R) (UPS)	Saints	114.0	5
189.	WR	Phillip Dorsett (2)	Colts	114.0	10
190.	RB	James White	Patriots	110.2	9
191.	RB	James Starks	Packers	105.4	4
192.	RB	CJ Spiller (IRSK)	Saints	105.4	5
193.	TE	Jordan Cameron (NO)	Dolphins	162.0	8
194.	TE	Vance McDonald (UPS)	49ers	161.4	8
195.	WR	Nelson Agholor (2)	Eagles	113.2	4
196.	WR	Kenny Stills	Dolphins	109.5	8
197.	WR	Sammie Coates (2) (UPS)	Steelers	108.4	8
198.	RB	Alfred Blue	Texans	103.8	9
199.	RB	Chris Thompson	Redskins	103.0	9
200.	RB	Tevin Coleman	Falcons	99.0	11

*Assumes the Week 1 Starter
(SUS4) = Assumes Tom Brady is suspended for the first 4-games of the season

Ranks reflect value based on 16 weeks of play. Ranks also reflect that a passing TD is worth 6 points for quarterbacks. Past performance was considered as were issues relating to each team's offense including the offense run by the team's offensive coordinator, any coaching changes and personnel changes, and which players are listed as starters and back-ups on the most recent depth charts. Historical draft patterns were considered to help assign players by position to each round.

KEY: (NO) = New Offense; (UPS) = Upside; (IRSK) = Injury Risk; (INJ) = Injured; (DNS) = Downside; (R) = Rookie; (2) = 2nd Year WR; (3) = 3rd Year WR

TOP 200
(Non-PPR / 6-point Pass TD Leagues)

	Pos	Player	Team	Value	Bye
1.	WR	Antonio Brown	Steelers	286.5	8
2.	RB	David Johnson	Cardinals	252.6	9
3.	RB	Todd Gurley	Rams	248.6	8
4.	RB	DeVonta Freeman	Falcons	246.2	11
5.	WR	Odell Beckham Jr. (3)	Giants	244.0	8
6.	RB	Le'Veon Bell (IRSK)	Steelers	241.5	8
7.	RB	Jamaal Charles	Chiefs	240.5	5
8.	WR	Julio Jones (IRSK)	Falcons	233.0	11
9.	RB	Lamar Miller (NO)	Texans	223.6	9
10.	WR	Allen Robinson (3)	Jaguars	222.0	5
11.	WR	Jordy Nelson	Packers	216.4	4
12.	TE	Rob Gronkowski (IRSK)	Patriots	204.3	9
---	----	---------------------------	--------------------	-------	---
13.	RB	Adrian Peterson (IRSK)	Vikings	222.4	6
14.	RB	Ezekiel Elliott (R)	Cowboys	222.1	7
15.	WR	Brandon Marshall	Jets	215.5	11
16.	WR	Dez Bryant	Cowboys	207.0	7
17.	RB	Doug Martin	Buccaneers	206.6	6
18.	WR	DeAndre Hopkins	Texans	205.8	9
19.	RB	LeSean McCoy	Bills	205.5	10
20.	RB	Jeremy Langford	Bears	203.0	9
21.	RB	Eddie Lacy	Packers	202.5	4
22.	WR	Keenan Allen	Chargers	195.0	11
23.	WR	Sammy Watkins (3) (INJ)	Bills	194.8	10
24.	WR	TY Hilton	Colts	194.7	10
---	----	---------------------------	--------------------	-------	---
25.	RB	Thomas Rawls (INJ) (UPS)	Seahawks	201.0	5
26.	RB	Carlos Hyde (NO) (UPS)	49ers	199.1	8
27.	RB	Mark Ingram	Saints	196.0	5
28.	RB	Matt Forte (NO)	Jets	195.6	11
29.	WR	Alshon Jeffrey	Bears	194.0	9
30.	RB	C.J. Anderson (UPS)	Broncos	193.5	11
31.	WR	Mike Evans (3)	Buccaneers	192.0	6
32.	WR	AJ Green	Bengals	188.1	9
33.	WR	Golden Tate	Lions	188.0	10
34.	WR	Brandin Cooks (3)	Saints	181.5	5
35.	WR	Randall Cobb	Packers	180.0	4
36.	QB	Cam Newton	Panthers	479.0	7
---	----	---------------------------	--------------------	-------	---
37.	RB	Ryan Mathews (NO) (UPS) (IRSK)	Eagles	186.5	4
38.	RB	Jonathan Stewart (IRSK)	Panthers	181.8	7
39.	RB	Latavius Murray	Raiders	180.0	10
40.	WR	Kelvin Benjamin (3)	Panthers	176.0	7

41.	WR	Amari Cooper (2)	Raiders	174.5	10
42.	QB	Aaron Rodgers	Packers	463.0	4
43.	WR	Jarvis Landry (3)	Dolphins	172.0	8
44.	RB	Melvin Gordon (NO)	Chargers	180.0	11
45.	RB	Ameer Abdullah (UPS)	Lions	178.8	10
46.	WR	Jeremy Maclin	Chiefs	169.6	5
47.	WR	Eric Decker	Jets	168.8	11
48.	WR	Allen Hurns (3)	Jaguars	168.0	5
---	----	-----------------------------	--------------------	-------	---
49.	QB	Drew Brees	Saints	444.5	5
50.	QB	Tom Brady (SUS4)	Patriots	440.0 (330.0)	9
51.	RB	Melvin Gordon (NO)	Chargers	180.0	11
52.	RB	Ameer Abdullah (UPS)	Lions	178.8	10
53.	RB	Jay Ajayi (R) (IRSK) (UPS)	Dolphins	178.3	8
54.	RB	Jeremy Hill	Bengals	177.7	9
55.	WR	John Brown (3)	Cardinals	162.7	9
56.	WR	Marvin Jones (NO)	Lions	161.1	10
57.	WR	Larry Fitzgerald	Cardinals	156.9	9
58.	TE	Gary Barnidge (NO)	Browns	148.4	13
59.	TE	Tyler Eiffert (INJ)	Bengals	147.6	9
60.	TE	Jordan Reed (IRSK)	Redskins	146.6	9
---	----	-----------------------------	--------------------	-------	---
61.	RB	Isaiah Crowell (NO) (UPS)	Browns	176.1	13
62.	RB	Matt Jones (IRSK) (UPS)	Redskins	172.0	9
63.	RB	DeMarco Murray (NO) (DNS)	Titans	172.0	13
64.	RB	LeGarrette Blount (IRSK)	Patriots	171.6	9
65.	RB	Duke Johnson (NO)	Browns	171.0	13
66.	QB	Russell Wilson	Seahawks	428.5	5
67.	QB	Andrew Luck	Colts	427.0	10
68.	WR	Tavon Austin	Rams	156.5	8
69.	WR	Steve Smith	Ravens	156.0	8
70.	WR	Torrey Smith (NO) (DNS)	49ers	156.0	8
71.	WR	Jordan Mathews (3) (NO) (UPS)	Eagles	154.2	4
72.	TE	Greg Olsen	Panthers	143.2	7
---	----	-----------------------------	--------------------	-------	---
73.	QB	Blake Bortles	Jaguars	409.5	5
74.	QB	Eli Manning	Giants	408.0	8
75.	TE	Coby Fleener (NO)	Saints	131.7	5
76.	RB	Justin Forsett (IRSK)	Ravens	168.9	8
77.	RB	Dion Lewis	Patriots	163.4	9
78.	RB	Frank Gore (IRSK)	Colts	159.5	10
79.	WR	DeVante Parker (2)	Dolphins	155.4	8
80.	RB	Danny Woodhead (NO)	Chargers	148.0	11
81.	RB	Karlos Williams	Bills	148.0	10
82.	WR	Donte Moncrief (3)	Colts	147.2	10
83.	WR	Tyler Lockett (2) (UPS)	Seahawks	145.0	5
84.	WR	Michael Crabtree	Raiders	143.5	10
---	----	-----------------------------	--------------------	-------	---
85.	QB	Kirk Cousins	Redskins	402.5	9
86.	QB	Carson Palmer	Cardinals	402.0	9

87.	QB	Ben Roethlisberger	Steelers	401.0	8
88.	RB	Chris Ivory (NO)	Jaguars	145.0	5
89.	WR	Michael Floyd	Cardinals	140.0	9
90.	WR	Julian Edelman	Patriots	137.4	9
91.	WR	Willie Snead (2)	Saints	137.2	5
92.	WR	Mike Wallace (NO)	Ravens	136.2	8
93.	WR	Markus Wheaton	Steelers	136.0	8
94.	RB	DeVontae Booker (R) (UPS)	Broncos	134.0	11
95.	TE	Jimmy Graham	Seahawks	124.2	5
96.	TE	Antonio Gates	Chargers	124.7	11
97.	DST	Cardinals DST	Cardinals	DST	9
98.	DST	Broncos DST	Broncos	DST	11
99.	TE	Delanie Walker	Titans	119.8	13
100.	TE	Julius Thomas	Jaguars	117.0	5
101.	TE	Zach Miller (UPS)	Bears	116.8	9
102.	TE	Dwayne Allen	Colts	116.0	10
103.	QB	Philip Rivers (NO)	Chargers	393.0	11
104.	QB	Andy Dalton	Bengals	391.0	9
105.	WR	Doug Baldwin	Seahawks	135.5	5
106.	WR	Vincent Jackson	Buccaneers	135.0	6
107.	WR	Travis Benjamin (NO)	Chargers	134.0	11
108.	WR	DeSean Jackson	Redskins	132.2	9
109.	DST	Texans DST	Texans	DST	9
110.	DST	Seahawks DST	Seahawks	DST	5
111.	RB	Rashad Jennings	Giants	131.6	8
112.	WR	Kevin White (2) (UPS)	Bears	126.0	9
113.	WR	Demaryius Thomas	Broncos	120.0	11
114.	WR	Corey Coleman (R) (UPS)	Browns	119.3	13
115.	WR	Bruce Ellington (3) (NO)	49ers	118.2	8
116.	RB	Wendell Smallwood (R) (UPS)	Eagles	118.0	4
117.	RB	Javorius 'Buck' Allen	Ravens	114.5	8
118.	RB	Paul Perkins (R)	Giants	111.0	8
119.	WR	Terrance Williams	Cowboys	113.5	7
120.	WR	Laquon Treadwell (R)	Vikings	111.6	6
121.	WR	Devin Funchess (3)	Panthers	110.8	7
122.	WR	Emmanuel Sanders	Broncos	110.2	11
123.	DST	Panthers DST	Panthers	DST	7
124.	DST	Bengals DST	Bengals	DST	9
125.	RB	Charles Sims	Buccaneers	108.4	6
126.	TE	Zach Ertz	Eagles	115.4	4
127.	TE	Travis Kelce (3)	Chiefs	115.2	5
128.	TE	Will Tye (2)	Giants	113.4	8
129.	QB	Derek Carr	Raiders	390.0	10
130.	QB	Ryan Fitzpatrick*	Jets	389.0	11
131.	QB	Matt Stafford	Lions	387.5	10
132.	WR	Brandon LaFell (NO)	Bengals	107.2	9

133.	WR	Sterling Shepard (R)	Giants	106.0	8
134.	RB	Derrick Henry (R) (UPS)	Titans	103.0	13
135.	K	Stephen Gostkowski	Patriots	K	9
136.	RB	T.J. Yeldon	Jaguars	102.3	5
137.	WR	Will Fuller (R)	Texans	101.5	9
138.	QB	Tyrod Taylor	Bills	382.0	10
139.	QB	Tony Romo (IRSK)	Cowboys	365.0	7
140.	TE	Lardarius Green (NO) (UPS)	Steelers	109.2	8
141.	TE	Jason Witten	Cowboys	107.0	7
142.	RB	Theo Riddick	Lions	100.0	10
143.	RB	Kenyan Drake (R)	Dolphins	97.5	8
144.	RB	Bilal Powell	Jets	96.9	11
---	----	--------------------------	-------------------	-------	---
145.	DST	Vikings DST	Vikings	DST	6
146.	DST	Chiefs DST	Chiefs	DST	5
147.	RB	Tevin Coleman	Falcons	94.0	11
148.	RB	Gio Bernard (UPS)	Bengals	91.5	9
149.	TE	Martellus Bennett (NO) (UPS)	Patriots	106.0	9
150.	WR	Marlon Moore (NO)	Browns	99.6	13
151.	WR	Rishard Matthews (NO)	Titans	99.0	13
152.	WR	Josh Doctson (R)	Redskins	98.0	9
153.	WR	Kendall Wright	Titans	96.6	13
154.	QB	Marcus Mariota	Titans	361.0	13
155.	QB	Jay Cutler	Bears	358.0	9
156.	TE	Jordan Cameron	Dolphins	102.0	8
---	----	--------------------------	-------------------	-------	---
157.	K	Steven Hauschka	Seahawks	K	5
158.	K	Justin Tucker	Ravens	K	8
159.	K	Graham Gano	Panthers	K	7
160.	RB	Alfred Blue	Texans	88.8	9
161.	DST	Patriots DST	Patriots	DST	9
162.	DST	Rams DST	Rams	DST	8
163.	DST	Steelers DST	Steelers	DST	8
164.	DST	Jets DST	Jets	DST	11
165.	TE	Vance McDonald (UPS)	49ers	101.4	8
166.	RB	DeAndre Washington (R)	Raiders	88.0	10
167.	RB	James Starks	Packers	85.4	4
168.	RB	Shane Vereen	Giants	78.5	8
---	----	--------------------------	-------------------	-------	---
169.	WR	Eddie Royal	Bears	96.0	9
170.	WR	Pierre Garcon	Redskins	94.8	9
171.	WR	Stefon Diggs (2)	Vikings	94.0	6
172.	WR	Kenny Britt	Rams	93.0	8
173.	K	Mason Crosby	Packers	K	4
174.	K	Blair Walsh	Vikings	K	6
175.	K	John Brown	Giants	K	8
176.	K	Chris Boswell	Steelers	K	8
177.	K	Dan Bailey	Cowboys	K	7
178.	K	Chandler Catanzaro	Cardinals	K	9
179.	K	Adam Vinatieri	Colts	K	10

180.	K	Brandon McManus	Broncos	K	11
---	----	------------------------------	--------------------	-------	---
181.	TE	Eric Ebron (3)	Lions	98.7	10
182.	TE	Jared Cook (UPS)	Packers	97.0	4
183.	TE	Crockett Gillmore (INJ)	Ravens	96.0	8
184.	WR	Dorial Green-Beckham (2) (UPS)	Titans	92.0	13
185.	QB	Joe Flacco	Ravens	356.0	8
186.	QB	Jameis Winston	Buccaneers	341.0	6
187.	QB	Brock Osweiler (NO)	Texans	331.0	9
188.	WR	Mohamed Sanu (NO) (UPS)	Falcons	89.0	11
189.	WR	Jermaine Kearse	Seahawks	86.4	5
190.	WR	Davante Adams (3) (DNS)	Packers	81.7	4
191.	WR	Robert Woods	Bills	81.0	10
192.	WR	Victor Cruz	Giants	78.0	8
---	----	------------------------------	--------------------	-------	---
193.	WR	Seth Roberts (2)	Raiders	80.0	10
194.	WR	Chris Hogan (NO)	Patriots	74.8	9
195.	WR	Phillip Dorsett (2)	Colts	74.0	10
196.	WR	Tajae Sharpe (R)	Titans	78.0	13
197.	RB	Benny Cunningham	Rams	72.0	8
198.	RB	Andre Ellington (IRSK)	Cardinals	70.2	9
199.	RB	James White	Patriots	70.2	9
200.	RB	C.J. Prosise (R) (UPS)	Seahawks	68.0	5

*Assumes the Week 1 Starter
(SUS4) = Assumes Tom Brady is suspended for the first 4-games of the season

Ranks reflect value based on 16 weeks of play. Ranks also reflect that a passing TD is worth 6 points for quarterbacks. Past performance was considered as were issues relating to each team's offense including the offense run by the team's offensive coordinator, any coaching changes and personnel changes, and which players are listed as starters and back-ups on the most recent depth charts. Historical draft patterns were considered to help assign players by position to each round.

KEY: (NO) = New Offense; (UPS) = Upside; (IRSK) = Injury Risk; (INJ) = Injured; (DNS) = Downside; (R) = Rookie; (2) = 2nd Year WR; (3) = 3rd Year WR

QFG RANKINGS
TOP 50 (PPR)

These are the players you want on your team in PPR leagues. **QFG** is a measurement of **"quality fantasy games"** during the 2015 season. For running backs and wide receivers, this is the number of games the player posted double-digit fantasy points. For quarterbacks, this is the number of games the player posted 240 yards passing and 2 pass TDs (4 points per TD) or its equivalent in fantasy points when including things like rush yards and rush TDs.

The ranks consider the actual fantasy points scored by the player, games played in a 16 week fantasy football season, and a valuation of the number of fantasy-relevant games played. Each player's **2016 Top 200 Rank** is noted so you can gauge the value of the player this year. In a real sense, these are players you can consider targeting as must-have players to have on your team. This doesn't mean, however, **Tom Brady** is a first round draft pick. It just means that after his four game suspension, he should give you quality fantasy games more often than not.

As you review the rankings, note **Marshawn Lynch** is listed, not because he's playing this season, (he announced his retirement), but to point out that whoever replaces him for the Seahawks stands to finish high in the rankings in terms of quality fantasy games.

Also, players who scored high in the QFG rankings last season but who are expected to drop out of the Top 50 rankings this season or are a back-up, have been excluded. A good example of the former is **Demaryius Thomas** whose new quarterback is expected to be **Mark Sanchez**. A good example of the latter are **DeAngelo Williams** and **Karlos Williams** who would likely need a game with **Le'Veon Bell** and **LeSean McCoy** injured to make an expected fantasy impact.

	Pos	Player	Team	Rec	Gm	QFG	Rat	Top 200
1.	WR	Brandon Marshall	Jets	101	15	15	1.00	6
2.	WR	Eric Decker	Jets	75	14	14	1.00	37
3.	WR	Julio Jones	Falcons	127	15	14	0.93	2
4.	WR	Jarvis Landry	Dolphins	105	15	14	0.93	29
5.	RB	Mark Ingram	Saints	50	12	11	0.92	23
6.	WR	Julian Edelman	Patriots	61	9	8	0.89	61
7.	WR	Keenan Allen	Chargers	67	8	7	0.88	15
8.	WR	DeAndre Hopkins	Texans	104	15	13	0.87	13
9.	WR	Allen Robinson	Jaguars	75	15	13	0.87	5
10.	QB	Tom Brady	Patriots	-----	15	13	0.87	57
11.	TE	Rob Gronkowski	Patriots	70	14	12	0.86	12
12.	TE	Delanie Walker	Titans	85	14	12	0.86	106
13.	RB	Matt Forte	Bears	41	12	10	0.83	34
14.	RB	LeSean McCoy	Bills	32	12	10	0.83	33
15.	WR	Antonio Brown	Steelers	123	15	12	0.80	1
16.	WR	Larry Fitzgerald	Cardinals	103	15	12	0.80	39
17.	WR	Calvin Johnson	Lions	78	15	12	0.80	UR
18.	WR	Martavis Bryant	Steelers	50	10	8	0.80	UR
19.	RB	Jamaal Charles (IR)	Chiefs	21	5	4	0.80	10
20.	WR	Odell Beckham, Jr.	Giants	91	14	11	0.79	3
21.	RB	DeVonta Freeman	Falcons	71	14	11	0.79	4
22.	WR	John Brown	Cardinals	62	14	11	0.79	52
23.	WR	Alshon Jeffery	Bears	54	9	7	0.78	17
24.	TE	Jordan Reed	Redskins	83	13	10	0.77	32
25.	RB	Adrian Peterson	Vikings	29	15	11	0.73	24

26.	WR	AJ Green	Bengals	82	15	11	0.73	19
27.	TE	Gary Barnidge	Browns	71	15	11	0.73	45
28.	WR	Golden Tate	Lions	86	15	11	0.73	14
29.	WR	Jeremy Maclin	Chiefs	84	14	10	0.71	28
30.	WR	Allen Hurns	Jaguars	61	14	10	0.71	38
31.	RB	Todd Gurley	Rams	21	14	10	0.71	20
32.	WR	Steve Smith	Ravens	46	7	5	0.71	53
33.	RB	Marshawn Lynch	Seahawks	13	7	5	0.71	UR
34.	QB	Andy Dalton	Bengals	-----	13	9	0.70	131
35.	TE	Antonio Gates	Chargers	53	10	7	0.70	78
36.	QB	Cam Newton	Panthers	-----	15	10	0.69	36
37.	WR	Brandin Cooks	Saints	79	15	10	0.67	25
38.	QB	Carson Palmer	Cardinals	-----	15	10	0.67	107
39.	TE	Greg Olsen	Panthers	75	15	10	0.67	54
40.	WR	Michael Crabtree	Raiders	82	15	10	0.67	63
41.	WR	Sammy Watkins	Bills	49	12	8	0.67	27
42.	WR	TY Hilton	Colts	65	15	10	0.67	16
43.	RB	Frank Gore	Colts	34	15	10	0.67	82
44.	RB	Le'Veon Bell (IR)	Steelers	24	6	4	0.67	7
45.	RB	Jonathan Stewart	Panthers	16	13	8	0.62	71
46.	RB	Danny Woodhead	Chargers	73	15	9	0.60	48
47.	QB	Blake Bortles	Jaguars	-----	15	9	0.60	76
48.	QB	Aaron Rodgers	Packers	-----	16	9	0.60	41
49.	RB	David Johnson	Cardinals	36	16	9	0.60	9
50.	WR	Amari Cooper	Raiders	70	16	9	0.60	30

On The Cusp: RB **Doug Martin**, Cardinals (0.60), and WR **Randall Cobb**, Packers (0.60).

Risers: RB **David Johnson**, Cardinals; QB **Aaron Rodgers**, Packers; QB **Andrew Luck**, Colts; RB **Lamar Miller**, Texans; WR **Jordy Nelson**, Packers; WR **Dez Bryant**, Cowboys; WR **Keenan Allen**, Chargers; RB **Carlos Hyde**, 49ers; and, **Golden Tate**, Lions.

QFG RANKINGS
TOP 50 (Non-PPR)

These are the players you want on your team in PPR leagues. **QFG** is a measurement of "**quality fantasy games**" during the 2015 season. For running backs and wide receivers, this is the number of games the player posted double digit fantasy points. For quarterbacks, this is the number of games the player posted 240 yards passing and 2 pass TDs (4 points per TD) or its equivalent in fantasy points when including things like rush yards and rush TDs.

The ranks consider the actual fantasy points scored by the player, games played in a 16 week fantasy football season, and a valuation of the number of fantasy-relevant games played. Each player's **2016 Top 200 Rank** is noted so you can gauge the value of the player this year. In a real sense, these are players you can consider targeting as must-have players to have on your team. This doesn't mean, however, **Tom Brady** is a first round draft pick. It just means that after his four game suspension, he should give you quality fantasy games more often than not.

As review the rankings, note **Marshawn Lynch** is listed not because he's playing this season, (he announced his retirement), but to point out that whoever replaces him for the Seahawks stands to finish high in the rankings in terms of quality fantasy games.

Also, players who scored high in the QFG rankings last season but who are expected to drop out of the Top 50 rankings this season or are a back-up, have been excluded. A good example of the former is **Demaryius Thomas** whose new quarterback is expected to be **Mark Sanchez**. A good example of the latter are **DeAngelo Williams** and **Karlos Williams** who would likely need a game with **Le'Veon Bell** and **LeSean McCoy** injured to make an expected fantasy impact.

	Pos	Player	Team	Games	QFG	Ratio	Top 200
1.	QB	Tom Brady (SUS4)	Patriots	15	13	0.87	50
2.	RB	Jamaal Charles	Chiefs	5	4	0.80	7
3.	WR	Brandon Marshall	Jets	15	11	0.73	15
4.	WR	Allen Robinson	Jaguars	15	11	0.73	10
5.	RB	Marshawn Lynch	Seahawks	7	5	0.72	UR
6.	RB	DeVonta Freeman	Falcons	14	10	0.71	4
7.	WR	Odell Beckham, Jr.	Giants	14	11	0.71	5
8.	TE	Rob Gronkowski	Patriots	14	10	0.71	12
9.	RB	Todd Gurley	Rams	14	10	0.71	3
10.	WR	Eric Decker	Jets	14	10	0.71	47
11.	QB	Andy Dalton	Bengals	13	9	0.70	129
12.	QB	Cam Newton	Panthers	15	10	0.69	36
13.	WR	DeAndre Hopkins	Texans	15	10	0.67	18
14.	RB	Adrian Peterson	Vikings	15	10	0.67	13
15.	QB	Carson Palmer	Cardinals	15	10	0.67	87
16.	RB	Matt Forte	Bears	12	8	0.67	28
17.	RB	LeSean McCoy	Bills	12	8	0.67	19
18.	RB	Le'Veon Bell	Steelers	6	4	0.67	6
19.	WR	Antonio Brown	Steelers	15	9	0.60	1
20.	WR	Julio Jones	Falcons	15	9	0.60	8
21.	QB	Blake Bortles	Jaguars	15	9	0.60	73
22.	QB	Aaron Rodgers	Packers	15	9	0.60	42
23.	WR	Sammy Watkins	Bills	12	7	0.58	23
24.	RB	Mark Ingram	Saints	12	7	0.58	27
25.	WR	Allen Hurns	Jaguars	14	8	0.57	55

26.	QB	Ben Roethlisberger	Steelers	11	6	0.55	74
27.	RB	David Johnson	Cardinals	15	8	0.53	2
28.	TE	Gary Barnidge	Browns	15	8	0.53	59
29.	RB	Chris Ivory	Jets	15	8	0.53	89
30.	QB	Eli Manning	Giants	15	8	0.53	86
31.	QB	Philip Rivers	Chargers	15	8	0.53	130
32.	QB	Derek Carr	Raiders	15	8	0.53	103
33.	TE	Tyler Eifert	Bengals	12	6	0.50	60
34.	WR	John Brown	Cardinals	14	7	0.50	56
35.	WR	Mike Evans	Buccaneers	14	7	0.50	31
36.	WR	Michael Floyd	Cardinals	14	7	0.50	90
37.	QB	Drew Brees	Saints	14	7	0.50	49
38.	QB	Tyrod Taylor	Bills	12	6	0.50	102
39.	WR	Martavis Bryant	Steelers	10	5	0.50	UR
40.	WR	DeSean Jackson	Redskins	8	4	0.50	108
41.	RB	Doug Martin	Buccaneers	15	7	0.47	17
42.	WR	Doug Baldwin	Seahawks	15	7	0.47	105
43.	WR	AJ Green	Bengals	15	7	0.47	32
44.	TE	Greg Olsen	Panthers	15	7	0.47	72
45.	QB	Russell Wilson	Seahawks	15	7	0.47	66
46.	WR	Brandin Cooks	Saints	15	7	0.47	34
47.	WR	Jarvis Landry	Dolphins	15	7	0.47	43
48.	WR	Amari Cooper	Raiders	15	7	0.47	41
49.	QB	Kirk Cousins	Redskins	15	7	0.47	85
50.	QB	Ryan Fitzpatrick	Jets	15	7	0.47	138

On The Cusp: TE **Jordan Reed**, Redskins (0.46) and RB **Jonathan Stewart**, Panthers (0.46).

Risers: QB **Andrew Luck**, Colts; RB **Lamar Miller**, Texans; WR **Jordy Nelson**, Packers; WR **Dez Bryant**, Cowboys; WR **Keenan Allen**, Chargers; WR **T.Y. Hilton**, Colts; WR **Alshon Jeffery**, Bears; and, **Golden Tate**, Lions.

QUARTERBACK HANDCUFFS

If you like to carry a back-up quarterback on your roster, are in a deeper league where it makes sense to have one, or are in a two quarterback league, here are the potential No. 1 quarterbacks for up to 16 team leagues paired with the quarterbacks you can handcuff them to as QB2s. The QB2's bye week opponents are noted.

Bye	QB	Handcuff	Opponent
4	**Aaron Rodgers, Packers**	Carson Palmer, Cardinals	Rams
		Tyrod Taylor, Bills	@Patriots
	Teams on the Bye: Eagles,	Derek Carr, Raiders	@Ravens
	Packers	Andy Dalton, Bengals	Dolphins
		Philip Rivers, Chargers	Saints
		Matt Stafford, Lions	@Bears
		Ryan Fitzpatrick, Jets	Seahawks
		Tony Romo, Cowboys	@49ers
		Jay Cutler, Bears	Lions
		Marcus Mariota, Titans	@Texans
		Matt Ryan, Falcons	Panthers
		Joe Flacco, Ravens	Raiders
		Jameis Winston, Buccaneers	Broncos
		Brock Osweiler, Texans	Titans
		Teddy Bridgewater, Vikings	Giants
		Josh McCown, Browns	@Redskins
		Blaine Gabbert, 49ers	Cowboys
		Ryan Tannehill, Dolphins	Bengals
		Alex Smith, Chiefs	@Steelers
		Mark Sanchez, Broncos	@Buccaneers
		Jared Goff, Rams	@Cardinals
5	**Blake Bortles, Jaguars**	Carson Palmer, Cardinals	@49ers
	Drew Brees, Saints	Tyrod Taylor, Bills	@Rams
	Russell Wilson, Seahawks	Derek Carr, Raiders	Chargers
		Andy Dalton, Bengals	@Cowboys
	Teams on the Bye: Chiefs,	Philip Rivers, Chargers	@Raiders
	Jaguars, Saints, Seahawks	Matt Stafford, Lions	Eagles
		Ryan Fitzpatrick, Jets	@Steelers
		Tony Romo, Cowboys	Bengals
		Jay Cutler, Bears	@Colts
		Marcus Mariota, Titans	@Dolphins
		Matt Ryan, Falcons	@Broncos
		Joe Flacco, Ravens	Redskins
		Jameis Winston, Buccaneers	@Panthers
		Brock Osweiler, Texans	@Vikings
		Teddy Bridgewater, Vikings	Texans
		Josh McCown, Browns	Patriots
		Blaine Gabbert, 49ers	Cardinals
		Ryan Tannehill, Dolphins	Titans
		Sam Bradford, Eagles	@Lions
		Mark Sanchez, Broncos	Falcons
		Jared Goff, Rams	Bills
6	**Jameis Winston, Buccaneers**	Carson Palmer, Cardinals	Jets
		Tyrod Taylor, Bills	49ers

	Teams on the Bye: Vikings,	Derek Carr, Raiders	Chiefs
	Buccaneers	Andy Dalton, Bengals	@Patriots
		Philip Rivers, Chargers	Broncos
		Matt Stafford, Lions	Rams
		Ryan Fitzpatrick, Jets	@Cardinals
		Tony Romo, Cowboys	@Packers
		Jay Cutler, Bears	Jaguars
		Marcus Mariota, Titans	Browns
		Matt Ryan, Falcons	@Seahawks
		Joe Flacco, Ravens	@Giants
		Brock Osweiler, Texans	Colts
		Josh McCown, Browns	@Titans
		Blaine Gabbert, 49ers	@Bills
		Ryan Tannehill, Dolphins	Steelers
		Alex Smith, Chiefs	@Raiders
		Sam Bradford, Eagles	@Redskins
		Mark Sanchez, Broncos	@Chargers
		Jared Goff, Rams	@Lions
7	**Cam Newton, Panthers**	Carson Palmer, Cardinals	Seahawks
	Tony Romo, Cowboys	Tyrod Taylor, Bills	@Dolphins
		Derek Carr, Raiders	@Jaguars
	Teams on the Bye: Cowboys,	Andy Dalton, Bengals	Browns
	Panthers	Philip Rivers, Chargers	@Falcons
		Matt Stafford, Lions	Redskins
		Ryan Fitzpatrick, Jets	Ravens
		Jay Cutler, Bears	@Packers
		Marcus Mariota, Titans	Colts
		Matt Ryan, Falcons	Chargers
		Joe Flacco, Ravens	@Jets
		Jameis Winston, Buccaneers	@49ers
		Brock Osweiler, Texans	@Broncos
		Teddy Bridgewater, Vikings	@Eagles
		Josh McCown, Browns	@Bengals
		Blaine Gabbert, 49ers	Buccaneers
		Ryan Tannehill, Dolphins	Bills
		Alex Smith, Chiefs	Saints
		Sam Bradford, Eagles	Vikings
		Mark Sanchez, Broncos	Texans
		Jared Goff, Rams	Giants
8	**Eli Manning, Giants**	Carson Palmer, Cardinals	@Panthers
	Ben Roethlisberger, Steelers	Tyrod Taylor, Bills	Patriots
		Derek Carr, Raiders	@Buccaneers
	Teams on the Bye: 49ers,	Andy Dalton, Bengals	Redskins
	Dolphins, Giants, Ravens,	Philip Rivers, Chargers	@Broncos
	Rams, Steelers	Matt Stafford, Lions	@Texans
		Ryan Fitzpatrick, Jets	@Browns
		Tony Romo, Cowboys	Eagles
		Jay Cutler, Bears	Vikings
		Marcus Mariota, Titans	Jaguars
		Matt Ryan, Falcons	Packers
		Jameis Winston, Buccaneers	Raiders

		Brock Osweiler, Texans	Lions
		Teddy Bridgewater, Vikings	@Bears
		Josh McCown, Browns	Jets
		Alex Smith, Chiefs	@Colts
		Sam Bradford, Eagles	@Cowboys
		Mark Sanchez, Broncos	Chargers
9	**Tom Brady, Patriots**	Tyrod Taylor, Bills	@Seahawks
	Carson Palmer, Cardinals	Derek Carr, Raiders	Broncos
	Kirk Cousins, Redskins	Philip Rivers, Chargers	Titans
	Andy Dalton, Bengals	Matt Stafford, Lions	@Vikings
	Jay Cutler, Bears	Ryan Fitzpatrick, Jets	@Dolphins
		Tony Romo, Cowboys	@Browns
	Teams on the Bye: Bears,	Marcus Mariota, Titans	@Chargers
	Bengals, Cardinals, Patriots,	Matt Ryan, Falcons	@Buccaneers
	Redskins, Texans	Joe Flacco, Ravens	Steelers
		Jameis Winston, Buccaneers	Falcons
		Teddy Bridgewater, Vikings	Lions
		Josh McCown, Browns	Cowboys
		Blaine Gabbert, 49ers	Saints
		Ryan Tannehill, Dolphins	Jets
		Alex Smith, Chiefs	Jaguars
		Sam Bradford, Eagles	@Giants
		Mark Sanchez, Broncos	@Raiders
		Jared Goff, Rams	Panthers
10	**Andrew Luck, Colts**	Carson Palmer, Cardinals	49ers
	Tyrod Taylor, Bills	Andy Dalton, Bengals	@Giants
	Derek Carr, Raiders	Philip Rivers, Chargers	Dolphins
	Matt Stafford, Lions	Ryan Fitzpatrick, Jets	Rams
		Tony Romo, Cowboys	@Steelers
	Teams on the Bye: Bills, Colts,	Jay Cutler, Bears	@Buccaneers
	Lions, Raiders	Marcus Mariota, Titans	Packers
		Matt Ryan, Falcons	@Eagles
		Joe Flacco, Ravens	Browns
		Jameis Winston, Buccaneers	Bears
		Brock Osweiler, Texans	@Jaguars
		Teddy Bridgewater, Vikings	@Redskins
		Josh McCown, Browns	@Ravens
		Blaine Gabbert, 49ers	@Cardinals
		Ryan Tannehill, Dolphins	@Chargers
		Alex Smith, Chiefs	@Panthers
		Sam Bradford, Eagles	Falcons
		Mark Sanchez, Broncos	@Saints
		Jared Goff, Rams	@Jets
11	**Philip Rivers, Chargers**	Carson Palmer, Cardinals	@Vikings
	Ryan Fitzpatrick, Jets	Tyrod Taylor, Bills	@Bengals
	Matt Ryan, Falcons	Derek Carr, Raiders	Texans
		Andy Dalton, Bengals	Bills
	Teams on the Bye: Broncos,	Matt Stafford, Lions	Jaguars
	Chargers, Falcons, Jets	Tony Romo, Cowboys	Ravens

		Jay Cutler, Bears	@Giants
		Marcus Mariota, Titans	@Colts
		Joe Flacco, Ravens	@Cowboys
		Jameis Winston, Buccaneers	@Chiefs
		Brock Osweiler, Texans	@Raiders
		Teddy Bridgewater, Vikings	Cardinals
		Josh McCown, Browns	Steelers
		Blaine Gabbert, 49ers	Patriots
		Ryan Tannehill, Dolphins	@Rams
		Alex Smith, Chiefs	Buccaneers
		Sam Bradford, Eagles	@Seahawks
		Jared Goff, Rams	Dolphins
13	**Marcus Mariota, Titans**	Carson Palmer, Cardinals	Redskins
		Tyrod Taylor, Bills	@Raiders
	Teams on the Bye: Browns,	Derek Carr, Raiders	Bills
	Titans	Andy Dalton, Bengals	Eagles
		Philip Rivers, Chargers	Buccaneers
		Matt Stafford, Lions	@Saints
		Ryan Fitzpatrick, Jets	Colts
		Tony Romo, Cowboys	@Vikings
		Jay Cutler, Bears	49ers
		Matt Ryan, Falcons	Chiefs
		Joe Flacco, Ravens	Dolphins
		Jameis Winston, Buccaneers	@Chargers
		Brock Osweiler, Texans	@Packers
		Teddy Bridgewater, Vikings	Cowboys
		Blaine Gabbert, 49ers	@Bears
		Ryan Tannehill, Dolphins	@Ravens
		Alex Smith, Chiefs	@Falcons
		Sam Bradford, Eagles	@Bengals
		Mark Sanchez, Broncos	@Jaguars
		Jared Goff, Rams	@Patriots

QUARTERBACK-DEFENSE PAIRINGS

Unless you must have two defenses/special teams on your fantasy football roster, draft one defense/special team in your fantasy football draft and play the waiver wire during the bye week.

Fantasy footballers should avoid the situation of your quarterback playing your defense. It is fantasy football quicksand. When playing your quarterback against your defense, as one does well in the game, the other does worse, and *vice versa*. Your fantasy football team never seems to get ahead. So to maximize your roster, consider drafting a defense that never has to play your quarterback. The table below will help.

The quarterbacks listed are quarterbacks that could reasonably be drafted as fantasy football starters in 10, 12, 14, and 16 team leagues and two quarterback leagues. The listed defenses are defenses they will not play during the season. These are defenses ranked in or about the top-sixteen. We've listed the defenses in order of ranking.

Player, Team	Defenses / Special Teams (BYE Week)
Cam Newton, Panthers	Texans, Bengals, Patriots, Steelers, Jets, Jaguars, Packers, Bills
Aaron Rodgers, Packers	Cardinals, Broncos, Panthers, Bengals, Chiefs, Patriots, Rams, Steelers, Jets, Raiders, Bills
Drew Brees, Saints	Texans, Bengals, Vikings, Patriots, Steelers, Jets, Jaguars, Packers, Bills
Tom Brady, Patriots	Panthers, Vikings, Chiefs, Patriots, Raiders, Jaguars, Packers
Russell Wilson, Seahawks	Broncos, Texans, Bengals, Vikings, Chiefs, Steelers, Raiders, Jaguars, Packers
Andrew Luck, Colts	Cardinals, Seahawks, Panthers, Bengals, Patriots, Rams, Bills
Blake Bortles, Jaguars	Cardinals, Seahawks, Panthers, Bengals Patriots, Rams, Steelers, Jets
Ben Roethlisberger, Steelers	Cardinals, Broncos, Texans, Seahawks, Panthers, Vikings, Rams, Raiders, Jaguars, Packers
Kirk Cousins, Redskins	Broncos, Texans, Seahawks, Chiefs, Patriots, Rams, Jets, Raiders, Jaguars, Bills
Eli Manning, Giants	Cardinals, Broncos, Texans, Seahawks, Panthers, Chiefs, Patriots, Jets, Raiders, Jaguars, Bills
Carson Palmer, Cardinals	Broncos, Texans, Bengals, Chiefs, Steelers, Raiders, Jaguars, Packers
Tyrod Taylor, Bills	Broncos, Texans, Panthers, Vikings, Chiefs, Packers
Derek Carr, Raiders	Cardinals, Seahawks, Bengals, Vikings, Patriots, Rams, Steelers, Jets, Packers
Andy Dalton, Bengals	Cardinals, Seahawks, Panthers, Vikings, Chiefs, Rams, Raiders, Jaguars, Packers, Bills
Philip Rivers, Chargers	Cardinals, Seahawks, Bengals, Vikings, Patriots, Rams, Steelers, Jets, Packers, Bills
Matt Stafford, Lions	Cardinals, Broncos, Seahawks, Panthers, Bengals, Chiefs, Patriots, Steelers, Jets, Raiders, Bills
Ryan Fitzpatrick, Jets	Broncos, Texans, Panthers, Vikings, Jets, Raiders, Jaguars, Packers
Tony Romo, Cowboys	Cardinals, Broncos, Texans, Seahawks, Panthers, Chiefs, Patriots, Rams, Jets, Raiders, Jaguars, Bills
Jay Cutler, Bears	Cardinals, Broncos, Seahawks, Panthers, Bengals, Chiefs, Patriots, Rams, Steelers, Jets, Raiders, Bills
Marcus Mariota, Titans	Cardinals, Seahawks, Panthers, Bengals, Patriots, Rams, Steelers, Jets, Bills
Matt Ryan, Falcons	Texans, Bengals, Vikings, Patriots, Steelers, Jets, Jaguars, Bills

QUARTERBACK RANKINGS
(4-point TD Leagues)

	Player	Team	Value	BYE
1.	Cam Newton	Panthers	409.0	7
2.	Aaron Rodgers	Packers	387.0	4
3.	Drew Brees	Saints	376.5	5
4.	Tom Brady (SUS4)	Patriots	375.0 (281.3)	9
5.	Russell Wilson	Seahawks	360.5	5
6.	Andrew Luck (UPS)	Colts	359.0	10
7.	Blake Bortles	Jaguars	345.5	5
8.	Ben Roethlisberger	Steelers	341.0	8
9.	Kirk Cousins	Redskins	338.5	9
10.	Eli Manning	Giants	338.0	8
11.	Carson Palmer	Cardinals	338.0	9
12.	Tyrod Taylor	Bills	334.0	10
13.	Derek Carr (UPS)	Raiders	334.0	10
14.	Andy Dalton	Bengals	331.0	9
15.	Philip Rivers (NO)	Chargers	329.0	11
16.	Matt Stafford	Lions	327.5	10
17.	Ryan Fitzpatrick*	Jets	323.0	11
18.	Tony Romo (IRSK)	Cowboys	320.0	7
19.	Jay Cutler	Bears	304.0	9
20.	Marcus Mariota	Titans	301.0	13
21.	Matt Ryan	Falcons	300.5	11
22.	Joe Flacco	Ravens	296.0	8
23.	Jameis Winston	Buccaneers	293.0	6
24.	Brock Osweiler (NO)	Texans	283.0	9
25.	Teddy Bridgewater	Vikings	283.0	6
26.	Josh McCown* (NO)	Browns	278.0	13
27.	Blaine Gabbert (NO)	49ers	277.0	8
28.	Ryan Tannehill (NO)	Dolphins	277.0	8
29.	Alex Smith	Chiefs	271.0	5
30.	Sam Bradford (IRSK)* (NO)	Eagles	253.0	4
31.	Mark Sanchez* (NO)	Broncos	241.0	11
32.	Jared Goff* (R)	Rams	238.0	8

*Assumes the Week 1 Starter
(SUS4) = Assumes Tom Brady is suspended for the first 4-games of the season

Ranks reflect value based on 16 weeks of play. Ranks also reflect that a passing TD is worth 4 points for quarterbacks. Ranks reflect value based on 16 weeks of play. Past performance was considered as were issues relating to each team's offense including the offense run by the team's offensive coordinator, any coaching changes and personnel changes, and which players are listed as starters and back-ups on the most recent depth charts.

KEY: (NO) = New Offense; (UPS) = Upside; (IRSK) = Injury Risk; (INJ) = Injured; (DNS) = Downside; (R) = Rookie

QUARTERBACK RANKINGS
(6-point TD Leagues)

	Player	Team	Value	Bye
1.	Cam Newton	Panthers	479.0	7
2.	Aaron Rodgers	Packers	463.0	4
3.	Drew Brees	Saints	444.5	5
4.	Tom Brady (SUS4)	Patriots	440 (330)	9
5.	Russell Wilson	Seahawks	428.5	5
6.	Andrew Luck (UPS)	Colts	427.0	10
7.	Blake Bortles	Jaguars	409.5	5
8.	Eli Manning	Giants	408.0	8
9.	Kirk Cousins	Redskins	402.5	9
10.	Carson Palmer	Cardinals	402.0	9
11.	Ben Roethlisberger	Steelers	401.0	8
12.	Philip Rivers (NO)	Chargers	393.0	11
13.	Andy Dalton	Bengals	391.0	9
14.	Derek Carr (UPS)	Raiders	390.0	10
15.	Ryan Fitzpatrick*	Jets	389.0	11
16.	Matt Stafford	Lions	387.5	10
17.	Tyrod Taylor	Bills	382.0	10
18.	Tony Romo (IRSK)	Cowboys	365.0	7
19.	Marcus Mariota	Titans	361.0	13
20.	Jay Cutler	Bears	358.0	9
21.	Joe Flacco	Ravens	356.0	8
22.	Jameis Winston	Buccaneers	341.0	6
23.	Brock Osweiler (NO)	Texans	331.0	9
24.	Teddy Bridgewater	Vikings	331.0	6
25.	Josh McCown* (NO)	Browns	326.0	13
26.	Matt Ryan	Falcons	325.5	11
27.	Ryan Tannehill (NO)	Dolphins	325.0	8
28.	Blaine Gabbert (NO)	49ers	323.0	8
29.	Alex Smith	Chiefs	319.0	5
30.	Sam Bradford (IRSK)* (NO)	Eagles	301.0	4
31.	Jared Goff* (R)	Rams	288.0	8
32.	Mark Sanchez* (NO)	Broncos	285.0	11

*Assumes the Week 1 Starter
(SUS4) = Assumes Tom Brady is suspended for the first 4-games of the season

Ranks reflect value based on 16 weeks of play. Ranks also reflect that a passing TD is worth 4 points for quarterbacks. Ranks reflect value based on 16 weeks of play. Past performance was considered as were issues relating to each team's offense including the offense run by the team's offensive coordinator, any coaching changes and personnel changes, and which players are listed as starters and back-ups on the most recent depth charts.

KEY: (NO) = New Offense; (UPS) = Upside; (IRSK) = Injury Risk; (INJ) = Injured; (DNS) = Downside; (R) = Rookie

QUARTERBACK PROFILES

1. Cam Newton, Panthers - BYE: 7

If you aren't ecstatic at the prospect of having **Cam Newton** on your team, I'm not sure what can be done for you. Newton provides a solid option as a quarterback (where he threw for 3,837 yards, 35 touchdowns and only ten interceptions) and running back (where he ran for 636 yards and ten touchdowns) at the time. You might not win your quarterback matchup every week, but if you have even an average running back, you will rake in the fantasy points because of your run game. Newton and the Panthers will chomp at the bit to prove their Super Bowl run wasn't a fluke, especially after Newton gets his favorite target in **Kevin Benjamin** back. Cam Newton is primed to have a season even better than his MVP campaign. (GC)

2. Aaron Rodgers, Packers - BYE: 4

Aaron Rodgers has set the bar high for himself, so when he finished last season with 31 regular season touchdowns and 8 interceptions, it was a "down season" for him. Even without the services of his top wide receiver, **Jordy Nelson**, having a running back who played out of shape**, Eddie Lacy**, and the offensive line suffering injuries to most of their starters throughout the season, Rodgers was still one of the top fantasy quarterbacks. Things should only improve for Rodgers this season. Nelson is on track to be back to full strength this season, which will only help the Packers No. 2 wide receiver **Randall Cobb** get back to where he was in the 2014 season. From all reports, Eddie Lacy has gotten himself back into shape this offseason, so if he gets back to where he was in 2013 and 2014, this will make teams respect the running game and open up the passing game for Rodgers. A healthy offensive line will allow Rodgers time in the pocket, which should scare opposing defenses. If all goes according to plan, there is no reason to believe Rodgers won't be a Top 5 quarterback once again. Bank on 4,400 yards and 35-plus TDs from Rodgers this season. (JW)

3. Drew Brees, Saints - BYE: 5

If it isn't broke, don't fix it. **Drew Brees** is one of the most consistent quarterbacks in the league. Brees almost tallied his fifth 5,000 yard season in 2015, and he tied his second lowest interception total as a starter with 11. He's thrown for 30-plus TDs in eight consecutive seasons now. Drew Brees remains one of the strongest quarterbacks to pick in nearly every fantasy format. In part, it's because the Saints throw the football a ton, averaging over 625 time the past three seasons. Though **Marques Colston** is no longer a Saint, Brees has never been one to home in on one specific receiver. There are a host of receivers waiting to break out on the Saints. Expect more of the same from Drew Brees in 2016. Brees remains a Top 5 fantasy QB. (GC)

4. Tom Brady, Patriots - BYE: 9

What more can be said about Tom Brady? He put up another tremendous season in 2015, throwing for 4,770 yards and 36 touchdowns to only seven interceptions. He's showing NO signs of slowing down at age 38 and entering his seventeenth season. Tom Brady has new tight end **Martellus Bennett** to add to his other offensive playmakers and third-round rookie, Malcolm Mitchell. The only thing that may slow Brady down is the potential four-game "Deflategate" suspension which is looming. Regardless, even if Brady must sit out a quartet of games, he is still in the upper-tier of fantasy quarterbacks (top five) you want on your team. Brady is a solid selection in round five or six of all fantasy drafts. (DG)

5. Russell Wilson, Seahawks - BYE: 5

Russell Wilson was nothing short of amazing beginning in Week 11 when he went on a tear throwing 24 touchdowns in 7 games. Because of this, Wilson dropped the talk of not carrying the offense with **Marshawn Lynch** on the shelf. He threw for a whopping 34 touchdowns to just eight interceptions on the season, while improving his completion average from 63.1% in 2014 to 68.1% in 2015. He also eclipsed the 4,000-yard barrier with 4,024 through the air. He scaled back the rushing totals a little bit as he dropped from 118 attempts to 103 attempts and his average of 7.2 yards in 2014 dropped to 5.4 yards in 2015. The Seahawks want to return to running the football. They drafted three running backs as proof of this. Wilson is a Top 5 quarterback option going into fantasy football drafts as the offense will rely on him to carry the load early while **Thomas Rawls** returns from injury and the Seahawks continue to work with their running game. An offensive line that allowed 46.0 sacks and the second most quarterback smacks (160.0) is a concern. Expect a small step back in yardage and/or touchdown passes (say 3,900 yards, 31 TDs) as a lot of his production came at the end of last season. (SB)

6. Andrew Luck, Colts - BYE: 10

There are some who believe **Andrew Luck** is this season's best QB. After his stellar 2014 year where he threw for 4,761 yards, 40 touchdowns and 16 interceptions, Luck struggled in 2015 due to injuries and was eventually shut down after Week 9. With a continuous string of injuries, Luck played in just 7 games where he produced 1,881 yards for 15 touchdowns on 12 interceptions. It was just an awful season for Luck and fantasy team managers who drafted him. Andrew Luck should bounce back for 2016. While the Colts may not throw the football as much, he should still zero in on 4,300 yards and thirty-plus TDs. He's a top six quarterback who you should get as a steal in Round 5 or later. (IE/JS)

7. Blake Bortles, Jaguars - BYE: 5

Everyone wants **Blake Bortles** to make an impact earlier than he will. People held high expectations for Bortles from the moment he stepped on the field. Last season was a breakout one for Blake Bortles. While he had solid numbers (4,428 yards, 35 TDs), two things beyond his high interception rate (18 total) are fairly concerning: he has one of the lower completion percentages in the league (58.6%), and he gets sacked an awful lot (2015: 51; 2014: 55). The latter is only partially his fault, but they're both roadblocks to consistent fantasy success. The Jaguars passed getting Bortles help along the offensive line in the draft. While Bortles will likely continue throwing a lot of interceptions, he should be able to offset them with quality numbers in the passing game to the tune of around 4,500 yards passing and 30-plus TDs. Blake Bortles is a Top 10 fantasy option this season. Target Bortles as a QB1 in Round 7 of fantasy drafts. (GC)

8. Ben Roethlisberger, Steelers - BYE: 8

Entering his thirteenth season, **Ben Roethlisberger** has taken his place among the elite quarterbacks in the league. Big Ben is coming off of a season where he threw for over 3,900 yards and 21 touchdowns in only 12 games. With a full complement of all-pro weapons surrounding him, including **Antonio Brown** and **LeVeon Bell**, Roethlisberger has fully grasped **Todd Haley**'s offense and is likely to exceed last year's lofty numbers. If, and this is a big if, Big Ben can stay healthy for 16 games, 4,500 yards and 35 touchdowns are numbers within reach in 2016. (RB)

9. Kirk Cousins, Redskins - BYE: 9

Last season, **Kirk Cousins** showed he can be a starting quarterback in the league. Cousins threw for 4,166 yards and 29 touchdowns to only 11 interceptions. His completion percentage was 69.8%, tops in the league. In the back half of the season, he showed he could fully throw multi-TD games (four of 3 TDs or more) and rushing for TDs with 5 on the season. The only thing that might worry fantasy team managers is that Cousins' quality fantasy game (QFG) rating was 47%. One way to view this is Cousins will help you win your fantasy games about half of the time. In his favor, Cousins should throw the football over 540 times this season, to a talented group of wide receivers. Kirk Cousins should pace 4,400 yards passing and 30-plus TDs. Cousins can be viewed as a low end QB1 in standard sized leagues. (IE/JS)

10. Eli Manning, Giants - BYE: 8

Eli Manning followed one of his best statistical seasons in 2014 (379/601 for 4,410 yards and 30 TDs) with a better one in 2015 (387/618 for 4,432 yards and 35 TDs). Manning had the highest quarterback rating (93.6), touchdowns thrown (35), and most completions (387) in his career last season. His average yards per game (277) was the second highest in his career. With back to back seasons throwing for thirty or more touchdowns and fewer than fifteen interceptions, Eli Manning is officially an elite quarterback. With the Giants expected to have a pass heavy offense once again, and throwing to **Odell Beckham, Jr.**, **Victor Cruz** and, rookie **Sterling Shepard**, expect Manning to at least replicate his stats from last season. Manning is a Top 10 fantasy option at quarterback. (AG)

11. Carson Palmer, Cardinals - BYE: 9

Having reached 36 years of age, **Carson Palmer** qualifies as 'old' in football terms. The former Heisman winner has also suffered a pair of devastating knee injuries, but has persevered to continue to play at a high level, arguably an MVP level. Palmer racked up his *best season as a pro* in 2015, notching a QBR over 104 while passing for 4,600 yards and 35 TDs against just 17 turnovers. Signed through 2017, Palmer has provided the stability and leadership the Cardinals have lacked since **Kurt Warner** retired. An unquestioned starter in one of the league's top offensive units, expect a healthy Palmer to be among the Top 10 QB options in fantasy. He'll be at or near the numbers he posted last season. The only hesitation with Palmer is in dynasty leagues where he should be paired with a younger option to build for the future. (CB)

12. Tyrod Taylor, Bills - BYE: 10

Coming off of a breakout season where **Tyrod Taylor** scored double digit fantasy points in all but one of the games he played in, he is expected to continue to threaten defenses with both his arm and his legs. A healthy **Sammy Watkins** (this is key) and a solid backfield should put the right offensive weapons at his disposal and help make Taylor a solid QB in fantasy leagues again. Tag Taylor for 3,400 yards passing and 20 pass TDs while chipping in an additional 600 yards on the ground and 4 rush TDs. He's in the conversation as a low-end QB1 in 12 team leagues or larger. He loses value if your league gives a full 6 points for passing TDs and he is a QB2 in those formats. (JQ)

13. Derek Carr, Raiders - BYE: 10

Derek Carr has emerged as an up-and-coming young quarterback in the league. Carr's second season stats comprised 3,987 yards with a completion percentage of 61.1%. His touchdown to interception ratio compared to future hall of fame quarterbacks. Carr threw 32 touchdowns and only 13 interceptions. He posted quality fantasy games (QFG rating) in at least 50% of his games. With a talented set of wide receivers and a solid running back, Carr is set to take the next step. View him as a quarterback capable of a 4,000-plus yard season and 32-plus TDs. He will likely need a play-maker who did not step up last season, to step up this season to help him improve from last season. Derek Carr is a border-line QB1 in 12-team leagues. (IE/JS)

14. Andy Dalton, Bengals - BYE: 9

Andy Dalton is a roller-coaster ride for any fantasy owner. In 2015, Dalton was pretty reliable, especially in the second half of the season before he was injured in Week 14. However, Dalton's third best receiver, Mohamed Sanu, is gone, and his best red zone target, **Tyler Eifert**, may not be ready for the start of the season. Marvin Jones, who missed the 2015 season, has moved on to the Lions. Some might argue that Dalton's success hinged on stellar offensive line and wide receiver play. So, be it. Dalton should bounce back for 4,000 yards and 30 TDs this season. It's his sixth year as a pro and the Bengals got him some help adding the often under-used veteran **Brandon LaFell** in free agency, and by adding rookie **Tyler Boyd**, and to a lesser extent rookie **Cody Core**, through the draft. If Eifert misses time, **Tyler Kroft** will be there to take his place. The Bengals top offensive line is a bonus. View Andy Dalton as a border-line QB1, better drafted as a high end QB2, in 12 team leagues, draftable in Round 9 or Round 10 of fantasy drafts. (GC/JS)

15. Phillip Rivers, Chargers - BYE: 11

Rivers has been a low-end QB1 for years. Even at age 35, there's no reason to believe he won't continue to produce. Despite a ghastly run game, injuries to his key receivers and a poor offensive line, **Philip Rivers** managed over 4,000 yards through the air and an average of 30 TDs for the past three seasons. The return of Offensive Coordinator **Ken Wisenhunt**, who helped lead the Chargers to the playoffs in 2013, adding veteran center **Matt Slauson** and speedster wide receiver **Travis Benjamin**, and the return of a healthy **Keenan Allen** should lead to another solid season for Rivers. If **Melvin Gordon** can pick up his run game, there's no reason not to expect Philip Rivers to continue to put up above average fantasy numbers. (GC)

16. Matthew Stafford, Lions - BYE: 10

Matthew Stafford looks to pick up where he left off last season after leading the Lions to a 6-2 finish, throwing 20 TDs and only 4 INTs after OC **Jim Bob Cooter** took over. The 28 year old gunslinger should be a productive QB with second year RB **Ameer Abdullah** settling in and WR **Golden Tate** ready to pick up the production as the Lions' top WR. Some may expect a sharp decline in Stafford's production with **Calvin Johnson** retired. While Stafford won't be better without Calvin Johnson, he shouldn't be much worse. Expect 4,200 yards and near 30 TDs as the Lions lean on the pass. Matt Stafford makes for a QB2 in standard leagues and a borderline QB1 in larger 16 team leagues. (JQ/JS)

17. *Ryan Fitzpatrick, Jets - BYE: 11

Fitzpatrick is coming off a career season, his best as a pro where he threw for 3,905 yards and 31 TDs. **Ryan Fitzpatrick** also set the Jets franchise record for touchdowns thrown in a season with 31. Despite the Jets having two former college football star quarterbacks on their roster, Fitzpatrick is still number one on their depth chart. Throwing to big targets like **Brandon Marshall** and **Eric Decker** has its advantages. Add to the mix speedster wide receiver **Devin Smith** and All Pro running back **Matt Forte**, and Fitzpatrick looks primed for at least a repeat of last season's statistical output. Now, the Jets must get him under contract. If they fail to do so, the Jets playmakers will be adversely affected to varying degrees. (IE/JS)

18. Tony Romo, Cowboys - BYE: 7

Tony Romo has had up and down seasons with the Cowboys ever since they drafted him in 2004. However, his quarterback numbers reflect otherwise. Over the years, Romo has consistently thrown for over 4,000 yards, or close to it. His 2015 campaign was a different season for him though. Due to injuries, Romo played in just 4 games. He had similar difficulties a few years before, in 2010, where he only played in 6 games. The year following that season in 2011, Romo threw for over 4,000 yards. History tells fantasy team managers to not overlook Romo because he could have another big post-injury year. Several quarterbacks have moved ahead of Romo in the rankings, however. View Romo as a solid QB2 draftable in Round 10. (IE)

19. Jay Cutler, Bears - BYE: 9

Nobody will be sold on **Jay Cutler** as a QB1. Cutler is simply too volatile and has no bevy of proven receivers. However, he had the highest quarterback rating of his career in 2015 due in large part to his lowest interception rate in a full season. Without **Matt Forte** in town, however, and with a new offensive coordinator, the task seems tall for Cutler to repeat last year's success if you want to call it that. However, Cutler has a group of running backs with a lot of potential. If Jay Cutler can continue to rely on quick passes, and get reliable running behind an improved offensive line, he could have a solid season. Factor in including **Kevin White**, a legitimate target alongside **Alshon Jeffery**, and Cutler has options. Cutler is a middle to low-end QB2 draftable in the later rounds of fantasy drafts for those who handcuff their quarterbacks in standard sized leagues. (GC)

20. Marcus Mariota, Titans - BYE: 13

The jury is still out whether **Marcus Mariota** can develop into a franchise quarterback. A concern is Mariota missed four games in 2015 (five if you want to count the lone quarter he played against the Patriots) as a rookie. This dampened what was a solid rookie season where he paced 3,300 yards passing and 25 TDs had he played a full season. Marcus Mariota's resume as it stands provides a nice TD/INT ratio with 19 touchdowns and 10 interceptions. However, Mariota was sacked 38 times including seven games where he was sacked 3-plus times. The Titans got help for the offensive line in the offseason. The receiving group was also subpar for the majority of 2015. So, Marcus Mariota should welcome the change to a more traditional run heavy offense this season. Mariota should make strides this season to becoming a better quarterback and he'll pick better spots in which to run the ball as his 7.4 yards per carry suggests he is explosive. The durability concerns and style of play the Titans will implement hurts his draft stock this season. He's a low-end QB2 and worth a later round draft pick for those who carry a second quarterback in standard sized leagues. (SB)

21. Matt Ryan, Falcons - BYE: 11

Matt Ryan has struggled to be something more than a 4,700 yard passer for over 29 TDs. Ryan has been consistent, however. He's thrown for over 4,500 yards in each of his last 4 seasons. Last season, Matt Ryan threw for 4,591 and 21 TDs and had a 66.3% completion percentage. Troubling, however, only one-third of Matt Ryan's games are quality fantasy games. The hope is Ryan feels much more comfortable in Offensive Coordinator **Kyle Shanahan's** offense in 2016. He should improve on last season's TD totals which will make him a low-end QB2 in 4-point passing TD formats. (IE)

22. Joe Flacco, Ravens - BYE: 8

A torn ACL ended **Joe Flacco**'s 2016 season six games early. Still, he completed a career high 64.4 percent of his passes despite throwing to a receiving group which was mostly young and missing its best players. In his first season in Marc Trestman's offense Flacco was on pace for 600-plus passing attempts and 4,400-plus yards. However, pacing 22 TDs was far short of his career high of 27 TDs. Joe Flacco and the Ravens say he will be ready for 'Day One' of training camp. As long as that's the case, Flacco should throw to a healthy **Steve Smith, Sr.,** a rejuvenated **Mike Wallace,** and emerging **Kamar Aiken,** and hopefully, an explosive and healthy **Breshad Perriman.** There's a lot to like about the passing offense under Marc Trestman. Ideally, Flacco should press for 30 TDs. Treat Joe Flacco like a low-end QB2 with upside, draftable late in fantasy drafts. (FG)

23. Jameis Winston, Buccaneers - BYE: 6

In his rookie season, Winston proved to skeptics he was passionate for football. The runner-up to the offensive rookie of the year tossed 22 touchdowns with over 4,000 yards, adding 6 rushing touchdowns to the mix. However, Winston endured growing pains, tossing 15 interceptions. He also showed his frustration when the offense struggled. Among fantasy quarterbacks, Winston ranked in the middle of the pack. He posted some big games too. Still, Winston is a QB2 going into the 2016 season. What could hold Winston back are a lack of options coming from the receiver position and running back position. With some mild improvement, Jameis Winston could post 4,400 yards and top last season's touchdown totals. Winston is a late-round grab but will likely land on many fantasy waiver wires to start the season. He's a hold in dynasty leagues. (EG)

24. Brock Osweiler, Texans - BYE: 9

Brock Osweiler's entrenchment as the Texans' starter does not equate to a tremendous boost in fantasy production. Osweiler's production with the Broncos, while impressive for his first snaps as a starter, were below average. Despite a completion percentage of 61.8%, his 10 passing touchdowns to six interceptions wasn't very good. Osweiler is a high end QB2 coming into a very complex offense. Besides, the Texans draft signaled that they will go more up-tempo this year and speed has become a priority as **Lamar Miller, Will Fuller** and **Tyler Ervin** all possess the ability to provide one or two highlight plays each week. The Texans will run the football a lot. The only difference for Osweiler is he is learning a new offense with new players. Expect similar numbers to those Osweiler could have posted last season as a full-time starter, around 3,900 yards and 24 TDs on 15 interceptions. Osweiler should go undrafted in fantasy drafts. (SB)

25. Teddy Bridgewater, Vikings - BYE: 6

Bridgewater will enter his second full season as the Vikings starting quarterback, his third overall. The best way to describe Bridgewater's performance during his first full season of starting would be inconsistent. If you review **Teddy Bridgewater**'s stats from each game he played in last season, the first thing that will pop out is that he threw no touchdown in 6 out of the 17 games he played in, including the playoff loss to the Seahawks. However, you will notice that not all of what Bridgewater did was average or below average last season. Bridgewater had 2 games (against the Lions and the Cardinals) that saw him throw for over 300 yards and a game against the Bears that saw him go 17-of-20 for 231 yards and 4 touchdown passes. This suggests Bridgewater is still a developing but has the potential to be a solid starting caliber quarterback. Besides running back **Adrian Peterson** and tight end **Kyle Rudolph**, the Vikings really haven't provided Teddy Bridgewater much of a supporting cast. Wide receiver **Stefon Diggs** had a solid rookie season and should improve in his second season. They also spent a first round pick on a wide receiver, Ole Miss wide receiver **Laquon Treadwell**. Bridgewater will need for his offensive line to step up this season and give him time in the pocket. Bridgewater isn't worth a draft pick for your fantasy team just yet. His yardage is expected to be below 4,000 yards and his TD total just over 20. (JW)

26. *Josh McCown, Browns - BYE: 13

The 36 year old veteran **Josh McCown** is expected to compete with **Robert Griffin III** for the starting job after McCown played in only 8 games in 2015. McCown posted reasonable numbers in his eight games, throwing for 2,109 yards with 12 TDs and only 4 INTs. McCown has shown that he can produce, but as of late has been hampered by injury. While indications are Robert Griffin III will win the starters' job, McCown's body of work shows he's likely more effective. (JQ)

27. Blaine Gabbert, 49ers - BYE: 8

Entering his sixth season, Blaine Gabbert was long considered a bust until he showed signs of being a competent starting QB last season. He started the final eight games in 2015 after Colin Kaepernick went on IR for shoulder surgery. In those contests, Gabbert posted 2,031 yards and 11 total touchdowns. Still only twenty-six year old, Gabbert has every opportunity to harness the reigns of the 49ers offense. Look for him to be a bye-week option if you need a QB in the pinch, especially if the 49ers are going up against a good offense as their defense is still in rebuild mode. (DG)

28. Ryan Tannehill, Dolphins. BYE 8

Despite the team not making much noise last season, Tannehill was still in the upper half of quarterbacks. He finished 9th in passing yards with 24 touchdowns (more than **Ben Roethlisberger** and **Matt Ryan**), and he only threw 12 interceptions (only one more than **Drew Brees**). However, because he threw the football 585 times (eighth most in the league), his QBR rating was low at 43.15, thirty-first overall. In fantasy, he was plain inconsistent. **Adam Gase** is said to be a quarterback guru, so this year Tannehill is supposed to be better. Tannehill will need to improve upon his touchdown total if he will make an impact. Otherwise, history is history, and he'll be available in the late rounds as a low-end QB2. (TA)

29. Alex Smith, Chiefs - BYE: 5

Alex Smith has thrown over 3,200 yards in all three of his most recent seasons with the Chiefs. One aspect that goes unnoticed with Smith is the use of his legs. Smith not only passed for almost 3,500 yards and 20 touchdowns in 2015, but he also rushed for 498 yards, averaging 31 yards per game, and 2 TDs. Alex Smith doesn't produce the fantasy points team managers want from their quarterbacks, including their back-up quarterbacks. The big reason for this is the Chiefs have a run first, ball control offense. (IE)

30. Sam Bradford, Eagles - BYE: 4

Sam Bradford finished 7-7 as the Eagles starter in 2015 where he had his best season as a pro despite missing two games (3,725 yards, 21 TDs, 14 INTs). He is the Eagles projected starter even with No. 2 overall pick **Carson Wentz** on the roster. New Head Coach **Doug Pederson** has quite the coaching history. Significantly, he was the Offensive Coordinator for the Chiefs from 2013 to 2015. Bradford threw for 3,725 yards and 19 TDs last year. The Eagles offense should be conservative. To see Bradford exceed last season's numbers in 16 games would be quite the fete. Besides, there is always the chance back-up **Chase Daniel** or **Carson Wentz** becomes the team's starter at some point this season. Sam Bradford also has quite the injury history. Bradford should be undrafted. (JQ/JS)

31. Mark Sanchez, Broncos - BYE: 11

Widely expected to open the season under center for the defending Super Bowl champions, **Mark Sanchez** could well exceed expectations in 2016. **Gary Kubiak** has a history of getting career seasons out of journeymen quarterbacks like **Matt Schaub** and **Jake Plummer**, and Sanchez played in an offensive scheme very similar to Kubiak's during his days at USC. However, given his proven habit of turning the ball over and with promising rookie **Paxton Lynch** waiting in the wings, Sanchez should only be a bye week waiver wire option. He's expected to post around 3,800 yards and 22 TDs should he start all season long. Mark Sanchez will go undrafted in most leagues. (DK)

32. Jared Goff, Rams - BYE: 8

Although the Rams haven't officially named **Jared Goff** the week 1 starter, Jared Goff will be the Week 1 starter. As a first overall draft pick, expectations are sky high for the California native. With **Todd Gurley** carrying the ground game, Goff is expected to be the savior of the newly relocated Rams. It is too early to tell how productive Goff will be. He's a low-end QB2 for fantasy in redraft leagues. Goff will be a high risk, high reward fantasy pick. Jared Goff is obviously a top five pick in dynasty leagues. If he throws for 3,400 yards and 25 TDs, that'd be a good season for the rookie quarterback. (JQ/JS)

33. *Robert Griffin III, Browns - BYE: 13

Robert Griffin III is hoping to resurrect his career in Cleveland. He will have to earn the starting spot by taking it away from **Josh McCown**, the 2015 starter. If Griffin is named the starter and recaptures his old form from his rookie season, he could add some explosiveness to a Browns offense that ranked thirtieth in points per game in 2015. It remains unclear whether the 2012 Offensive Rookie of the Year can reclaim the success he had early in his career with the Redskins. RGIII should begin the season on fantasy pines in most leagues. He hasn't played in a regular season game in over a year. (JQ)

34. Jimmy Garoppolo, Patriots - BYE: 9

Unless things change, **Jimmy Garoppolo** will be the starting quarterback for the Patriots for the first four weeks of the season. He'll have games against the Cardinals, Dolphins, Texans, and Bills with only the Cardinals game on the road. The Patriots will likely go run heavy with their offense. While it wouldn't surprise for Jimmy Garoppolo to play well for a back-up, with two games of 200-plus yards passing and two multi-TD games, it would surprise for Garoppolo to do much better. He's not worth a fantasy pick even to play him for four games. Don't waste a valuable bench spot on Jimmy Garoppolo. If he does better than expected, you can always pick-up-and-play him. For fantasy football purposes, this is **Tom Brady**'s team and Garoppolo is just keeping the seat warm. (JS)

35. Colin Kaepernick, 49ers - BYE: 8

The script of Colin Kaepernick's career the last few years could be sold in Hollywood as a soap opera, it's been so topsy-turvy. From the heights of stardom after leading the 49ers to the 2012 Super Bowl to Blaine Gabbert's backup two years later. Coming back from three off season surgeries, 'Captain K' hasn't seen the field yet in OTAs, but should be ready for training camp. He'll be behind the eight ball in new coach Chip Kelly's system and have to battle with Gabbert to be the team's starting signal caller. Consider Kaep in the high-risk, high-reward late round flier option in deeper leagues who might boom for you if he returns to his prior form. In smaller leagues, he's undraftable. (DG)

36. Paxton Lynch, Broncos - BYE: 11

Selected with the 26th overall pick in the 2016 draft, Lynch could well be the Broncos future franchise quarterback. Although his size (6'-7", 244 pounds) immediately provokes comparisons to former Denver QB **Brock Osweiler**, that's where they end. Lynch has a more compact throwing motion and much better athleticism and mobility than the current Texans signal-caller, which make him an ideal fit for the **Gary Kubiak** offense. Despite his immense upside, however, Lynch played in a spread offense in college which means he'll probably need a year on the sidelines to fine-tune his mechanics and football IQ before he's ready to take the field as a pro. While it is true the Broncos want to speed up that learning curve, the team has clarified they will not risk stunting his growth by rushing him into action too soon. **Paxton Lynch** is a worthwhile investment in dynasty leagues. (DK)

37. Carson Wentz, - Eagles BYE: 4

All indications are **Carson Wentz** will spend his first season on the pine holding a clipboard and learning about football as it is played at a professional level. However, don't be surprised if the Eagles passing game falters, they don't turn to the rookie sooner rather than later. It's the nature of the pro game when your passing game struggles, to see if another player can give the offense a spark. Wentz played in a pro-style offense and should be better ready than most. He won't be a draft pick in fantasy re-draft leagues. Carson Wentz is obviously a top add in dynasty drafts. (JS)

38. Jeff Driskel, 49ers - BYE: 8

Jeff Driskel is a sixth round rookie from Louisiana Tech and will battle free agent signee Thad Lewis for the third-string QB position. Expect Driskel to beat out Lewis in training camp. Driskel lit up Conference USA last year, putting up 4,033 passing yards and 28 TDs to earn conference newcomer of the year and All-Conference honorable mention. Driskel has the size (6 foot 4, 234 pounds) and speed (4.56 40-yard dash, a QB best at the NFL Combine), to be an absolute perfect fit in **Chip Kelly**'s offense. This is why some have high hopes for Driskel, as the QB competition in front of him is very unsettled. Consider Driskel an off-the-radar deep sleeper and more of a dynasty project. (DG)

RUNNING BACK RANKINGS (PPR)

	Player	Team	Value	BYE
1.	DeVonta Freeman	Falcons	323.2	11
2.	Le'Veon Bell	Steelers	311.5	8
3.	David Johnson	Cardinals	302.6	9
4.	Jamaal Charles	Chiefs	300.5	5
5.	Todd Gurley	Rams	268.6	8
6.	Lamar Miller (NO)	Texans	263.6	9
7.	Ezekiel Elliott (R)	Cowboys	257.1	7
8.	Mark Ingram	Saints	256.0	5
9.	Adrian Peterson (IRSK)	Vikings	252.4	6
10.	LeSean McCoy	Bills	250.5	10
11.	Matt Forte (NO)	Jets	245.6	11
12.	Jeremy Langford (DNS)	Bears	243.0	9
13.	Eddie Lacy	Packers	242.5	4
14.	Doug Martin	Buccaneers	236.6	6
15.	Thomas Rawls (INJ) (UPS)	Seahawks	236.0	5
16.	Dion Lewis (DNS)	Patriots	235.4	9
17.	C.J. Anderson (UPS)	Broncos	228.5	11
18.	Carlos Hyde (NO) (UPS)	49ers	224.1	8
19.	Danny Woodhead (NO)	Chargers	223.0	11
20.	DeMarco Murray (IRSK)	Titans	222.0	13
21.	Latavius Murray	Raiders	220.0	10
22.	Jay Ajayi (NO) (UPS) (IRSK)	Dolphins	213.2	8
23.	Duke Johnson (NO)	Browns	211.0	13
24.	Ryan Mathews (NO) (IRSK) (UPS)	Eagles	206.5	4
25.	Melvin Gordon (NO)	Chargers	205.0	11
26.	Ameer Abdullah (UPS)	Lions	203.8	10
27.	Jonathan Stewart (IRSK)	Panthers	200.8	7
28.	Matt Jones (UPS)	Redskins	197.0	9
29.	Isaiah Crowell (NO)	Browns	196.1	13
30.	Jeremy Hill	Bengals	192.7	9
31.	Frank Gore	Colts	189.5	10
32.	Javorius "Buck" Allen	Ravens	184.5	8
33.	Justin Forsett (DNS)	Ravens	183.9	8
34.	LeGarrette Blount	Patriots	181.6	9
35.	Theo Riddick	Lions	180.0	10
36.	Chris Ivory	Jaguars	175.0	5
37.	T.J. Yeldon	Jaguars	167.3	5
38.	Rashad Jennings	Giants	161.6	8
39.	Charles Sims	Buccaneers	158.4	6
40.	DeVontae Booker (R) (UPS)	Broncos	154.0	11
41.	Karlos Williams	Bills	153.0	10
42.	Bilal Powell	Jets	141.9	11
43.	Gio Bernard	Bengals	141.5	9
44.	Paul Perkins (R)	Giants	141.0	8
45.	Wendell Smallwood (R) (UPS)	Eagles	138.0	4
46.	Shane Vereen	Giants	128.5	8
47.	DeAndre Washington (R)	Raiders	128.0	10

48.	Kenyan Drake (R)	Dolphins	122.5	8
49.	Benny Cunningham	Rams	117.0	8
50.	Derrick Henry (R) (UPS)	Titans	113.0	13
51.	James White	Patriots	110.2	9
52.	James Starks	Packers	105.4	4
53.	CJ Spiller (IRSK)	Saints	105.4	5
54.	Alfred Blue	Texans	103.8	9
55.	Chris Thompson	Redskins	103.0	9
56.	Tevin Coleman	Falcons	99.0	11
57.	Andre Ellington (IRSK)	Cardinals	94.2	9
58.	Darren McFadden (IRSK)	Cowboys	88.4	7
59.	C.J. Prosise (R)	Seahawks	88.0	5
60.	Jerick McKinnon	Vikings	87.5	6
61.	Kenneth Dixon (R)	Ravens	78.0	8
62.	Darren Sproles (NO)	Eagles	74.0	4
63.	Cameron Artis-Payne	Panthers	71.0	7
64.	Mike Tolbert	Panthers	70.5	7
65.	Khiry Robinson (NO)	Jets	64.0	11
66.	Charcandrick West	Chiefs	63.0	5
67.	Robert Turbin (NO) (UPS)	Colts	63.0	10
68.	Ronnie Hillman	Broncos	63.0	11
69.	Tim Hightower	Saints	63.0	5
70.	Alfred Morris	Cowboys	57.8	7
71.	Brandon Bolden	Patriots	57.8	9
72.	Shaun Draughn (NO)	49ers	56.5	8
73.	Jonathan Grimes	Texans	54.0	9
74.	Chris Johnson	Cardinals	50.2	9
75.	Ka'Deem Carey	Bears	48.5	9
76.	DeAngelo Williams (UPS)	Steelers	48.1	8
77.	Branden Oliver	Chargers	39.8	11
78.	Matt Asiata	Vikings	39.0	6
79.	Keith Marshall (R)	Redskins	37.0	9
80.	Damien Williams (NO)	Dolphins	35.5	8

Ranks reflect value based on 16 weeks of play. Past performance was considered as were issues relating to each team's offense including the offense run by the team's offensive coordinator, any coaching changes and personnel changes, and which players are listed as starters and back-ups on the most recent depth charts.

KEY: (NO) = New Offense; (UPS) = Upside; (IRSK) = Injury Risk; (INJ) = Injured; (DNS) = Downside; (R) = Rookie

RUNNING BACK RANKINGS (Non-PPR)

	Player	Team	Value	BYE
1.	David Johnson	Cardinals	252.6	9
2.	Todd Gurley	Rams	248.6	8
3.	DeVonta Freeman	Falcons	246.2	11
4.	Le'Veon Bell (IRSK)	Steelers	241.5	8
5.	Jamaal Charles	Chiefs	240.5	5
6.	Lamar Miller (NO)	Texans	223.6	9
7.	Adrian Peterson (IRSK)	Vikings	222.4	6
8.	Ezekiel Elliott (R)	Cowboys	222.1	7
9.	Doug Martin	Buccaneers	206.6	6
10.	LeSean McCoy	Bills	205.5	10
11.	Jeremy Langford (DNS)	Bears	203.0	9
12.	Eddie Lacy	Packers	202.5	4
13.	Thomas Rawls (INJ) (UPS)	Seahawks	201.0	5
14.	Carlos Hyde (NO) (UPS)	49ers	199.1	8
15.	Mark Ingram	Saints	196.0	5
16.	Matt Forte (NO)	Jets	195.6	11
17.	C.J. Anderson (UPS)	Broncos	193.5	11
18.	Ryan Mathews (NO) (UPS) (IRSK)	Eagles	186.5	4
19.	Jonathan Stewart (IRSK)	Panthers	181.8	7
20.	Latavius Murray	Raiders	180.0	10
21.	Melvin Gordon (NO)	Chargers	180.0	11
22.	Ameer Abdullah (UPS)	Lions	178.8	10
23.	Jay Ajayi (R) (IRSK) (UPS)	Dolphins	178.3	8
24.	Jeremy Hill	Bengals	177.7	9
25.	Isaiah Crowell (NO) (UPS)	Browns	176.1	13
26.	Matt Jones (IRSK) (UPS)	Redskins	172.0	9
27.	DeMarco Murray (NO) (DNS)	Titans	172.0	13
28.	LeGarrette Blount (IRSK)	Patriots	171.6	9
29.	Duke Johnson (NO)	Browns	171.0	13
30.	Justin Forsett (IRSK)	Ravens	168.9	8
31.	Dion Lewis	Patriots	163.4	9
32.	Frank Gore (IRSK)	Colts	159.5	6
33.	Danny Woodhead (NO)	Chargers	148	11
34.	Karlos Williams	Bills	148.0	10
35.	Chris Ivory (NO)	Jaguars	145.0	5
36.	DeVontae Booker (R) (UPS)	Broncos	134	11
37.	Rashad Jennings	Giants	131.6	8
38.	Wendell Smallwood (R) (UPS)	Eagles	118.0	4
39.	Javorius 'Buck' Allen	Ravens	114.5	8
40.	Paul Perkins (R)	Giants	111.0	8
41.	Charles Sims	Buccaneers	108.4	6
42.	Derrick Henry (R) (UPS)	Titans	103.0	13
43.	T.J. Yeldon	Jaguars	102.3	5
44.	Theo Riddick	Lions	100	10
45.	Kenyan Drake (R)	Dolphins	97.5	8
46.	Bilal Powell	Jets	96.9	11
47.	Tevin Coleman	Falcons	94.0	11

48.	Gio Bernard (UPS)	Bengals	91.5	9
49.	Alfred Blue	Texans	88.8	9
50.	DeAndre Washington (R)	Raiders	88.0	10
51.	James Starks	Packers	85.4	4
52.	Shane Vereen	Giants	78.5	8
53.	Benny Cunningham	Rams	72.0	8
54.	Andre Ellington (IRSK)	Cardinals	70.2	9
55.	James White	Patriots	70.2	9
56.	C.J. Prosise (R)	Seahawks	68.0	5
57.	C.J. Spiller (IRSK)	Saints	65.4	5
58.	Chris Thompson	Redskins	63.4	9
59.	Jerick McKinnon	Vikings	62.5	6
60.	Mike Tolbert	Panthers	55.5	7
61.	Darren Sproles (NO)	Eagles	54.0	4
62.	Khiry Robinson (NO)	Jets	54.0	11
63.	Charcandrick West	Chiefs	53.0	5
64.	Darren McFadden	Cowboys	48.4	7
65.	Tim Hightower	Saints	48.0	5
66.	Robert Turbin (NO) (UPS)	Colts	48.0	10
67.	Ronnie Hillman	Broncos	48.0	11
68.	Kenneth Dixon (R)	Ravens	48.0	8
69.	Alfred Morris (NO)	Redskins	47.8	9
70.	Cameron Artis-Payne	Panthers	46.0	7
71.	Ka'Deem Carey	Bears	43.5	9
72.	DeAngelo Williams (UPS)	Steelers	43.1	8
73.	Shaughn Draughn (NO)	49ers	41.5	8
74.	Brandon Bolden	Patriots	35.8	9
75.	Chris Johnson	Cardinals	35.2	9
76.	Jonathan Grimes	Texans	34.0	9
77.	Damien Williams (NO)	Dolphins	30.5	8
78.	Brandon Oliver	Chargers	29.8	11
79.	Keith Marshall (R)	Redskins	27.0	9
80.	Matt Asiata	Vikings	24.0	6

Ranks reflect value based on 16 weeks of play. Past performance was considered as were issues relating to each team's offense including the offense run by the team's offensive coordinator, any coaching changes and personnel changes, and which players are listed as starters and back-ups on the most recent depth charts.

KEY: (NO) = New Offense; (UPS) = Upside; (IRSK) = Injury Risk; (INJ) = Injured; (DNS) = Downside; (R) = Rookie

RUNNING BACK PROFILES

1. David Johnson, Cardinals - BYE: 9

Very few rookies had a better 2015 season than David Johnson. The obscure rookie third round pick out of Northern Iowa began the year as a kick return specialist and third-string RB. By the end of the season, he was in the offensive rookie of the year discussion and drawing comparisons to some of the best running backs in pro football history. The converted former collegiate WR scored 13 total TDs in the regular season, and seized the opportunity created by the injury to **Chris Johnson** to establish himself as the Cardinals' clear three-down back of the present. Johnson must continue to work on his in-game decision making and ball control, but his size, speed, and natural instincts make him a very dangerous weapon for the Cardinals and their high-powered offense. Johnson figures to be the bell cow for the Cardinals in 2016, and will be ranked high among RBs. He is a virtual must-have in dynasty leagues, and a nice RB1 option across the board. David Johnson is a top-three running back in all formats who will push for 1,800 all-purpose yards and double-digit TDs. He is arguably No. 1 in non-PPR formats. (CB)

2. Le'Veon Bell, Steelers - BYE: 8

When on the field, **Le'Veon Bell** is unquestionably the most prolific fantasy running back in the league today. Entering his fourth season, Bell has averaged just short of 80 rushing yards per game along with just short of 40 receiving yards per game. Simply, Bell is the top running back in fantasy football, especially in PPR formats. The only concern with Bell is his ability to stay on the field. He is coming off of a 2015 campaign where he played in only 6 games due to a suspension and serious knee injury. All indications are that the knee is healthy and Bell is ready to roll. While these issues may give fantasy owners pause, Le'Veon Bell's potential is too good to pass up and he'll be one of the top three running backs selected in the first round of draft. Bell is a player expected to produce 1,600 all-purpose yards and double digit TDs. (RB)

3. Todd Gurley, Rams - BYE: 8

The reigning offensive Rookie of the Year had a great rookie campaign, rushing for 1,106 yards in only 13 games. With a rookie QB likely under center and a relatively unproven receiving corps, Gurley will get as many touches (mostly rushes) as he can handle as the team's workhorse running back. Think **Adrian Peterson** not **Le'Veon Bell**. A Top 5 running back, Gurley should pace 1,700 all-purpose yards and double digit TDs. He'll be drafted in all formats in the first round. (JQ)

4. Devonta Freeman, Falcons - BYE: 11

It was believed **Devonta Freeman** could not be a premier running back in the league at 5'8" tall, 206 pounds Freeman's rookie season was unremarkable with 95 touches for 473 all-purpose yards and 2 TDs. The Falcons even added top running back prospect **Tevin Coleman** in last year's draft. Yet, Freeman exploded for 1,634 all-purpose yards (578 yards receiving) and 14 TDs in 15 games, finishing his 2015 campaign as one of the league's elite running backs. Devonta Freeman has established himself as a dual threat running back who will be selected in the first round of all fantasy drafts. (IE)

5. Adrian Peterson, Vikings - BYE: 6

Adrian Peterson will be 31 years old when this season starts. Last season, at the age that most running backs decline, he carried the ball 327 times for 1,485 yards and 11 touchdowns. Not all of Peterson's game was perfect as he fumbled the ball 7 times, three of which were lost. But, that goes with the territory. **Teddy Bridgewater** will be asked to do more this season, but the majority of the Vikings offense will still run through Adrian Peterson. If you have the first overall pick in a non-PPR draft, Peterson will be in the discussion. He's guaranteed to project as a 300-plus *rush* running back for over 1,300 yards and double digit TDs in 2016. What limits his upside is his limited involvement in the passing game. Also, his production is bound to fall off sooner or later because of his age (due to injury or otherwise) and he is coming off a season with a high workload. (JW/JS)

6. Jamaal Charles, Chiefs - BYE: 5

Jamaal Charles is one of the most elusive and speedy running backs in the league. This playmaker makes big plays out of anything defenses give him. Charles is exceptional because he not only runs effectively for the Chiefs, but he also catches screens and turns small gains into touchdowns. Regardless of this past season's ACL tear, Charles is expected to come back healthy, just as he did a few years ago from his first ACL tear, on his other knee. What makes Jamaal Charles particularly appealing in fantasy is his 80% QFG rating ("Quality Fantasy Games"). On a modest 225 rushes and 60 receptions, Charles should top 1,600 all-purpose yards and double digit TDs. He remains a Top 5 running back who'll be drafted at the top of Round 2 in most fantasy drafts. (IE/JS)

7. Lamar Miller, Texans - BYE: 9

When **Lamar Miller** was with the Dolphins, his touches were at a premium. The last two years have provided some ridiculous highlight runs and catches from Miller, but he averaged 15.9 touches per game in 2014 (1,374 total yards and 9 touchdowns) and even fewer in 2015, averaging 15.1 touches per game (1,269 yards and 10 touchdowns). Miller has a frame smaller than former Texans All-Pro running back **Arian Foster,** but if he's given anywhere near the touches Foster was getting when he was the primary back (23.6 touches per game), Lamar Miller should entrench himself as a top eight fantasy running back. The Texans have a better offensive line than the Dolphins. Miller will finish Top 15 barring injury and should be a Top 10 RB in PPR leagues. Miler should pace 1,500 to 1,600 all-purpose yards and double digit TDs. He's a second round draft pick in all fantasy formats. (SB)

8. LeSean McCoy, Bills - BYE: 10

After enduring a slow start to the 2015 season, **LeSean McCoy** rushed for 100 yards in seven consecutive games before suffering a season ending MCL injury. McCoy only appeared in 12 games last season. If the shifty running back can pick up where he left off before his injury, he can carry a Bills run game that led the league in rush yards per game (152.0). LeSean McCoy is an RB1 in all fantasy formats. If he stays healthy, 1,600 plus all-purpose yards and six or more TDs is reachable. Draft McCoy in the third round of all fantasy drafts. (JQ)

9. Ezekiel Elliott, Cowboys - BYE: 7

Ezekiel Elliott had an infamous career at Ohio State where he led the Buckeyes to a national championship in his sophomore campaign. After Elliot went his senior year, the Cowboys selected him as the fourth overall pick in this year's draft. Fantasy team managers should remember the Cowboys' offensive line is the best offensive line in the league. The Cowboys' offensive line plus Elliott should mean a fantastic year statically for Zeke. This crop top running back will fit right into Jerry Jones' organization. If he remains healthy, Ezekiel Elliott could dance with 1,500 all-purpose yards and double digit TDs. Target Elliott in Round 2 of fantasy drafts. (IE)

10. Thomas Rawls, Seahawks - BYE: 5

In the six games he started last season, **Thomas Rawls** blew up the gridiron for 780 all-purpose yards and 5 TDs. No rocket science is needed to see that at that pace, Rawls could top 2,000 all-purpose yards and double digit TDs easily. However, it is a small sample size. The verdict is out whether he'll truly be ready to play in Week 1 as he is rehabbing a fractured ankle sustained in Week 14 of the 2015 season. If he is healthy, he's expected to be the team's workhorse running back. He's not a super reliable pass catcher. However, the nine receptions he had in 2015 as a rookie should jump to 20-25 this season, which provides a little added value. If healthy, he'll push for 1,800 all-purpose yards and double digit TDs in the offensive system the Seahawks run. Thomas Rawls is easily a Top 10 running back in PPR leagues, Top 5 running back in non-PPR leagues. Rawls is sure to be over-drafted. So, if you want him, you must likely select him in the late second round or early third round of fantasy drafts. However, you really need to draft another fringe RB1 candidate if Rawls' injury takes longer than expected to come back from. Ideally, you'll want to draft him as an RB2 unless he is healthy and ready to play in Week 1. We'll know soon enough.

11. Jeremy Langford, Bears - BYE: 9

Let me begin with a caveat: it's very possible there were huge improvements in Langford's game over the offseason. It happens every year, where a running back comes out of nowhere and surprises us all. With **Matt**

Forte's departure, the time is now or never for **Jeremy Langford**. Unfortunately, it's unclear whether it's "now." To begin, Langford runs inefficiently as he only had 3.6 yards per carry last season. This means his yards after contact aren't very good. He's not a great receiver, but not a bad one either, as he had an 83 yard reception last season. His blocking can only improve. His fantasy value relies on touchdowns which can be a volatile statistic. Last, Head Coach **John Fox** likes to use multiple backs run throughout the game to give a defense looks at different styles of running. All this said, it's genuinely unclear who this "second" running back on the Bears will be. It's fairly clear, however, Langford is right now in the lead. View Langford as an RB2, borderline RB1 capable of 1,300 all-purpose yards and five-plus TDs, but who carries downside. You may be able to nab Jeremy Langford with a mid-round pick in some leagues. (GC/JS)

12. Doug Martin, Buccaneers - BYE: 6

Doug Martin had a bounce back 2015 season after struggling the previous two seasons due to many injuries. Last season, Martin returned and finished as the second leading rusher in the league. He was the Buccaneers work horse back the Buccaneers needed, rushing for 1,402 yards and 6 touchdowns. People who took a chance on Martin last season were rewarded. His best game came against the Jaguars and Eagles, which included a 235-yard rushing effort against the Eagles. Doug Martin should score more TDs this season as quarterback **Jameis Winston** probably will not run for 6 touchdowns again. Martin should have a good season. Look for Doug Martin to top 1,100 yards rushing and to push for double-digit TDs. (EG)

13. Matt Forte, Jets - BYE: 11

Matt Forte is coming off of a fantastic set of seasons playing for the Bears. Forte rushed for over 1,000 yards in 5 out of his 8 seasons for the Bears. At age 30, he's still in fantastic shape. One asset of his is that he is a dual running back, able to catch passes arguably better than any other running back in the league. He projects as a 1,000-plus yard rusher with over 400 yards receiving who could push for double digit TDs. Matt Forte is still a top option in fantasy, a border-line RB1 in PPR leagues. Forte should be selected by the end of the third round in most leagues. (IE)

14. Eddie Lacy, Packers - BYE: 4

In 2013, his rookie season, **Eddie Lacy** had 11 touchdowns on the ground. He followed that up in 2014 with 9 touchdowns. Last season Lacy just had only 3 rushing touchdowns, a number that made fantasy team owners wince. What's worse, his rush yards fell from an average of 1,119 yards per season to 758 in 2015. The former offensive rookie of the year also wasn't the weapon in the passing game the Packers had envisioned, only catching 20 balls for 188 yards and 2 touchdowns. 2015 was a season that Lacy wants to quickly put behind him. Edie Lacy spent this offseason getting into shape with reports indicating things went well. But one solid offseason doesn't guarantee that Lacy will produce like he did in 2013 and 2014. Even with so many questions, the prospects of Lacy's ability is too hard to pass up for fantasy team managers in the late second round of fantasy drafts. In 2014 Lacy was on the verge of becoming an all-around dominate running back. If coming into training camp in better shape is the answer, Eddie Lacy should have no problem getting to his projected 1,300 all-purpose yards and double digit TDs. (JW)

15. Mark Ingram, Saints - BYE: 5

Mark Ingram is a tough runner who keeps his feet moving and can create a lot of havoc after first contact. Before his season ended in Week 13 following a shoulder injury, Ingram's numbers were well above average for him with 769 yards rushing and six touchdowns, with an additional 405 yards receiving. He was on track for 1,500 all-purpose yards. His numbers were consistently solid. In PPR leagues, his QFG rating ("Quality Fantasy Games") was above 90%, above 55% in non-PPR leagues. In over half his games, he scored double-digit fantasy points in PPR leagues, scoring less than nine just once. In 2016, Mark Ingram should be used in much the same way as he was in 2015. This means, he'll be a low-end RB1 in PPR leagues and solid RB2 in non-PPR leagues. You can select him in the third round of PPR leagues and the fourth round of non-PPR leagues. (GC/JS)

16. Carlos Hyde, 49ers - BYE: 8

Last season was supposed to be Carlos Hyde's breakout. Frank Gore had left, leaving Hyde as the work horse running back. Unfortunately, Hyde broke out more than any running back in the league to open the season Week 1 vs. Minnesota posting 168 yards on 26 attempts scoring a pair of touchdowns. Hyde was well on his way to achieving that fantasy stardom so many had hyped heading into the year. Then, he suffered a foot injury a few weeks later which hampered him the next six games until he was subsequently put on Injured Reserve in Week 9. Look for Hyde to triumph in 2016 finally eclipsing the 1,000 yard mark, scoring upwards of 10 touchdowns while contributing in the receiving game. (DG)

17. C.J. Anderson, Broncos - BYE: 11

A first-round pick in most fantasy leagues last August, **C.J. Anderson** disappointed with essentially a repeat performance of his 2014 coming-out party: a sluggish first half of the season marred by lingering injuries, followed by an explosive second half. Despite Anderson's heroic performance in Super Bowl 50, the Broncos almost did not match the offer sheet the Dolphins signed him to as a restricted free agent this offseason. It is without question Anderson is a gifted player who might put up amazing numbers (1,300 all-purpose yards, near double digit TDs) in the **Gary Kubiak** system. However, he is yet to show he can stay healthy and carry a full workload for a full season, so you should not invest too early in this high-ceiling prospect with a relatively low floor. Target Anderson in the fourth round of your fantasy draft. (DK)

18. Latavius Murray, Raiders - BYE: 10

In his first year as a starter, Latavius Murray had a good year with 1,066 rushing yards and 6 TD scores. He chipped in an additional 232 yards receiving. Despite adding the diminutive **DeAndre Washington** in this year's draft, the Raiders seem content that Latavius Murray will be their starting running back this season. Behind what is being touted as one of the better offensive lines in the league, Murray could break through. Consider last season's stat line a minimum this season. Latavius Murray is a solid RB2 in all fantasy formats, draftable beginning in Round 4 of drafts. (IE/JS)

19. Jonathan Stewart, Panthers - BYE: 7

Stewart is a fine running back as 989 yards and six touchdowns on 4.1 yards per carry isn't anything to write home about, but it isn't anything to complain about either. However, two factors prevent **Jonathan Stewart** from being a coveted fantasy running back this season. First, he's getting to the age (29) where running backs break down. Stewart has had a dubious injury past already (only three full seasons in his career, and none in the last four seasons), and he's still dealing with an ankle injury from the Super Bowl four months ago. Jonathan Stewart doesn't project as a player who can play a full season. Second, and **Cam Newton** takes away a lot of goal line chances. When you have a 6' 5" tall QB who is more than willing to bruise for a touchdown on the ground, your RB will take some statistical hits. While there are no real legitimate RB threats on the Panthers, Jonathan Stewart is a limited option in fantasy. (GC)

20. Demarco Murray, Titans - BYE: 13

This will be the second season in which **DeMarco Murray** is playing with a new team. It's also the second season in a row Murray's new team has relatively high expectations of him to play well. Calling his 2015 season with the Eagles a bad one is an understatement. A poor fit in Chip Kelly's system, Murray's health, and his poor play in which he lost snaps to both **Ryan Mathews** and **Darren Sproles** all contributed to last season's meager numbers of 193 rushes for 702 yards (a career-low 3.6 yards per carry) and 44 receptions for 322 yards. Plus, the seven TDs he scored seemed few and far between. DeMarco Murray is still a three-down back and he's going to a Titans team which added help to its offensive line in the offseason. It's clear the Titans are looking to bully teams and use a direct run first approach which bodes well for Murray. In terms of fantasy production, Murray should be a quality RB2 approaching 1,300 total yards with six or more touchdowns next season. However, it's important to remember Murray has had durability issues throughout his career. Murray is draftable beginning in Round 4. (SB)

21. Jay Ajayi, Dolphins. BYE 8

Many Dolphins fans were disappointed the team didn't add a big name running back with the departure of **Lamar Miller**, despite the team's effort to sign free agent **C.J. Anderson** from the Broncos. Even though his snaps were limited last season due to injuries, anyone that watched **Jay Ajayi** play saw his potential. He's got a big frame (6'0" tall, 230 pounds), but moves like a smaller, shiftier running back. We all saw the records Ajayi set in his time at Boise State, and **Adam Gase** has featured a running back in his offense before, so it's not a bad idea to take a chance on him. Ajayi is not quite RB1 material, but he's an RB2 with upside (1,300 APY, 8 TDs) with an injury risk. Target Ajayi in the middle of the fifth round in all fantasy drafts. (TA)

22. Ryan Mathews, Eagles - BYE: 4

Ryan Mathews is set up to succeed in 2016 with **Demarco Murray** off to Titans. Mathews only ran for 6 TDs last season but, if he remains healthy, he is expected to carry the workload for the Eagles. Significantly, new Head Coach **Doug Pederson** was the Offensive Coordinator for the Chiefs from 2013 to 2015. The Chiefs offense has, under **Andy Reid** and Pederson, run through the rushing attack. Cutting against Ryan Mathews is his injury history. If Mathews can stay healthy, he could exceed 1,300 all-purpose yards and push for double digit TDs. He's in line for 225 rushes. Ryan Mathews projects as a borderline RB3 in PPR leagues, and a solid RB2 in non-PPR leagues. He's a risky fantasy selection in Rounds 5 or 6 of fantasy drafts, but the upside is there. (JQ/JS)

23. Matt Jones, Redskins - BYE: 9

Matt Jones had a decent rookie season in 2015 as the backup running back to Alfred Morris. Jones rushed the football 144 times for 490 yards and found the end zone three times. He also chipped in 19 receptions for 304 yards and 1 TD. It's disconcerting, however, that Jones averaged just 3.4 yards per carry. The good news for Matt Jones is that he is expected to be the bell cow running back for the Redskins as **Alfred Morris** is now in Dallas and there seem to be no serious contenders to steal touches from him. With Jones as the Redskins primary running back, he has some serious upside. He projects for 1,300 all-purpose yards and 7 TDs but could do much better if he can get his rushing numbers up. He's a border-line RB2 with upside who'll likely be over-drafted in most leagues. (IE/JS)

24. Jeremy Hill, Bengals - BYE: 9

Last offseason, some believed **Jeremy Hill** would continue with the 20.2 carry per game pace Hill maintained in the last nine games of 2014 where he totaled 1,339 yards and 9 TDs. Fantasy team managers who thought this way too were burned by Hill, as his average plummeted to 13.9 carries per game, finishing with 873 yards, on a meager 3.6 yards per rushing attempt. Still, he tied for the league lead in rushing TDs (11) which is never something to scoff at. As TheFantasyGreek.com noted last preseason, "Expect the Bengals to continue splitting the work [between Jeremy Hill and Gio Bernard] in a similar manner." Fantasy team owners should continue to be cautious to believe Hill will return to his earlier 2014 form. Especially concerning is that he's sharing a backfield with **Giovani Bernard**, who has proven himself to be a more reliable receiver and who has the potential to be a more solid running back. View Jeremy Hill as a low-end RB2 in non-PPR leagues and a high-end RB3 in PPR leagues who should push for 1,000 all-purpose yards and double digit TDs. (GC/JS)

25. Ameer Abdullah, Lions - BYE: 10

Ameer Abdullah is returning from offseason shoulder surgery. He is expected to be healthy for the start of his second season as a pro. Abdullah still has a lot to prove after totaling 780 all-purpose yards for 3 TDs on 168 touches. Beginning in Week 12, he went on a tear with near 400 all-purpose yards, 5.0 yards per carry. There's no one else to really challenge Abdullah for the bulk of the carries except maybe **Stevan Ridley**, if healthy. Otherwise, Ameer Abdullah has a ton upside. He's earmarked for 1,300 all-purpose yards and 8 TDs. A borderline RB2, you'll be able to select Abdullah in the middle rounds. (JQ/JS)

26. Isaiah Crowell, Browns - BYE: 13

Isiah Crowell led the Browns in rushing in 2015 with 706 yards on 185 rushing attempts but scored just 5 TDs, four rushing. With the Browns not drafting a single running back in this year's draft, Crowell is expected to hold the top spot on the RB depth chart and continue to dominate the rushes. New Head Coach **Hue Jackson** likes to run the football. While the Bengals offensive coordinator, the Bengals ran the football over 450 times the last two seasons. Crowell stands to see a significant increase in rushes. Crowell is in line to top 1,000 yards rushing with an additional 150 to 200 yards receiving. It'd be no surprise if he double his touchdown scores from last season. Crowell is a border-line RB2 whose value slides in PPR leagues to a RB3. (JQ/JS)

27. Dion Lewis, Patriots - BYE: 9

Lewis tore his ACL last year and has been rehabbing his way back. Reports suggest he's early and expected to be ready for Week 1. Dion Lewis was very productive putting up 622 total yards with four touchdowns in seven games before going down to injury. Lewis is an excellent complement to **LeGarrette Blount** in the backfield. Lewis is a better grab in PPR leagues where he is being drafted in the fourth round as he could easily haul in 70 receptions. In standard leagues, you can select Lewis towards the eighth round. Lewis should be in line for 1,000 all-purpose yards if he can stay healthy. (DG)

28. Danny Woodhead, Chargers - BYE: 11

Woodhead is basically a wide receiver in running back's clothing. He set career highs in catches (80), receiving yards (755) and touchdowns (9) last season, but his run game is subpar as he averaged 3.4 yards per carry behind a disappointing offensive line. **Danny Woodhead** thrived in Offensive Coordinator **Ken Wisenhunt**'s offense in 2013 where he posted 1,000-plus all-purpose yards and 8 TDs. Woodhead is a solid option as your second running back in PPR leagues where he should haul in 75 receptions on the season. In non-PPR leagues, he's a more of an RB3. (GC)

29. Melvin Gordon, Chargers - BYE: 11

The most frustrating thing about **Melvin Gordon** is the wealth of potential he possesses. While Gordon was a fairly one-dimensional running back at Wisconsin, he averaged almost eight yards per carry behind an excellent offensive line. That success, however, didn't translate to the NFL, where the Chargers averaged only 3.5 yards per carry. To be a successful running back, Melvin Gordon must become more valuable at the goal line, where he struggled last season, as he could not punch any touchdowns in during his rookie campaign. The Chargers drafted his college fullback, **Derek Watt**, who should help. As long as Gordon can keep his fumbles down (he had six in 2015) and as long as his return from a micro-fracture in his knee heals, he should be a solid running back for Philip Rivers, who loves to dump the ball to running backs when he's in trouble. (GC)

30. Duke Johnson, Browns - BYE: 13

Second year running back **Duke Johnson** will likely remain the number two rusher behind **Isaiah Crowell**. But, Johnson's main role is a pass catcher out of the backfield. Johnson could haul in 61 receptions for 534 yards and two TDs during his 2015 rookie campaign. In new Head Coach **Hue Jackson's** offense, which employs a pass catching running back like Johnson, his touches from 165 in 2015 to upwards of 210 in 2016. Duke Johnson is in line for 1,000 all-purpose yards and 5 TDs. Johnson should even get more rushing work spelling Isaiah Crowell. Duke Johnson is a borderline RB2 in PPR leagues. (JQ/JS)

31. Frank Gore, Colts - BYE: 10

Despite **Frank Gore** being 33 years of age, he should still be on your fantasy radar. Gore rushed for 967 yards last season and scored 7 TDs behind a subpar offensive line. The Colts addressed the offensive line this offseason but nothing significant regarding the backfield. This means Gore should be in line for a repeat performance of last season, assuming he can stay healthy. Gore is best drafted as an RB3 this season. Some will overdraft him. If you don't have to, don't draft Gore any earlier than the seventh round. (IE/JS)

32. LeGarrette Blount, Patriots - BYE: 9

Blount is sitting pretty as the Patriots main option at running back after the Patriots didn't address the position in the draft. LeGarrette Blount is fully healthy coming off a hip injury that cut short his 2015 season. He'll get the lion's share of red-zone touches. Free agent RB signee **Donald Brown** figures to add into the mix as does **Dion Lewis** and **James White**. But expect the Patriots backfield to play out with Blount leading the way in touches and touchdowns. Blount should easily boast a line of 200-plus carries, 1,000-plus yards and 7-plus touchdowns. His line be better with Brady set to miss the first four games of the season. (DG)

33. Chris Ivory, Jaguars - BYE: 5

Chris Ivory has been underrated his entire career. Ivory averaged 5.4 yards per carry on 278 attempts over his three years with the Saints, and finally showed his true colors last season with the Jets, breaking out for almost 1,300 yards from scrimmage and eight TDs, which placed him seventh among running backs in standard leagues. His consistency was an issue, however. While Ivory was a great signing for the Jaguars this offseason, it was a bad one for fantasy managers. This signing eliminates two 'workhorse' running backs, who ate up carries and yards for fantasy teams last season, as Ivory will split touches with **T.J. Yeldon**. Chris Ivory is in line for 1,000-plus all-purpose yards with at least a handful of TDs. The Jaguars are still expected to pass the football in a **Greg Olson** run offense with a talented young quarterback at the helm. You can target him beginning in Round 7 of fantasy drafts. Chris Ivory will likely fluctuate between playing like an RB2 or RB3 this season. (GC)

34. Justin Forsett, Ravens - BYE: 8

After a breakthrough season in 2014, **Justin Forsett** was largely unimpressive over a nine-game span last season as he scored just 2 touchdowns on 151 rushing attempts for 768 total combined yards. Forsett will return from a broken right arm and is 30 years old to start the season. Despite a back-up group full of young running backs, all indications are he will be given every opportunity to remain the team's number one running back. Perhaps with a steady offensive line, Forsett will regain the composure and consistency of the player who led the Ravens rushing attack two years ago. Tread lightly with Forsett, however, as his upside is minimal and the younger running backs in the group should press him for playing time. He'll be over-drafted by some. Treat Justin Forsett as an RB3 in standard sized leagues who should not be drafted any earlier than the seventh round. (FG)

35. Rashad Jennings, Giants - BYE: 8

In what was his best season as a pro, **Rashad Jennings** played all sixteen games in 2015 and posted over 1,000 all-purpose yards (APY), the most in his career. Jennings scored three rushing touchdowns and a receiving touchdown, also a career first. Jennings may have been held back statistically by a pass first offense. This won't change in 2016. With the undeniable expectation that Jennings flirts with around 1,000 APY and a handful of touchdowns again, Jennings makes for a low end RB3, with W/R flex possibilities in deeper leagues, draftable in Rounds 8 or 9 of most fantasy drafts. (AG)

36. Karlos Williams, Bills - BYE: 10

Williams showed some promising ability in his 2015 rookie season, but is projected to remain behind McCoy on the RB depth chart. Even in a backup role, **Karlos Williams** has the ability to put up respectable fantasy numbers despite getting minimal touches as he has been a touchdown hawk with 9 in 2015. But, while a worthwhile reserve, his fantasy performances may be uneven and it will likely take an injury to **LeSean McCoy** for Williams' value to be realized. View Williams as a borderline RB3/4 in all formats who loses value in PPR formats. (JQ/JS)

37. Javorius "Buck" Allen, Ravens - BYE: 8

Javorius Allen is the principal "back-up" running back who could overtake Justin Forsett as the starter. After Forsett went down to injury, Allen totaled 627 all-purpose and scored 3 TDs over the last seven games of his rookie season of 2015. He also chipped in 37 catches out of the backfield, and shined against the Dolphins with 170 combined yards and 1 TD. Allen should get enough touches (5 to 10 per game) to be a worthwhile fantasy draft pick if **Justin Forsett** begins the season as the Ravens starting running back. Allen projects as a low-end

RB3 in PPR leagues and a high end RB4 in non-PPR leagues. You can target him in Round 10 of fantasy drafts which is quite the value given his upside. (FG)

38. Devontae Booker, Broncos - BYE: 11

Selected by the Broncos in the fourth round at 136 overall, rookie Devontae Booker might be one of the best value picks of the 2016 draft. Widely ranked within the top 50 to 75 prospects on most big boards, this explosive, yet powerful running back from Utah drew comparisons to **Arian Foster** and **Terrell Davis**, two of **Gary Kubiak**'s most decorated running backs. Also, the Broncos reportedly had a first round grade on him and would've considered him at 31 overall had they been unable to trade up for Paxton Lynch. However, Booker is coming off a torn meniscus and it may take him a while to make an impact this season. Still, those that draft **C.J. Anderson** are highly recommended to select Booker as his handcuff. Devontae Booker, who should be drafted in the latter part of fantasy drafts, could see his stock rise as preseason wears on. (DK)

39. Derrick Henry, Titans - BYE: 13

There isn't a better fit for a smash mouth offense than **Derrick Henry**. The 2015 Heisman Trophy winner was the Titans second round pick in the April draft, which seemed a little confusing after signing **DeMarco Murray** to be the team's premier rusher. While Henry shouldn't overtake Murray (at least initially) as the team's number one rusher, the Titans will implement an offense which requires two physical running backs. Derrick Henry had a historic junior season in which he rushed 395 times for 2,219 yards and 28 touchdowns. He's not going to provide any help in the passing game. Henry should complement Murray and chip in near 700 all-purpose yards and 6 TDs. However, if Murray struggles again or is injured, Henry's role in the offense could increase exponentially. Henry is worth a later round draft pick in the twelfth or thirteenth rounds of most drafts. (SB)

40. T.J. Yeldon, Jaguars - BYE: 5

T.J. Yeldon raises the same concerns as **Chris Ivory**: he's trusted and reliable when healthy, but will split touches this season with Ivory. However, Yeldon saw a distinct *lack of touches* in the red zone, which limited his fantasy value last season greatly. With Chris Ivory on board, this will likely continue into 2016 with Yeldon's game action mostly on passing downs. T.J Yeldon is in line for near 1,000 all-purpose yards and six TDs and could push for 60 receptions. He's a solid reserve who gets a bump in PPR leagues as a low end RB3. (GC)

41. Giovani Bernard, Bengals - BYE: 9

The last time a running back tandem ran for over 1,000 yards each, it was DeAngelo Williams and Jonathan Stewart of the Panthers, back in 2009. It's a rare fete, done only five other times. The question begged to be answered: who will shine in the Bengals backfield, Gio Bernard or **Jeremy Hill**? Hill had a higher value last season due to his league-leading 11 touchdowns on the ground. However, he saw a huge drop in rushing efficiency, meaning if he sees any decline in touchdowns his value drops dramatically. Gio Bernard, for himself, ran for a pair of touchdowns last season which was a disappointment after scoring 15 combined over the two years before. However, in nearly every other metric he improved: yards per carry, total yards from scrimmage, and yards per catch. While Hill may continue to be a TD-scoring running back, Gio Bernard seems more reliable. Still, he's no better than a high end RB4 whose 1,000 all-purpose yard ceiling is further capped by the number of touchdowns he scores, which last season was a season low of two. (GC)

42. Wendell Smallwood, Eagles - BYE: 4

Wendell Smallwood should get several touches per week, both rushing and receiving. Whether he could be an every down running back remains to be seen, but the opportunity will likely be there given **Ryan Mathews** injury history. The Eagles likely wouldn't make **Darren Sproles** their every down running back should injury strike Mathews. 900 all-purpose yards and four to six TDs wouldn't be out of the question for the rookie Wendell Smallwood in an offense which wants to emphasize its running backs. View Smallwood as a late round pick. The upside is too good to pass up. (JQ/JS)

43. Charles Simms, Buccaneers - BYE: 6

In his second season, **Charles Simms** proved to be a dynamic change-of-pace running back, rushing for 529 yards and adding 561 yards receiving for 4 touchdowns on the season. The best fantasy value Simms provides for team managers is in PPR leagues where he hauled in 50 receptions in 2015. View Sims as a borderline RB3 who'll serve mostly as a bye week replacement unless **Doug Martin** is injured. (EG)

44. Theo Riddick, Lions - BYE: 10

Riddick is primarily known for his pass catching ability out of the backfield piling up more receptions (118) than carries (72) in his young pro career, with 80 receptions and 43 rushes just last season. In 2016, expect more of the same from **Theo Riddick** with some added touches on the ground because of an injury-ridden backfield this offseason. He'll push for 800 all-purpose yards and a handful of TDs. Riddick makes for a low-end flex-play in PPR leagues. (JQ/JS)

45. Bilal Powell, Jets - BYE: 11

Bilal Powell is expected to be the second string running back for the Jets this upcoming season. Powell rushed for 313 yards on 70 carries in 2015 and chipped in an additional 388 yards receiving on 47 receptions with 3 total touchdowns. If there is a concern, it's that the newly acquired Matt Forte could eat into Powell's reception total which is where he earned his keep last season. But, with the way the Jets used Powell from Week 11 on (32 receptions), you should continue a role in the offense to at least be fantasy-relevant as an RB4. (IE)

46. Paul Perkins, Giants - BYE: 8

Expectations are high for rookie **Paul Perkins**, a fifth round draft pick from UCLA. With back-to-back seasons of over 1,300 yards, the 2015 Alamo Bowl offensive MVP is playing to be the future of the Giants rushing attack. Despite being **Rashad Jennings**' back-up, **Paul Perkins** could have quite a role in the offense with possibly 5 to 8 touches per game. The Giants won't want to lean on the thirty-one year old Rashad Jennings. Monitor his progress in the Giants' offense this offseason. For fantasy football purposes, he should be available in the late rounds of most drafts. (AG)

47. Shane Vereen, Giants - BYE: 8

Shane Vereen has more career yards receiving (1,517) than rushing (1,167). With that in mind, Vereen is a third down utility back used more for blocking and short yardage purposes. He had less than 800 all-purpose yards with 4 receiving TDs in 2015, despite playing in a full 16 games. With **Paul Perkins** likely to eat into some of Vereen's touches, Vereen makes for a waiver wire fill in for the bye weeks in certain match-ups. (AG)

48. Kenyan Drake, Dolphins - BYE: 8

Rookie **Kenyan Drake** could split time with **Jay Ajayi** until one of them proves they deserve more carries. However, considering Drake spent most of his time at Alabama a back-up to **Derrick Henry**, he'll likely serve as a compliment to Ajayi rather than a work horse who can carry the backfield. There's no need to draft him on draft day if you don't have to. However, he projects as an RB4 (750 APY, 4 TDs) especially in PPR leagues. (TA)

49. DeAndre Washington, Raiders - BYE: 10

DeAndre Washington was a fifth round draft pick in this year's draft. Washington had a solid career playing for Texas Tech in their high passing offense. Despite the offense's orientation, he totaled 233 rushes for 1,492 yards and 14 rushing TDs. To that, Washington added 41 receptions for 385 yards and 2 TDs. DeAndre Washington is a great route runner from the backfield and he has serious upside if the Raiders can use him correctly. At 5'8" tall and 204 pounds, Washington shouldn't challenge **Latavius Murray** for the starter's job, even though the slight stature seemed to work well for the Falcons **Devonta Freeman** who at 5'8" and 206 pounds rushed for 1,061 yards and tied for a league high 11 rushing TDs. Washington will likely replace **Roy Helu** as a change-of-pace back, especially on passing downs. Helu did little in his first season with the Raiders with just 26 touches in 9 games. He's nursing a hip injury. View Washington as an RB4 in 12-team PPR leagues. He should carve out a role in the offense which could produce 600 all-purpose yards and 4 TDs if all goes well. (IE/JS)

50. Darren McFadden, Cowboys - BYE: 7

Darren McFadden will be in his second season with the Cowboys, ninth in the league. This 28-year-old running back compiled his best stats in nearly 5 years last season behind the Cowboys' top-ranked offensive line. McFadden led the Cowboys in rushing in 2015 with 1,089 yards on 239 carries. It is fairly clear that **Ezekiel Elliot** is going to be the starting running back this season for the Cowboys. This will cause McFadden's statistics to decrease significantly in 2016. He should remain a factor in the passing game, giving him some PPR bye week value. (IE)

51. James Starks, Packers - BYE: 4

James Starks proved to be a reliable and valuable backup to **Eddie Lacy** in 2013 and 2014. As Lacy's primary backup in 2013, Starks rushed for 493 yards with 3 rushing touchdowns. In 2014, again as Lacy's backup, Starks churned out 333 yards on the ground with 2 rushing touchdowns. In 2015 Starks saw his role change, as Starks was thrust into the starting role and rushed for 601 yards with 2 touchdowns. Starks might not have been the weapon in the running game that Lacy was in 2013 and 2014, but Starks was a valuable weapon in the Packers' passing game. Starks had 43 receptions for 392 yards and 3 receiving touchdowns. It isn't a guarantee that Lacy will be back to where he was in 2013 and 2014. If he isn't, James Starks will once again be asked to step into the Packers starting running back role. Starks projects as a high-end WR5 in twelve-team leagues. His fantasy value is predicated on how Eddie Lacy plays in 2016 which makes him no better than a late round grab in fantasy drafts. (JW)

52. Alfred Blue, Texans - BYE: 9

Blue is a handcuff to **Lamar Miller**, but he should also get five to eight touches per game. If Lamar Miller has durability issues, Blue will have decent value. In 2015, he made a noticeable jump in his yards per carry from 3.1 in 2014 to 3.8 in 2015 on only 14 more carries. Still, it's not very good and Blue was inconsistent trading a good fantasy game for several bad ones last season. Plus, rookie **Tyler Ervin** should eat into his touches. Again, Alfred Blue is nothing more than a handcuff this season, who will go undrafted in standard sized leagues. (SB)

53. Tevin Coleman, Falcons - BYE: 11

Tevin Coleman is the Falcons second string running back after the monster statistical season **Devonta Freeman** had in 2015. Coleman rushed for 392 yards on 87 rushes (4.5 YPC), well behind Freeman. It will be hard for Coleman to surpass Devonta Freeman on the depth chart short of an injury. Coleman should have similar stats to what he had last year based on a similar role in the offense. He's a late round pick in deeper leagues. (IE)

54. Andre Ellington, Cardinals - BYE: 9

In previous seasons, at least some analysts thought **Andre Ellington** could come in and carry the load on the ground for the Cardinals. That has simply not been true in the past, nor will it be the case in 2016. The former sixth-round selection out of Clemson, with his speedy but slight frame, is best suited for spot-duty and third down work. Ellington is now in the final year of his rookie deal, and has a lot to play for this season. Figuring to back up both **David Johnson** and **Chris Johnson**, Ellington can bring an instant spark to the game, but he must stay healthy. Depending on how the season goes, it would not be surprising to have the Cardinals bring him back into the fold. Regardless, because of his speed, instincts, and pass-catching ability, Ellington figures to be around for a while as a specialty back. He should out-play Chris Johnson, statistically speaking. (CB)

55. C.J. Prosise, Seahawks - BYE: 5

Prosise an early favorite to be the third down back for the Seahawks in 2016. He was always an explosive athlete, but struggled to get on the field at Notre Dame until his sophomore year where he caught 29 passes for 516 yards on an insane 17.9 yard per catch average. **C.J. Prosise** was the featured back in 2015 and his 1,032 yards rushing to go with 308 yards receiving proved that he was worth a third round selection as a dual-threat RB with limited mileage. Prosise will battle with **Christine Michael** and **Alex Collins** for reps, but neither of them can play his role. He has the ceiling of Lions' third down running back **Theo Riddick**. For now, expect around 500 all-purpose yards and a handful of TDs for Prosise. This makes him a later round fantasy draft pick. His value will rise exponentially should Rawls miss time. (SB)

56. Chris Thompson, Redskins - BYE: 9

Chris Thompson is entering his fourth season as a pro, all with the Redskins. His last three seasons haven't been impressive. He's spent time injured. The running back finally made progress in 2015 where he rushed for 216 yards on 35 rushes (6.0 YPC). Thompson would be expected to get work spelling **Matt Jones**, so 500 all-purpose yards and two TDs aren't out of the question. It's not enough to draft Chris Thompson in fantasy. (IE/JS)

57. Jordan Howard, Bears - BYE: 9

While there may be reasons to get excited about rookie **Jordan Howard**, there also are reasons not to. Howard ran for over 1,200 yards and nine touchdowns on just 196 carries last season for Indiana. However, he also missed four games because of injury. It's well-known that RB has one of the shortest shelf lives of any position, so injuries are virtually expected. However, Jordan Howard can bring power and pop to the Bears backfield. He postures well as the Bears second running back in the offense. However, this is not the year to spend a fantasy draft pick on him in standard sized leagues. Howard is a dynasty league hold because of his potentially future with the Bears as a highly involved second running back. If he carves out a role in the offense, he could see 500 to 600 yards of production and five or more TDs if he's used in goal line situations. (GC/JS)

58. James White, Patriots - BYE: 9

White ended last season on a high note, drawing 16 targets and catching for 45 yards in the AFC Championship Game versus the Broncos. Due to the Bronco's vaunted pass rush, Brady was forced to check down throughout. Don't expect White to draw such attention and targets this season. He is behind **LeGarrette Blount** and **Dion Lewis** while mixing in on third downs for passing down work. White will get first and second down carries occasionally as he mixed into the offense. But, he won't get the bulk of the work unless one of the two bodies in front of him go down. White is worth monitoring on the waiver wire and snagging him if injuries hit the Pats backfield. (DG)

59. Chris Johnson, Cardinals - BYE: 9

Despite suffering a season-ending leg injury against the 49ers last season in November, the thirty year old Johnson racked up 814 rushing yards and 3 TDs while serving as the Cardinals' featured running back to that point in 2015. **Bruce Arians**' downhill rushing scheme is a perfect match for Johnson's running style. But gone are the days of CJ2K and CJ1K. But, Johnson remains a serviceable backup and three-down fill-in option for the Cardinals. Returning on a 1-year deal, Chris Johnson figures to backup **David Johnson**, and be in the mix with **Andre Ellington** for additional work out of the backfield. 600 yards from scrimmage and a few more TDs is not out of the question. (CB)

60. Mike Tolbert, Panthers - BYE: 7

Tolbert is part of a dying breed of fullbacks. When the Panthers played the Broncos in Super Bowl 50, the Broncos didn't even carry a fullback on their roster. Yet, he's mentioned because the Panthers have faith in him to be part of the rushing game when their featured running backs have been injured. In this way, he's been effective in fantasy. View Tolbert as strictly a potential injury replacement for **Jonathan Stewart** and/or **Cameron Artis-Payne**. (GC/JS)

61. Darren Sproles, Eagles - BYE: 4

Darren Sproles is coming off of a year of career lows in yards per carry and yards per reception. While 33 years old, Sproles should still have a role in the offense but its scope is unknown. Plus, rookie **Wendell Smallwood** is in the wings and expected to challenge for playing time from day one. Even if Sproles recaptures the role he had just two seasons ago, his numbers wouldn't exceed 700 all-purpose yards and a handful of TDs. Sproles' bigger role could be on special teams as a returner. Quality fantasy games should be sporadic. Look for other options in your fantasy draft than Darren Sproles. (JQ/JS)

62. Charcandrick West, Chiefs - BYE: 5

Charcandrick West had a great year once **Jamaal Charles** injured his ACL last season. In the 10 games West played after Charles went down, he found the end zone 5 times with 586 rushing and 205 receiving yards. Although Charles will be back, West has proven to be dependable. His role with the Chiefs will change. West will be given more opportunities on the field, even with the 30-year-old Charles healthy. However, it likely won't be enough for him to be fantasy-relevant. Charcandrick West started 9 games last season. (IE)

63. Robert Turbin, Colts - BYE: 10

Adding Robert Turbin was one of the few key personnel moves the Colts made in free agency. He could also be one of the least talked about sleepers in in the league. Turbin is coming off a four year stint with the Seahawks where he totaled over 1,100 all-purpose yards through those three seasons. He primarily served as **Marshawn Lynch's** back-up which means he's got minimal wear and tear on the legs, rushing 80 or less times per season. Robert Turbin will likely have a minimal role behind veteran Frank Gore. If Gore goes down to injury, Turbin should have little in his way to becoming the starter. (IE/JS)

64. Ronnie Hillman, Broncos - BYE: 11

After an abysmal performance in the playoffs (1.7 YPC), Ronnie Hillman barely found any suitors in free agency, and he re-signed with the Broncos for a one-year deal. Also, two-year practice squad member **Kapri Bibbs** is poised to give him a push for the third RB spot. Yet, Hillman was the Broncos leading rusher in 2015 (863 rushing yards and 7 TD) thanks to **C.J. Anderson**'s lingering health issues. Should Hillman hang onto his job, Anderson's medical issues resurface, and **Devontae Booker** struggles to pick up the offense, the stars could align for Hillman to surprise again. He is a later round draft pick in larger leagues for teams looking for depth. (DK)

65. De'Angelo Williams, Steelers - BYE: 8

Most running backs are over the hill at 33 years of age. Williams has little mileage on him, and not only did he fill in for the injured **Le'Veon Bell** last season, but he was magnificent logging 4.5 yards a carry (200 rushes, 907 yards) and scoring 11 touchdowns. **DeAngelo Williams** looks to be a backup in 2016. But, with the propensity of Le'Veon Bell getting injured, Williams makes for a valuable handcuff in any league. No predictions here, but if you draft Bell, look for Williams earlier rather than later. He'll likely be drafted by Round 10 in most drafts. (RB)

66. Cameron Artis-Payne, Panthers - BYE: 7

After an excellent final season at Auburn, many expected **Cameron Artis-Payne** to make an impact bigger than he did in his rookie season. **Jonathan Stewart** proved reliable enough in the backfield that Artis-Payne saw little playing time until Stewart went down to injury. While Artis-Payne flashed, his overall body of work didn't impress either. Unless Stewart goes down to injury, expect no significant fantasy impact from Artis-Payne, especially with Newton taking many goal-line plays in to his own hands. (GC)

67. Tre Mason, Rams - BYE: 8

Tre Mason is having an offseason where he has missed OTAs due to an off-the-field issue. It is questionable whether the former Auburn Tiger can regain his spot atop the Rams RB depth chart behind **Todd Gurley.** Monitor his situation in the preseason as he is Gurley's back-up. In the meantime, Mason is a high risk fantasy option. (JQ)

68. C.J. Spiller, Saints - BYE: 5

C.J. Spiller has the potential to thrive in the Saints offense. His style of running fits well with the Saints' offense and Spiller is of the mind he could flourish if given the chance. However, it doesn't appear he'll get the chance. C.J. Spiller has no defined role on the team, other than as the third running back on the depth chart. Last season, the once starter, had 70 touches *on the season*. Avoid Spiller until he gets a defined role or there are injuries. (GC)

69. Jerick McKinnon, Vikings - BYE:

Jerick McKinnon is strictly a change of pace running back to **Adrian Peterson** who last season had 52 rushes for 271 yards and 21 receptions for 173 yards and 3 TDs. McKinnon's role would grow if Adrian Peterson were to be injured, but **Matt Asiata** would likely get the bulk of the workload like he did in 2014 when Peterson missed the season. (JS)

70. Benny Cunningham, Rams - BYE: 8

Bennie Cunningham is getting much of the snaps at OTAs with **Tre Mason** out. He's more of a receiving running back. Although Cunningham may see more action than expected, his production likely won't be enough for him to contribute to a fantasy roster unless he becomes the starter. (JQ)

71. Spencer Ware, Chiefs - BYE: 5

Coming into last season, **Spencer Ware** was the third string running back. That changed when both **Jamaal Charles** and **Charcandrick West** went down to injuries. Ware stepped in and produced. Fantasy owners around all leagues were itching to grab him. Ware finished with 403 yards on 72 carries and 6 scores. Ware proved that he could produce numbers at the NFL level. With Jamaal Charles back, however, Ware's role will be reduced. He'll be a factor if Charles is injured again. (IE)

72. Khiry Robinson, Jets - BYE: 11

Khiry Robinson is not a typical running back. Robinson is a short down yardage runner that is not afraid to lower his shoulder and run through defenders to get a few extra yards. This may cause skepticism in some fantasy owner's eyes, but it shouldn't. Robinson may not have over 10 yards rushing in a game, but there is a high possibility that Robinson is the RB the Jets use in goal line situations to score touchdowns. Monitor Robinson's progression and let's see if he carves out a role for himself. (IE/JS)

73. Tim Hightower, Saints - BYE: 5

In four games without **Mark Ingram** last season, **Tim Hightower** ran for 327 yards and three touchdowns. Hightower is the clear number two in the Saints' offense, leaving **CJ Spiller** the odd man out. Some people like to use RB 'cuffs' in fantasy football, banking a late pick or a free agent pick on essentially a secondary running back who can steal some points. Hightower will get touches this season and wouldn't be a terrible cuff. However, he'll be on your bench taking the place of fantasy player you might use in any week. (GC)

74. Alfred Morris, Cowboys - BYE: 7

Alfred Morris is coming off a disappointing season with the Redskins. Morris' statistics have plummeted since his rookie year in 2012 where he rushed for 1,610 yards. In the years following, he has compiled 1,275 yards in 2013, 1,074 yards in 2014, and 751 yards in 2015. He resides as the third running back on the Cowboys depth chart. Unless there is an injury to Ezekiel Elliott, Morris could struggle to get touches this season, continuing the downward trend. (IE)

75. Kadeem Carey, Bears - BYE: 9

Too many running backs are on the Bears to get excited about **Ka'Deem Carey**. Any residual excitement from last season has dulled after the Bears drafted **Jordan Howard.** Carey's stats from last season are underwhelming (159 yards, two touchdowns, 3.7 YPC). Of the running backs in the Bears system, Carey will get the third or fourth most touches. This is not a recipe for fantasy success. (GC)

76. Shaun Draughn, 49ers - BYE: 8

The 28 year-old Draughn is the early favorite to back up Carlos Hyde. After Hyde went down last season, the 49ers plucked him off the scrap heap and plugged him into the offense where he performed to the tune of 273 yards on 78 rushes over 11 games, good for a 3.5 yard average. While respectable, these are not the numbers of a world beater. Granted, his line in front of him didn't do him any favors. Shaun Draughn also has adequate hands hauling in 27 receptions good for 176 yards. If Hyde goes down again like last year, Draughn is the primary option to lead the team in carries. Therefore, he's a late-round depth option. (DG)

77. Christine Michael, Seahawks - BYE: 5

After leaving the Cowboys in the middle of 2015, **Christine Michael** returned to the Seahawks who were in desperate need of running back help with injuries to Marshawn Lynch and Thomas Rawls. Michael had impressive starts in three of the last five games of the season (including one playoff game) where he produced 70-plus yards in each game, topping out at 102 yards rushing on 17 attempts in Week 17. However, he's not a super reliable pass catcher and he's failed earn over 39 rushing attempts in a season. Christine Michael is also expected to lose value with the additions of **C.J. Prosise** and **Alex Collins** who each posted impressive 2015 collegiate campaigns and provide both third down and goal line carry potential. Trouble is looming for Michael if both impress early. (SB)

78. Brandon Bolden, Patriots - BYE: 9

Bolden is more of the 'scat back' for the Patriots. He contributed in 15 games rushing for 207 yards on 63 catches but no touchdowns. Bolden hauled in 19 grabs for 180 yards and a pair of TDs, however. He is a depth option for this team and one that won't stand out fantasy-wise. Expect similar numbers in 2016 unless Bolden is forced into full-time active duty. (DG)

79. Branden Oliver, Chargers - BYE: 11

Oliver cannot deliver any serious fantasy numbers unless there's a major injury to Melvin Gordon or Danny Woodhead. Branden Oliver showed fantastic potential following major injuries in 2014. In week three, he ran for 182 yards and a pair of touchdowns. He followed that up with 124 yards and a touchdown the next week. But after that, Oliver was dead in the water, running for only 333 yards and one touchdown the rest of the season. Last year his value was limited, and so were his touches: he saw the ball only 44 times. Avoid Branden Oliver in fantasy drafts. (GC)

80. Keith Marshall, Redskins - BYE: 9

Keith Marshall was drafted in the final round of this year's draft with the Redskins' final pick. His college career was fairly unremarkable mostly because of injuries. But, he flashed. Marshall's combine results, however, were extraordinary. Marshall ran a blazing forty-time of 4.31 and benched 225 pounds 25 times. Keith Marshall is fast and athletic and could surprise if given the opportunity. He's not worth a fantasy pick. (IE)

81. Alex Collins, Seahawks - BYE: 5

C.J. Prosise is getting a lot of love because he has an established role as the primary pass catcher out of the backfield, but **Alex Collins** deserves recognition. Collins posted 1,000-plus yards rushing in all three of his seasons at Arkansas and ran for an impressive average of 5.4, 5.4 and 5.8 yards per carry, each season, respectively. His 20 touchdowns in 2015 suggests he has a nose for the end zone. If **Thomas Rawls'** return does not go as planned, Collins could well become the '2016 Touchdown Vulture' in fantasy leagues everywhere. Don't draft Collins yet, but keep an eye on his progress this preseason. (SB)

82. Mike Davis, 49ers - BYE: 8

Second-year running back Mike Davis looked like a potential first round pick lighting up the SEC for 1,183 rushing yards on 203 carries, and scoring 11 touchdowns in his sophomore season. Then, after an underachieving junior season he declared for the NFL draft where the 49ers selected him in the fourth round. Davis struggled to adjust to the NFL running for 58 yards on 35 carries. A broken hand forced Davis to miss 10 games during the season. Look for Davis to be out to prove critics wrong this season. Davis is a late round grab in deeper leagues. (DG)

83. Jacquizz Rodgers, Bears - BYE: 9

Jacquizz Rodgers only played five games last season. In those five games, he never saw the ball over four times, and never ran for over 16 yards, with no touchdowns. Throughout his career he could never really be labeled a feature back. While Rodgers could carve out a role for himself as a change-of-pace option, too many other moving parts are on the offense to view his role as anything but minor. (GC)

84. Zach Zenner, Lions - BYE: 10

The former undrafted free agent showed promise in his rookie season with the Lions, but his season was cut short by a trip to the injured reserve list. If **Zach Zenner** can remain healthy, he could prove to be a nice option in short yardage situations and a contributor on special teams. But, despite the hype he might garner, he should be off fantasy football radars to start the season. (JQ)

85. Tyler Ervin, Texans - BYE: 9

If you are in a deep dynasty league or keeper league, **Tyler Ervin** is a sneaky good stash. His speed and quickness led him to a prolific career at San Jose State with 2,374 kickoff return yards and 2,586 yards of total offense. His role expanded as the years went on, and last season, Ervin produced 1,601 yards on the ground with 13 touchdowns to go with 45 catches and 334 yards through the air. Tyler Ervin reminds of **Dexter McCluster** or **Darren Sproles** specializing as a return and receiving specialist. He's deadly when he gets his hands on the ball in space. Head Coach **Bill O'Brien** will get creative with Ervin, but his fantasy value will be limited as a rookie. (SB)

86. Kenneth Dixon, Ravens - BYE: 8

The rookie from Louisiana Tech was a TD-machine his senior year, totaling 26 TDs both rushing and passing on just over 1,500 all-purpose yards, with about one-third of his yards being receiving yards. **Kenneth Dixon** should add explosiveness to the Ravens' offense. Dixon and **Buck Allen** could totally move **Justin Forsett** off the field and to the sideline by mid-season. Kenneth Dixon has a lot of upside, but not enough to garner a draft pick in standard sized leagues. Look for Dixon to be a potential mid-season free agent pickup. (FG)

87. Daniel Lasco, Saints - BYE: 5

There is room for **Daniel Lasco** on the Saints' roster. However, most teams use seventh round picks on good athletes as opposed to position specific athletes. Lasco's pedigree is uneven. While he displayed qualities of being an every down running back (like being a good blocker) when he played for California, he also spent a part of his college career injured (7 games). In his junior year, Daniel Lasco played all 12 games, rushing for 1,115 yards and scoring 12 TDs, while adding 356 yards and 2 TDs in the passing game. Lasco averaged five-plus yards per carry his junior and senior years. Despite reasons to feel good about Lasco prospects for the future, his exact role in the Saints offense is unknown. He'll be undraftable in fantasy. (GC/JS)

88. Mike Gillislee, Bills - BYE: 10

Mike Gillislee did not see action in 2015 until week 13. Gillislee will likely be third on the RB depth chart. While he'll be undrafted in all fantasy formats, he makes the most of the minimal chances he gets, averaging 5.7 yards per carry and scoring 3 total TDs in 2015. (JQ)

89. Kenjon Barner, Eagles - BYE: 4

You'd like to think **Kenjon Barner** should see more action this year than he received last season with only 28 carries. However, he's struggled so far to find a place in two seasons on two teams in the pros. Barner won't be drafted in fantasy. (JQ)

90. DaJuan Harris, 49ers - BYE: 8

The 49ers are Harris' fifth team in four years as the 49ers plucked him off the Ravens' practice squad last season. With the myriad of injuries to the 49ers' backfield, the Troy University product stepped up with 153 total yards in Week 17 versus a staunch Rams defense. The 49ers signed the 27 year-old Harris to a two-year extension as he'll fight with Mike Davis for the No. 3 RB spot. Harris will be a must-get if Hyde or Draughn go down with injury. (DG)

WIDE RECEIVER RANKINGS (PPR)

	Player	Team	Value	Bye
1.	Antonio Brown	Steelers	444.5	8
2.	Julio Jones (IRSK)	Falcons	363.0	11
3.	Odell Beckham Jr. (3)	Giants	349.0	8
4.	Allen Robinson (3)	Jaguars	317.0	5
5.	Brandon Marshall	Jets	315.5	11
6.	Jordy Nelson	Packers	311.4	4
7.	Dez Bryant	Cowboys	297.0	7
8.	DeAndre Hopkins	Texans	295.8	9
9.	Golden Tate	Lions	288.0	10
10.	Keenan Allen	Chargers	285.0	11
11.	TY Hilton	Colts	284.7	10
12.	Alshon Jeffrey	Bears	284.0	9
13.	Mike Evans (3)	Buccaneers	282.0	6
14.	AJ Green	Bengals	273.1	9
15.	Brandin Cooks (3)	Saints	271.5	5
16.	Randall Cobb	Packers	270.0	4
17.	Sammy Watkins (3) (INJ)	Bills	267.8	10
18.	Jeremy Maclin	Chiefs	264.6	5
19.	Jarvis Landry	Dolphins	264.0	8
20.	Amari Cooper (2)	Raiders	259.5	10
21.	Kelvin Benjamin (3)	Panthers	256.0	7
22.	Eric Decker	Jets	253.8	11
23.	Allen Hurns (3)	Jaguars	248.0	5
24.	Larry Fitzgerald	Cardinals	246.9	9
25.	Marvin Jones (NO)	Lions	246.1	10
26.	Jordan Mathews (3) (NO)	Eagles	239.2	4
27.	John Brown (3)	Cardinals	237.7	9
28.	Steve Smith	Ravens	236.0	8
29.	Julian Edelman	Patriots	227.4	9
30.	Donte Moncrief (3)	Colts	227.2	10
31.	Michael Crabtree	Raiders	223.5	10
32.	Torrey Smith (NO) (DNS)	49ers	221.0	8
33.	Tavon Austin	Rams	216.5	8
34.	DeVante Parker (2)	Dolphins	215.4	8
35.	Willie Snead (2)	Saints	212.2	5
36.	Mike Wallace (NO)	Ravens	206.2	8
37.	Doug Baldwin	Seahawks	205.5	5
38.	Markus Wheaton	Steelers	196.0	8
39.	Michael Floyd	Cardinals	195.0	9
40.	Vincent Jackson	Buccaneers	195.0	6
41.	Corey Coleman (R) (UPS)	Browns	189.3	13
42.	DeSean Jackson	Redskins	186.2	9
43.	Kevin White (2) (UPS)	Bears	186.0	9
44.	Travis Benjamin	Chargers	184.0	11
45.	Tyler Lockett (2) (UPS)	Seahawks	184.0	5
46.	Demaryius Thomas	Broncos	180.0	11
47.	Bruce Ellington (3) (UPS)	49ers	178.2	8
48.	Brandon LaFell (NO)	Bengals	172.2	9
49.	Laquon Treadwell (R)	Vikings	171.6	6
50.	Terrance Williams	Cowboys	163.5	7
51.	Kendall Wright	Titans	161.6	13
52.	Pierre Garcon	Redskins	159.8	9
53.	Rishard Matthews (NO) (UPS)	Titans	159.0	13
54.	Sterling Shepard (R) (UPS)	Giants	156.0	8
55.	Devin Funchess (2)	Panthers	155.8	7

56.	Emmanuel Sanders	Broncos	155.2	11
57.	Stefon Diggs (2)	Vikings	149.0	6
58.	Josh Doctson (R)	Redskins	148.0	9
59.	Will Fuller (R)	Texans	146.5	9
60.	Eddie Royal	Bears	146.0	9
61.	Kenny Britt	Rams	143.0	8
62.	Mohamed Sanu (NO)	Falcons	139.0	11
63.	Robert Woods	Bills	134.0	10
64.	Dorial Green-Beckham (2) (UPS)	Titans	128.0	13
65.	Davante Adams (3) (DNS)	Packers	126.7	4
66.	Jermaine Kearse	Seahawks	126.4	5
67.	Chris Hogan (NO)	Patriots	124.8	9
68.	Breshad Perriman (2) (INJ)	Ravens	123.5	8
69.	Seth Roberts (2)	Raiders	120.0	10
70.	Tajae Sharpe (R) (UPS)	Titans	118.0	13
71.	Victor Cruz	Giants	118.0	8
72.	Michael Thomas (R) (UPS)	Saints	114.0	5
73.	Phillip Dorsett (2)	Colts	114.0	10
74.	Nelson Agholor (2)	Eagles	113.2	4
75.	Kenny Stills	Dolphins	109.5	8
76.	Sammie Coates (2) (UPS)	Steelers	108.4	8
77.	Marqis Lee (3)	Jaguars	108.0	5
78.	Andrew Hawkins	Browns	107.0	13
79.	Cecil Shorts	Texans	106.5	9
80.	Corey Brown (3)	Panthers	106.0	7
81.	Stevie Johnson	Chargers	104.0	11
82.	Cole Beasley	Cowboys	104.0	7
83.	Rashad Greene (2) (UPS)	Jaguars	99.0	5
84.	Justin Hardy (2)	Falcons	94.8	11
85.	Brian Quick	Rams	93.0	8
86.	Albert Wilson (3)	Chiefs	92.0	5
87.	Kolby Listenbee (R)	Bills	92.0	10
88.	Rueben Randle (NO)	Eagles	87.6	4
89.	TJ Jones (2)	Lions	87.0	10
90.	Jarius Wright	Vikings	86.5	6
91.	Danny Amendola	Patriots	83.6	9
92.	Jamison Crowder (2)	Redskins	83.0	9
93.	Tyler Boyd (R) (UPS)	Bengals	81.6	9
94.	Marquess Wilson (INJ)	Bears	80.4	9
95.	Jaelen Strong (2)	Texans	76.5	9
96.	Quinton Patton	49ers	75.4	8
97.	Kamar Aiken	Ravens	70.7	8
98.	Quincy Enunwa (3)	Jets	68.4	4
99.	Josh Huff (3)	Eagles	62.0	4
100.	Leonte Carroo (R)	Dolphins	43.0	8

Ranks reflect value based on 16 weeks of play. Past performance was considered as were issues relating to each team's offense including the offense run by the team's offensive coordinator, any coaching changes and personnel changes, and which players are listed as starters and back-ups on the most recent depth charts.

KEY: (NO) = New Offense; (UPS) = Upside; (IRSK) = Injury Risk; (INJ) = Injured; (DNS) = Downside; (R) = Rookie

WIDE RECEIVER RANKINGS (Non-PPR)

	Player	Team	Value	Bye
1.	Antonio Brown	Steelers	286.5	8
2.	Odell Beckham Jr. (3)	Giants	244.0	8
3.	Julio Jones (IRSK)	Falcons	233.0	11
4.	Allen Robinson (3)	Jaguars	222.0	5
5.	Jordy Nelson	Packers	216.4	4
6.	Brandon Marshall	Jets	215.5	11
7.	Dez Bryant	Cowboys	207.0	7
8.	DeAndre Hopkins	Texans	205.8	9
9.	Keenan Allen	Chargers	195.0	11
10.	Sammy Watkins (3) (INJ)	Bills	194.8	10
11.	TY Hilton	Colts	194.7	10
12.	Alshon Jeffrey	Bears	194.0	9
13.	Mike Evans (3)	Buccaneers	192.0	6
14.	AJ Green	Bengals	188.1	9
15.	Golden Tate	Lions	188.0	10
16.	Brandin Cooks (3)	Saints	181.5	5
17.	Randall Cobb	Packers	180.0	4
18.	Kelvin Benjamin (3)	Panthers	176.0	7
19.	Amari Cooper (2)	Raiders	174.5	10
20.	Jarvis Landry (3)	Dolphins	172.0	8
21.	Jeremy Maclin	Chiefs	169.6	5
22.	Eric Decker	Jets	168.8	11
23.	Allen Hurns (3)	Jaguars	168.0	5
24.	John Brown (3)	Cardinals	162.7	9
25.	Marvin Jones (NO)	Lions	161.1	10
26.	Larry Fitzgerald	Cardinals	156.9	9
27.	Tavon Austin	Rams	156.5	8
28.	Steve Smith	Ravens	156.0	8
29.	Torrey Smith (NO) (DNS)	49ers	156.0	8
30.	DeVante Parker (2)	Dolphins	155.4	8
31.	Jordan Mathews (3) (NO) (UPS)	Eagles	154.2	4
32.	Donte Moncrief (3)	Colts	147.2	10
33.	Tyler Lockett (2) (UPS)	Seahawks	145.0	5
34.	Michael Crabtree	Raiders	143.5	10
35.	Michael Floyd	Cardinals	140.0	9
36.	Julian Edelman	Patriots	137.4	9
37.	Willie Snead (2)	Saints	137.2	5
38.	Mike Wallace (NO)	Ravens	136.2	8
39.	Markus Wheaton	Steelers	136.0	8
40.	Doug Baldwin	Seahawks	135.5	5
41.	Vincent Jackson	Buccaneers	135.0	6
42.	Travis Benjamin (NO)	Chargers	134.0	11
43.	DeSean Jackson	Redskins	132.2	9
44.	Kevin White (2) (UPS)	Bears	126.0	9
45.	Demaryius Thomas	Broncos	120.0	11
46.	Corey Coleman (R) (UPS)	Browns	119.3	13
47.	Bruce Ellington (3) (NO)	49ers	118.2	8
48.	Terrance Williams	Cowboys	113.5	7
49.	Laquon Treadwell (R)	Vikings	111.6	6
50.	Devin Funchess (3)	Panthers	110.8	7
51.	Emmanuel Sanders	Broncos	110.2	11
52.	Brandon LaFell (NO)	Bengals	107.2	9
53.	Sterling Shepard (R)	Giants	106.0	8
54.	Will Fuller (R)	Texans	101.5	9

55.	Rishard Matthews (NO)	Titans	99.0	13
56.	Josh Doctson (R)	Redskins	98.0	9
57.	Kendall Wright	Titans	96.6	13
58.	Eddie Royal	Bears	96.0	9
59.	Pierre Garcon	Redskins	94.8	9
60.	Stefon Diggs (2)	Vikings	94.0	6
61.	Kenny Britt	Rams	93.0	8
62.	Dorial Green-Beckham (2) (UPS)	Titans	92.0	13
63.	Mohamed Sanu (NO)	Falcons	89.0	11
64.	Jermaine Kearse	Seahawks	86.4	5
65.	Davante Adams (3) (DNS)	Packers	81.7	4
66.	Robert Woods	Bills	81.0	10
67.	Seth Roberts (2)	Raiders	80.0	10
68.	Victor Cruz	Giants	78.0	8
69.	Tajae Sharpe (R)	Titans	78.0	13
70.	Chris Hogan (NO)	Patriots	74.8	9
71.	Phillip Dorsett (2)	Colts	74.0	10
72.	Breshad Perriman (INJ) (2)	Ravens	73.5	8
73.	Nelson Agholor (2) (NO)	Eagles	73.2	4
74.	Michael Thomas (R) (UPS)	Saints	69.0	5
75.	Sammie Coates (2) (UPS)	Steelers	68.4	8
76.	Corey Brown (3)	Panthers	66.0	7
77.	Cole Beasley	Cowboys	64.0	7
78.	Stevie Johnson	Chargers	64.0	11
79.	Brian Quick	Rams	63.0	8
80.	Marqis Lee (3)	Jaguars	63.0	5
81.	Cecil Shorts	Texans	61.5	9
82.	Kenny Stills	Dolphins	59.5	8
83.	Rashad Greene (2) (UPS)	Jaguars	59.0	5
84.	Rueben Randle (NO)	Eagles	57.6	4
85.	Albert Wilson (3)	Chiefs	57.0	5
86.	Kolby Listenbee (R)	Bills	57.0	10
87.	Andrew Hawkins	Browns	57.0	13
88.	TJ Jones (2)	Lions	57.0	10
89.	Justin Hardy (2)	Falcons	54.8	11
90.	Marquess Wilson (INJ)	Bears	52.4	9
91.	Jarius Wright	Vikings	51.5	6
92.	Jamison Crowder (2)	Redskins	48.0	9
93.	Tyler Boyd (R) (UPS)	Bengals	46.6	9
94.	Jaelen Strong (2)	Texans	46.5	9
95.	Kamar Aiken	Ravens	45.7	8
96.	Quinton Patton	49ers	45.4	8
97.	Danny Amendola	Patriots	43.6	9
98.	Quincy Enunwa (3)	Jets	38.4	11
99.	Josh Huff (3) (NO)	Eagles	37.0	4
100.	Leonte Carroo (R)	Dolphins	23.0	8

Ranks reflect value based on 16 weeks of play. Past performance was considered as were issues relating to each team's offense including the offense run by the team's offensive coordinator, any coaching changes and personnel changes, and which players are listed as starters and back-ups on the most recent depth charts.

KEY: (NO) = New Offense; (UPS) = Upside; (IRSK) = Injury Risk; (INJ) = Injured; (DNS) = Downside; (R) = Rookie; (2) = 2nd Year WR; (3) = 3rd Year WR

WIDE RECEIVER PROFILES

1. Antonio Brown, Steelers - BYE: 8

In the last two seasons, **Antonio Brown** has cemented his position as the best wide receiver in the NFL. Coming off of a season where he hauled in 136 passes for over 1,800 yards and 10 touchdowns, there is no question Brown is the key piece of the prolific Steelers offense. What is interesting to note is that Brown put up those 2015 numbers while playing four games with the likes of **Michael Vick** and **Landry Jones** at quarterback. If Ben **Roethlisberger** can play 16 games, expect Antonio Brown to make a serious push for the 2,000 yard plateau in 2016. Brown is this season's No. 1 draft pick in all fantasy formats. (RB)

2. Julio Jones, Falcons - BYE: 11

Julio Jones exploded in 2015 catching 136 passes for a whopping total of 1,871 receiving yards, bringing his average to 116.9 yards per game. Unfortunately, Jones could find the end zone just 8 times, all low numbers when you consider the number of yards and catches. **Kyle Shanahan's** offense suits Julio Jones well. Jones will continue to thrive at a similar level. Julio Jones is a Top 3 fantasy wide receiver who'll be drafted in the first round of all fantasy drafts. (IE)

3. Odell Beckham, Jr., Giants - BYE: 8

After just two seasons, **Odell Beckham, Jr.** is already considered one of the best wide receivers in the league. His 2015 statistics were incredible with 96 receptions on 158 targets for 1,450 yards and 13 TDs. Beckham accounts for over 35% of the TD passes thrown by **Eli Manning**. His accomplishments over the 2015 season were many, including most touchdowns of fifty yards or more yards and most number of games receiving of one hundred or more yards. The only negative blemish in his 2015 season was his suspension for one game due to multiple personal fouls in the game against Panthers' cornerback **Josh Norman** in week 15 of the season. That one game suspension may have caused fantasy football players to lose their championship league game due to his absence. Expect more of the same this season. Odell Beckham, Jr. is a Top 5 pick in all fantasy football formats. (AG)

4. Allen Robinson, Jaguars - BYE: 5

Allen Robinson was probably one of two things for fantasy team managers last year: a sleeper who carried you to improbable success on the back of a breakout 1,400 yard, 14 TD season; or, somebody else's sleeper who made them hate themselves the whole season. Either way, many people are big on Robinson this season: he's projected to come off the board in the first round. This is somewhat shocking given his career expectations and productivity. And while one could say he's due to let fantasy team managers down, it's a new era for wide receivers where star wide receivers tend to progress rather than regress, especially in their third year as a pro. Robinson should again be the Jaguars most targeted and leading receiver with 1,400-plus yards, double digit TDs, and 80-plus receptions. (GC)

5. Brandon Marshall, Jets - BYE: 11

Brandon Marshall's first season with the Jets was outstanding as he caught 109 receptions for 1,502 yards and 14 touchdowns. It was his second best season in yardage and his best season in touchdowns. His 109 receptions was an added boost in PPR leagues. Add wide receiver **Devin Smith** and running back **Matt Forte**, and it makes it difficult for Marshall to put numbers up better than he did in 2015. Although this will be Marshall's eleventh year in the league, he still knows what it takes to be a dominant receiver. With 1,400 yards and double digit TDs still doable, Brandon Marshall remains a Top 10 wide receiver in all formats with **Ryan Fitzpatrick** as his quarterback. Marshall will be drafted in the early rounds of all leagues. (IE/JS)

6. Jordy Nelson, Packers - BYE: 4

In a preseason game last year, **Jordy Nelson** suffered a season ending knee injury. In 2014, Nelson had his best season, catching 98 balls for 1,519 yards and 13 touchdowns. To expect Nelson to duplicate those numbers in 2016 is a stretch, but if Nelson is at 100%, which from early reports indicates he is, he'll once again be a Top 10 wide receiver ear-marked for 90-plus receptions for 1,400-plus yards and double digit TDs. With coming off an injury like Nelson suffered, some fantasy owners might be reluctant to spend a high draft pick on Nelson, which makes him quite a steal in the late first round or second round of fantasy drafts. Jordy Nelson is the Packers No. 1 fantasy player. (JW)

7. Dez Bryant, Cowboys - BYE: 7

Dez Bryant has been a top wide receiver in the league ever since he was drafted in the first round out of 2010. Bryant has had over 1,200 receiving yards in 3 of his last 4 seasons. The one season where he didn't have over 1,200 yards was last season as **Tony Romo** was injured or hampered by injury. Bryant only compiled 401 receiving yards in 2015 because of injury. He will be limited during preseason activities, but Bryant should be good to go for another spectacular year. Dez Bryant is a Top 10 wide receiving option whose upside is tied mostly to Romo's health. (IE)

8. DeAndre Hopkins, Texans - BYE: 9

DeAndre Hopkins is a special player who took the next step in 2015 after a breakout 2014 campaign. He is coming off of a season in which he caught 111 receptions for 1,521 yards and 11 TDs with several quarterbacks. With Osweiler at the helm, Hopkins should get even more targets in the short and intermediate parts of the field which bodes well for him in PPR formats. Even with **Lamar Miller** in the backfield, the Texans best red zone play will be fades and back-shoulder throws to Hopkins who has become a true master of each. The additions of **Will Fuller** and **Braxton Miller** in the draft are enticing because in theory, this would take away from Hopkins' insane amount of targets, 192 in 2015. The truth is the Texans are looking to play faster and take away double teams from Hopkins in 2016. Regardless, DeAndre Hopkins should thrive even though the reception totals should drop a little bit, in line for double digit TDs and 1,400-plus yards. He's a Top 10 wide receiver and will be drafted in the first round of most fantasy drafts. (SB)

9. Golden Tate, Lions - BYE: 10

Golden Tate is poised for a breakout 2016 season. Last season was a down year as Tate only piled up 813 yards compared to his 1,331 in 2014. He has the opportunity and ability to put up great numbers like he did in 2014 (99 rec., 1,331 yards, 4 TDs) with superstar WR **Calvin Johnson's** retiring. Expect Golden Tate to do exactly that while adding several more touchdowns to the mix. Tate is a solid WR2 who should post numbers like a WR1 in PPR leagues. He's easily a fourth round pick in all fantasy formats. (JQ/JS)

10. Keenan Allen, Chargers - BYE: 11

In the 37 total games he's played, **Keenan Allen** has averaged almost six catches per game for 69 yards and 0.43 touchdowns, which averages to around 15 points per game in standard fantasy leagues. Before his injury last season, he was among the league's elite. His resume places him as a back-end first WR1, but he has the potential for much more. Keenan Allen safely projects for 100 catches and 1,400 yards, with the potential for double digit touchdowns as Rivers seeks a consistent target. As for his injury, while it sounds gruesome, a lacerated kidney is a fluke injury and should be nothing to worry about. Keenan Allen will be off fantasy draft boards by the end of Round 2. (GC)

11. TY Hilton, Colts - BYE: 10

T.Y. Hilton is the go-to receiver the Colts expected to have a breakout season in 2015, but injuries to **Andrew Luck** took their toll. Hilton still hauled in 69 receptions (a career low) for 1,124 yards and 5 TDs. With Luck back, T.Y. Hilton should bounce back this season and be on track for 1,400 yards receiving and 8 TDs, pushing for 90 receptions. He's a low-end WR1 in 12 team or larger leagues, but will be drafted by most as a WR2. Hilton will be a steal if selected in Round 3. (IE/JS)

12. Alshon Jeffery, Bears - BYE: 9

Alshon Jeffery is an elite wide receiver, arguably the best in the league when healthy. And there's the caveat: *when* he's healthy. Jeffery has only played in two full seasons, where he was clearly banged up and didn't perform at 100%, while playing in ten or less games in his *other two seasons*. Alshon Jeffery is playing for a new contract, a great motivator for players. Regardless of his contract status, Jeffery has been and will continue to be **Jay Cutler's** number one option in the passing game. Ear-mark Jeffery for around 1,400 yards receiving, 7 to 9 TDs, on 85 to 90 receptions. He's a solid pick in Round 2 of fantasy drafts. (GC)

13. WR Mike Evans, Buccaneers - BYE: 6

The second year wide receiver continued to prove to be the number one passing option for the Buccaneers as he ranked eleventh in overall receiving, with 1,206 yards, despite missing the first two games of the season. What lacked, however, was Evans' touchdown total. In 2014, he caught 12 touchdowns, while in 2015, he caught an unimpressive 3 touchdowns. During the Buccaneers 0-4 finish, it was evident Mike Evans was frustrated with the offense and often the officiating, which led to a game ejection against the Panthers. Looking forward to the 2016 season, Evans is still a borderline WR1 in standard sized leagues. He'll look to improve his relationship with **Jameis Winston**. One of the best things going for Mike Evans is the lack of other options in the Bucs passing game. Look for Evans to breakout in his third-year as a pro. He should lead the team in receptions and post 1,400-yards with 8 to 10 touchdowns. (EG)

14. AJ Green, Bengals - BYE: 9

The Bengals will go as far as **Andy Dalton** and **A.J. Green** take them. Since being drafted in Cincinnati, Green has been consistently dominant: he's garnered over 1,000 yards every season and caught double-digit TDs in three of the last five seasons, and he's finished at or near top-ten for fantasy receivers every full season he's played, at least in PPR leagues. While it may feel like the fantasy football world has grown tired of Green's continued excellence, it boils down to Green's effectiveness in PPR versus non-PPR leagues. In PPR leagues, Green had a 2015 QFG rating (Quality Fantasy Games) of 73%. This means in 73% of his games he's posting some combination of yards and TDs which equate to double digit fantasy points. In non-PPR leagues, the rating drops to 47%. In case, he's still a top receiver carrying WR2 value in part, because other wide receivers are expected to do better. A.J. Green is still pegged to post 1,200 yards or more, double digit TDs, and 85 receptions or more. He's a solid second round pick in PPR leagues and a solid third round pick in non-PPR leagues. (GC/JS)

15. Brandin Cooks, Saints - BYE: 5

Entering his third year as a pro, **Brandin Cooks** is a borderline number one wide receiver in all leagues, worth drafting once your fantasy draft hits round three or four. Cooks snagged 84 passes for 1,138 yards and nine touchdowns last season. He is the number one receiving threat in the Saints offense. If you're going to draft a wide receiver from the Saints, make it Cooks. He and **Willie Snead** have made it a goal to become one of the best receiving duos in the league. If Snead can show comparable improvement, teams will struggle picking just one receiver to double cover on the Saints. (GC)

16. Randall Cobb, Packers - BYE: 4

Without **Jordy Nelson** lining up opposite **Randall Cobb**, Cobb saw his receiving numbers drop in 2015. Cobb played banged up for a good part of the season. In 2014, with Nelson in the starting lineup, Cobb had his best season of his career, catching 91 passes for 1,287 yards with 12 touchdowns. But without Nelson, Cobb saw his numbers drop to 79 receptions for 829 yards and 6 touchdowns. His 2015 numbers weren't awful by any means, but they still weren't the numbers you would expect from a team's presumed number one passing option. With Nelson returning this season, Randall Cobb should get back to where he was in 2014. When Randall Cobb has Nelson playing opposite of him, Cobb is arguably the best slot wide receiver in the league. A 1,200-plus yard season with near 10 TDs would be a good bounce back season for Cobb. You can target him with a third or fourth round draft pick. (JW)

17. Sammy Watkins, Bills - BYE: 10

Sammy Watkins put up a stellar 1,047 receiving yards and 9 TDs in his sophomore season, playing in just 13 games. Watkins will be **Tyrod Taylor's** top target once again in 2016. Unfortunately, he suffered a broken foot during OTAs. While he's expected to be ready for the regular season, the situation must be monitored. If Watkins misses any time, it impacts the value of Tyrod Taylor negatively. If Watkins is healthy, he can be an above average choice for WR1 in non-PPR leagues and for WR2 in PPR leagues. Sammy Watkins will likely be off most draft boards by the end of Round 3. (JQ)

18. Jeremy Maclin, Chiefs - BYE: 5

Jeremy Maclin is the Chiefs go to wide receiver. Despite a Chiefs offense which utilizes its tight end in the passing game, Maclin was still a favorite of **Alex Smith.** Maclin totaled 87 receptions with 1,088 and 8 touchdowns in his first season with the Chiefs. He finished as the leading receiver on the team. That the Chiefs have a strong running game and incorporate more than one tight end in many formations will leave Maclin on an island with a corner back more times than not. Long story short, Jeremy Maclin wins these battles. Maclin should again be good for 85 receptions for 1,100 yards and 9 TDs. He's a solid WR2 in all formats. (IE)

19. Jarvis Landry, Dolphins. BYE 8

Jarvis Landry set a league record for most receptions in his first two seasons with 194. Landry has some of the best hands in the league, and his crisp routes always give Tannehill a reliable target to throw to. Jarvis Landry will draw more attention from defenses this season. Still, he is one of the best playmakers in the league. Landry is a solid WR2 in all fantasy formats, ranked higher in PPR leagues. Jarvis Landry is the best fantasy player the Dolphins have. (TA)

20. Amari Cooper, Raiders - BYE: 10

As a rookie, selected fourth overall in last year's draft, **Amari Cooper** blew up the gridiron for 72 receptions for 1,070 yards and 6 TDs, tops among rookie wide receivers last season. Expect Cooper to take the next step in his maturation with a bigger role in the offense: 85 receptions, 1,200-plus yards, and 8 TDs. Amari Cooper is a solid WR2 who you can draft in the third round of PPR leagues or the fourth round of non-PPR leagues. (IE)

21. Kelvin Benjamin, Panthers - BYE: 7

Kelvin Benjamin is slotted as the twenty-first best receiver on the board in PPR leagues, eighteenth in non-PPR leagues. Benjamin showed a sliver of his potential during his rookie year in 2014, when he netted over 1,000 yards and nine touchdowns. With last season's ACL injury behind him, he's a steal if he falls to you in the fourth or fifth round of your fantasy draft. **Cam Newton** loves Benjamin, and he will be a big part of the offense. A repeat of 2014's 73-1,008-9 stat line is easily doable. (GC)

22. Eric Decker, Jets - BYE: 11

Eric Decker played a major role in Fitzpatrick's franchise record breaking season as he compiled 80 receptions for 1,027 yards and 12 scores. Eric Decker's 6'3" frame makes him a large target for **Ryan Fitzpatrick**, which is why they succeeded in 2015. Decker's status will remain the same on the depth chart, but his fantasy football statistics may decrease slightly with the moves they made this offseason. Still, Decker is in line for 1,000-plus yards receiving and double digit TDs. View Decker as a solid WR2 in all formats. (IE)

23. Allen Hurns, Jaguars - BYE: 5

Allen Hurns got a well-deserved payday this offseason, rewarding a key part of one of the league's youngest offensive powerhouses. His 10 TDs and 1,000-plus yards are a reasonable prediction for what he'll see in 2016. While **Blake Bortles** is likely to regress in his number of touchdowns, counter-part wide receiver **Allen Robinson** is also likely to garner a lot of double teams after the season he had. This leaves Hurns as a solid option for your WR2 position, and one that won't break the bank. (GC)

24. Larry Fitzgerald, Cardinals - BYE: 9

Cardinals fans can thank former Head Coach **Dennis Green** for two things. First, the epic "The Bears are who we thought they were" rant *and* Larry Fitzgerald. The 2004 draft was actually good for the Cardinals, as they secured the likes of **Darnell Dockett** and **Karlos Dansby** with the future Hall of Famer Fitzgerald. Number "11" is a legend in the Valley of the Sun, but he has truly thrived when the Cardinals have had a competent QB under center. Fantasy-wise, Fitz was a 'Renaissance Man' in 2015, posting a career high in catches (109) to go with 1,215 yards and 9 TDs. Paired with **Carson Palmer**, a healthy Fitzgerald could put up similar but *lesser* numbers once again in 2016 probably a few less catches, but perhaps another TD or two. A free agent-to-be after the season, Larry Fitzgerald's long-term future is unclear. That aside, Fitzgerald is only 32 years old, and is a solid WR2 option in redraft leagues with more than enough upside to offset potential risks. (CB)

25. Marvin Jones, Lions - BYE: 10

Marvin Jones arrives in Detroit after spending the last few seasons in the shadow of WR **A.J. Green**, much like **Golden Tate** was with **Calvin Johnson**. With both Jones and Tate out from under their superstar counterparts, they should complement one another in a balanced Lions offense. Pairing Jones ability to stretch the secondary and Stafford's arm could make for a good season for the former Bengal. There's genuinely good opportunity here for Marvin Jones where he should reach 80 receptions for 1,000 yards and five-plus TDs. Jones is a borderline WR2 for fantasy draft purposes. (JQ)

26. Jordan Matthews, Eagles - BYE: 4

After racking up nearly 1,000 yards last season and 8 touchdowns, **Jordan Mathews** could average near double digit fantasy points in standard leagues. Expect the third year pass catcher to be the Eagles top wide receiver. He should post numbers at least similar to last season but will likely do better with there being no other real competition for receptions besides **Zach Ertz**. Matthews is a WR3 with upside who likely won't make it past the fifth round of all drafts. (JQ/JS)

27. John Brown, Cardinals - BYE: 9

The sure-handed speedster continues to grow and thrive in **Bruce Arians**' vertical passing attack. In just his second season, Brown surpassed 1,000 yards and grabbed 7 TDs for the Cardinals, and an argument could be made he was the best player on the field in his 10 catch, 196 yard receiving performance against the Steelers. Brown is unique because, despite his slight build and speed, he routinely operates in the middle of the field as a possession receiver. Brown has focused on strength and conditioning, and continues to improve his release. With all of the competition at WR for the Cardinals, it's more art than science to determine the pecking order, but Brown has WR2 skills and the ability to take any play to the house. Give Brown a slightly higher rating in dynasty formats, as he takes a little hit in PPR leagues. (CB)

28. Steve Smith, Sr., Ravens - BYE: 8

After tearing his Achilles in week eight last season, it's hard to believe that the thirty-seven year old **Steve Smith** has anything left in the tank. But, if anyone can return to play at an elite level, it's the cantankerous Smith who was on pace for over 1,500 yards receiving and 6 TDs at the time of his injury. Steve Smith did enough to earn the trust of Joe Flacco as he was pacing 100-plys receptions at the time of injury. With some new faces added to the offense, however, it's safe to view Smith as a high-end WR3, worth 80 catches for 1,000 yards and 6 TFDs. (FG)

29. Julius Edelman, Patriots - BYE: 9

Another rehabilitating Patriots playmaker, **Julian Edelman** is coming off two foot surgeries this offseason, but is expected to be ready for training camp. Edelman disappointed last year with only 693 receiving yards, but hauled in a career-high 7 touchdowns. His fantasy prospects are a little darker this year with the competition around him, so don't jump to draft him in the early rounds. He projects better as a WR3 this season. (DG)

30. Donte Moncrief, Colts - BYE: 10

Donte Moncreif is coming off of a toe injury and has missed OTAs. With **Andrew Luck** at quarterback last season, Moncreif caught 32 passes (out of 64 on the season) for 331 yards (out of 733 on the season) and 5 TDs (out of 6 on the season) in the 7 games the two played together. Entering his third season as a pro, Donte Moncrief is ear-marked to have a breakout season. This 6'2" tall, 220 lb. wide-out could show he is the most talented wide receiver the Colts have on their roster. Pencil Moncrief in for 1,100-plus yards and 6 to 8 TDs on 80 receptions. He likens to a high end WR3, with upside, who should be drafted before draft picks end in Round 7 end. (IE/JS)

31. Michael Crabtree, Raiders - BYE: 10

Michael Crabtree surprised all with his production last season, his first season in the Raiders' offense. Crabtree impressed by gaining the trust of **Derek Carr** early, being targeted a team high 146 times on the season. Crabtree caught 85 passes for 902 yards and 9 touchdowns. With defenses focusing coverage on **Amari Cooper**, Crabtree found his place in this offense. Crabtree has the potential to have an even better year with the Raiders. But, as other weapons in the offense emerge, Crabtree may have hit his ceiling. Michael Crabtree is a low-end WR3 in all formats. (IE/JS)

32. Torrey Smith, 49ers - BYE: 8

In his inaugural 49ers season, Smith predictably posted career lows in catches, yards and touchdowns. This took place on the league's thirty-second ranked offense in points scored. Smith is the clear cut #1 WR option which makes him a candidate for 100 targets this year. He still has home-run ability and speed to burn. Whomever the quarterback is just has to be accurate enough to set Smith up for success. In Chip Kelly's offense, expect Smith to put up numbers similar to the Baltimore days of 60 catches, 950 yards and 10 touchdowns. (DG)

33. Tavon Austin, Rams - BYE: 8

Tavon Austin is a dual threat wide receiver who can beat you in the passing game and the running game. Combined, Austin totaled 907 all-purpose yards and 9 TDs. His primary problem is his quality fantasy games rating (QFG Rating) is undesirable, mostly. In PPR leagues, it's just above 50% while in non-PPR leagues, it's below 50%. He definitely has WR3 appeal in PPR leagues but is better used as a flex player given his uneven production. The Rams want to get Tavon Austin the football behind the dynamic **Todd Gurley**. He's already the Rams' primary playmaker in the passing game with 52 receptions in 2015. At a minimum, expect more of the same for Tavion Austin in 2016. At a maximum, he could take a big step forward with consistent quarterback play. He'll be a solid pick early in the final third of fifteen round fantasy drafts in PPR leagues. (JQ/JS)

34. DeVante Parker, Dolphins. BYE 8

Parker blossomed in the last six games of 2016. In those games, Parker showed he could perform at the pro-level and he made a few highlight catches. Parker can run crisp routes and get the deep ball. This season, with **Jarvis Landry** drawing even more attention, look for Parker to be the primary red zone threat. Because of an abundance of wide receivers expected to produce in the WR2/WR3 range, **DeVante Parker** projects as a great WR3 with upside, fully capable of a 1,000 yard-plus season and six TDs on 60 interceptions. (TA)

35. Willie Snead, Saints - BYE: 5

Willie Snead's impressive 984 yards receiving were offset by a paltry three touchdowns. At a minimum, Snead should produce 1,000 yards receiving and increase his number of touchdowns. At a maximum, he and Brandin Cooks become one of the league's most improbable top receiving duos. Snead will provide excellent value in fantasy drafts. He possesses low-end WR3 value but will likely be drafted when many WR4s are, in the tenth or eleventh rounds. He and Cooks should be a solid duo. While neither should be spectacular, both should be above average. (GC)

36. Mike Wallace, Ravens - BYE: 8

After a down year with the pass-challenged Vikings (39 catches, 473 yards, 2 TDs), the worst in his seven-year career, **Mike Wallace** gets a new opportunity to show off his wares on a team which could definitely use him. Wallace has extreme downfield ability which **Joe Flacco** should be able to take advantage of. Flacco's strength is the long ball, so look for Wallace to resurrect his career in Baltimore. He should fit in nicely as the team's touchdown maven in the passing game. In fantasy, Mike Wallace is a border-line WR3 capable of 70 receptions for near 900 yards and 8 TDs. (FG)

37. Doug Baldwin, Seahawks - BYE: 5

Doug Baldwin established himself as the Seahawks No. 1 wide receiver in 2015. Baldwin led the team with 78 receptions, 1,069 yards, and 14 touchdowns. He finished as a Top 10 wide receiver last year and some people think he's there to stay. With the Seahawks getting back to running the football, **Jimmy Graham** (the second most targeted Seahawks player in 2015 despite missing 5 games) returning, and **Tyler Lockett** stepping up in the offense, it's more likely Baldwin reverts to the numbers he posted in 2013 and 2104. Scoring another 14 touchdowns seems highly unlikely. Defenses should give more attention to Baldwin in 2016. So, he may be over drafted in some leagues. Doug Baldwin projects for 65 to 70 receptions nearing 900 yards and six to eight touchdowns. This season, he's a low end WR3 or flex play. To land him, you must likely draft him in the late fourth to early fifth round of your fantasy draft, which would be a few rounds too early. (SB)

38. Markus Wheaton, Steelers - BYE: 8

Markus Wheaton should have come into his own by now. With **Martavis Bryant** suspended, one would think this could be a breakout year for Wheaton. While his production could slightly take a turn for the better, fantasy team managers should expect more of the same. Wheaton does not seem to have the unspoken chemistry with Roethlisberger. Expect an emergence of **Sammie Coates** with Bryant gone for the season. For Wheaton, expect around 60 catches and 850 yards this season with 6 to 8 touchdowns. (RB)

39. Michael Floyd, Cardinals - BYE: 9

Floyd might be one of the more intriguing storylines for the Cardinals in 2016. In the last year of his rookie contract, Floyd has all of the talent needed to be a solid number one receiver in the league. But, his inconsistent play and injury history made him trade bait during this year's draft. In 2015, Floyd suffered a gruesome hand injury in the preseason. While he missed none of the regular season, he didn't really become a consistent weapon in the offense until Week 6. During the middle of the season, Floyd was arguably the Cardinals' best receiver as he put up huge games against the Browns, Vikings and at Seattle, where his 7-113-2 stat line keyed the Cardinals victory over the Seahawks. Let's be honest, **Michael Floyd** could be a star, which makes him a very interesting dynasty pick. For 2016 purposes, Floyd is a low-end WR3 in a good offense with plenty of potential to surprise to the upside. (CB)

40. WR Vincent Jackson, Buccaneers - BYE: 6

An injury-plagued 2015 season resulted in a less than impressive finish for veteran Vincent Jackson, where he only played in 11 of 16 games. Even when healthy, Jackson was not much of a factor in the Buccaneers offense where he recorded 543 yards on the season and where he had 3 catches or less in six games. Overall it is hard to predict what the 33 year old wide receiver has left in the tank. So, he'll be selected in the later rounds of fantasy drafts, in the ninth or tenth rounds. However, he's still the team's second option in the passing game especially with no other player stepping up. If things go well, Vincent Jackson could again dance with 1,000 yards receiving and 5 or more TDs. (EG)

41. Corey Coleman, Browns - BYE: 13

The rookie first round draft pick has a lot of potential even in his first year in the league. **Corey Coleman** must work hard to prove himself and stand out in the crowded WR group in Cleveland. But he will, without a doubt, be one of the more talented options after hauling in 3,009 yards and 33 TDs last season at Baylor. If there is any single rookie wide receiver who could make a big impact, it's Coleman. Someone must catch the football 60 to 70 times among the wide receivers in Hue Jackson's offense, an offense that's thrown the football a little over 480 times over the past two seasons. Consider Corey Coleman to be in line for 850 yards or more and 6 TDs or more as a rookie. Top wide receivers have done well whether **Josh McCown** or **Robert Griffin III** was under center. Coleman is a WR4 in twelve team leagues. (JQ/JS)

42. DeSean Jackson, Redskins - BYE: 9

DeSean Jackson had a disappointing 2015 season as he missed 7 games due to injury. Jackson will enter his eighth season as a pro. He's mostly been a low reception, high production player. However, DeSean Jackson is in a contract year so he should play hard. Jackson should again pace 1,000 yards receiving on 55 receptions for 7 TDs. He's a WR4 who you can draft in Round 9 in standard sized leagues. (IE/JS)

43. Kevin White, Bears - BYE: 9

Kevin White has the potential to be one of the steals of this year's fantasy drafts. All signs point to him having the potential to be a number one wide receiver in the league, and with him slotting up next to **Alshon Jeffery,** who will draw double coverage, White could have a monster season. There's the concern of durability, given he was on IR for the entirety of his rookie season. While that rightfully raises a red flag, it also means that White could fall off the face of some fantasy draft boards. If you've seen Kevin White's college film, the electric wide receiver is a speedster capable of catching any pass. It'd be no surprise if White posts 900 yards receiving, 6 TDs, on 60 receptions in his first season playing. White presents an opportunity to get a fantasy reserve with WR2/3 upside in the middle rounds of drafts in standard sized leagues. (GC/JS)

44. Travis Benjamin, Chargers - BYE: 11

Initially, **Travis Benjamin** will likely be a counter-balance to **Keenan Allen**, who will often see double teams hoping to curtail his production. Benjamin approached 1,000 yards receiving last year with the Browns, but he will no longer be the primary target. It's debatable whether he'll see a sizable decline in his production because Keenan Allen will likely draw opponents' best coverage. Travis Benjamin makes for a TD target much like **Malcolm Floyd** or **Eddie Royal** before him. Benjamin is a tempting pick for fantasy owners, but Rivers will likely spread the ball out between **Keenan Allen, Stevie Johnson, Antonio Gates, Danny Woodhead,** and Benjamin. Far from a safe bet, Benjamin can be view as a WR4 in three wide receiver leagues of 12-teams or less. He's capable of 850 yards receiving and five to eight TDs. (GC)

45. Tyler Lockett, Seahawks - BYE: 5

Lockett became one of the more dangerous weapons in the league last season with 51 receptions for 664 receiving yards and receiving 6 TDs. It further illustrates that he's more than a kick return specialist, which is what he made the 2015 Pro Bowl for, after returning punts and kicks for over 1,200 yards on 73 attempts (16.4 yards per attempt) and scoring 2 return TDs. **Tyler Lockett** is bound for an increase in production entering his second season as a pro. Lockett is at his best in the slot and when put in motion to create match-up problems. He edged out **Jermaine Kearse** in fantasy production in PPR leagues and his stock continued to rise with big weeks against the Vikings, Ravens, and Browns near the end of the season. Tyler Lockett continued his success into the playoffs against the Panthers where he reeled in three catches for 75 yards and a touchdown. Lockett should see a rise in targets from 68 in 2015 and 850 yards receiving is well within reach, even with similar catches, to go with his over five touchdowns. View him as a flex play with upside draftable in the seventh round of most fantasy drafts. (SB)

46. Demaryius Thomas, Broncos - BYE: 11

Even though many (including Thomas himself) consider his 2015 campaign a down year, Thomas was still productive (105 receptions, 1,304 receiving yards, 6 TDs), especially when you consider he was playing for the league's thirty-first ranked passing offense. He looked rusty last season since he held out for most of the offseason program amidst his contract dispute, and was learning a new scheme on the fly. Now, with a full offseason program in the Kubiak offense under his belt, Thomas is primed for a more efficient season *if the quarterback play accommodates him*. It's difficult to say whether **Mark Sanchez** or **Paxton Lynch** will get Thomas the ball often enough or consistently enough for Thomas to make an every week impact. He'll be overdrafted in most fantasy leagues. Keep your fingers crossed "Bay-Bay" makes for a useful fantasy asset as he may struggle to get to 1,000 yards as he has in seasons past when the quarterback play for the Broncos was under-average, i.e., pre-Peyton Manning. (DK)

47. Bruce Ellington, 49ers - BYE: 8

Ellington was a fourth round pick in 2013 out of the University of South Carolina. He is highly athletic with the ability to return kicks and punts, but could never stay on the field consistently. In his first two seasons as a pro, Ellington would either miss time due to injuries or be in the coaches' doghouse due to fumbles. His traits make him seem like a tailor made fit for Chip Kelly's offense. Pluck Ellington up in the later rounds for WR depth on your bench. He has breakout written all over him, especially in Chip Kelly's offense. Expect him to put up a surprising blend of receiving (700 yards) to go with a handful of touchdowns (at least). (DG)

48. Brandon LaFell, Bengals - BYE: 9

Last season, there was no point in **Brandon LaFell** being on any fantasy football team. LaFell didn't grab a single touchdown and was an after-thought down the stretch. However, he showed he had reliable hands as recently as 2014, in which he caught 74 passes for 953 yards and 7 TDs. This means he has value in the right system. Brandon LaFell fills a need after the Bengals lost **Marvin Jones** and **Mohamed Sanu**. But, he must compete for touches, especially in the red zone, with **A.J. Green** and **Tyler Eifert**. The Bengals also spent a high draft pick on **Tyler Boyd**, indicating LaFell's time even as a No. 2 may be limited to this season. Around 850 yards and 4 or 5 TDs is expected of him. Lafell is worth a late round grab as a low-end WR4 or high-end WR5 in PPR and non-PPR leagues, respectively. Just know he may have to fight to remain relevant all season long in the Bengals offense. (GC)

49. Laquon Treadwell, Vikings - BYE: 6

This past season while at the University of Mississippi, **Laquon Treadwell** led arguably the best college football conference (SEC) in receiving. Not blessed with elite speed, Treadwell used his 6'2" frame to outmuscle cornerbacks for catches, something the Vikings are hoping he does during his rookie season. Treadwell is a perfect match for Teddy Bridgewater. Bridgewater struggles with the deep ball and instead relies on precision passing. Laquon Treadwell's game is built the same way. Treadwell doesn't have the speed to beat opposing defenses deep. Instead, he uses precise routes and uses his strength to beat opposing pass defenders. The Vikings need somebody to step up and become the top receiving option for their young quarterback and Treadwell has the talent to be that person. Don't expect Treadwell to catch 100 balls and have 1,200 yards receiving, but he could be a sleeper this season. He's got a better chance of posting several TDs when the team is in the red zone. View Treadwell as a borderline flex-play in standard sized leagues. Treadwell could push for 60 receptions for 750 yards and at least 6 TDs. He might be the best sleeper of this year's draft. (JW)

50. Terrance Williams, Cowboys - BYE: 7

Terrance Williams has spent all three of his seasons in the league with the Cowboys. With **Dez Bryant** out seven games, Williams set career highs in 2015 with 52 passes for 840 yards. One issue was he scored just 3 touchdowns last season, significantly lower than his 8 touchdowns in 2014. We have likely seen the best Terrance Williams must offer. With **Tony Romo** back, Williams' numbers should increase slightly in 2016 to near 850 yards and 5 TDs. (IE)

51. Kendall Wright, Titans - BYE: 13

Kendall Wright is coming off of his worst year as a pro in which he caught 36 passes for 408 yards and three touchdowns. Wright was another Titans fantasy option who couldn't stay healthy as he missed six games in 2015. His breakout 2013 sophomore season where he caught 94 passes for 1,079 yards feels like so long ago. Kendall Wright is entering the "what could've been" category for wide receivers with superior talent who never put everything together. Wright should still put up enough stats to be fantasy-relevant, around 700 yards and a handful of touchdowns. But, his ceiling is capped so much that you'd be better served trying to find a breakout rookie candidate elsewhere. (SB)

52. Pierre Garcon, Redskins - BYE: 9

Pierre Garcon has been a reliable wide receiver for the Redskins over the past few seasons. Garcon posted a similar stat line in both 2014 and 2015. In 2014, Garcon caught 68 passes for 752 yards and 3 touchdowns, and in 2014, he caught 72 passes for 777 yards and 6 touchdowns. Garcon's playing time and stats should diminish (or at least stay the same) with **DeSean Jackson** returning healthy and with highly touted rookie **Josh Doctson** now in the field. Don't overdraft Garcon. He's strictly a reserve. Pierre Garcon can be drafted in the bottom third of fifteen round drafts. (IE)

53. Rishard Matthews, Titans - BYE: 13

It was an interesting move by the Dolphins to let **Rishard Matthews** walk and sign with the Titans. It's just as intriguing that Matthews signed with a team full of second wide receiver options. Rishard Matthews had a nice 2015 season with the Dolphins in which he caught 43 receptions for 662 yards and four touchdowns in just 11 games played. What makes it more impressive is that he only had 61 targets. Matthews was easily on pace for 60-plus receptions and near 1,000 yards receiving last season. What's more, the offseason reports on Rishard Matthews have been positive and he looks to be in line to start. If he nears 100 targets, 60 catches and nearly 700 to 800 yards isn't too far of a stretch for Matthews. However, there are still too many 'ifs' to grade him higher than a late round WR5 or WR6. (SB)

54. Sterling Shepard, Giants - BYE: 8

Oklahoma rookie Sterling Shepard will be the perfect complement to Odell Beckham, Jr. as he's expected to be the Giants new No. 2 receiving option. Shepard's senior year is similar to elite numbers posted by NFL receivers: 86 receptions for 1,288 yards and 11 TDs. Shepard's ability to create separation at the line of scrimmage against the defender and to change direction quickly in coverage make him a prime candidate to be the Giants slot receiver. Despite high expectations, it's difficult viewing Shepard as making the fantasy impact which garners a high draft pick. View him as a WR5 with upside for fantasy. If all goes well, Sterling Shepard is in line for 700 yards and 6 TDs on 50 receptions. In larger leagues, target Shepard with a twelfth or thirteenth round pick. (AG)

55. Devin Funchess, Panthers - BYE: 7

Second round draft picks often carry a lot of expectations. And perhaps, this is why **Devin Funchess** struggled in the first half of the season as he only produced 90 yards receiving over the first seven games of the 2015 season. However, in the second half of the season, Funchess punched it and finished the season with 31 receptions for 473 yards and 5 TDs. Perhaps he took a while to grasp the playbook, or to gain the trust of his team. Now that Devin Funchess has more of a defined role on the team, he's a solid sleeper pick in the later rounds of fantasy drafts, projecting to somewhere around 700 yards and seven touchdowns. (GC)

56. Emmanuel Sanders, Broncos - BYE: 11

After two career seasons in the Mile High City, perhaps **Emmanuel Sanders** is the best wide receiver in the Broncos' stable. He may not be as big as **Demaryius Thomas**, but Sanders has a better route-tree, better hands, and plays with more physicality than Thomas. Those skills could well make him the go-to target for whoever lines up under center for the Broncos in 2016. Also, in the playoffs last season, opponents doubted him as opposed to Thomas, and he still was the Broncos' leading receiver in January and February. Emmanuel Sanders might have a higher fantasy floor…and ceiling…than Demaryius Thomas. However, like Thomas, it's unclear what we'll get from Sanders given the quarterback situation for the Broncos. He could struggle to be a consistent every week fantasy asset. Reaching 1,000 yards receiving could be difficult too for Sanders. (DK)

57. Stefon Diggs, Vikings - BYE: 6

For some unknown reason, Vikings offensive coordinator **Norv Turner** waited until the third game of the season to involve **Stephon Diggs** in the offensive game plan. But when Turner got Diggs involved, Diggs made Vikings fans wonder where he had been. Against the eventual Super Bowl champion Broncos, Stephon Diggs had 6 catches for 87 yards. Diggs would register 2 games of 100 yards or more receiving, and he finished the season as the second leading receiver for the Vikings. Diggs should be helped out this coming season with rookie **Laquon Treadwell** lining up opposite of him. Although Stephon Diggs isn't number one receiving option, he should be a solid number two. Diggs should at least come close to last season' numbers, pacing 50 receptions for 700 yards and 4 to 5 TDs. He's a WR5 worth a late round pick in twelve team leagues or bigger. (JW)

58. Josh Doctson, Redskins - BYE: 9

Josh Doctson was the twenty-second overall pick in this year's draft. For some, he was the No. 1 wide receiver in this year's draft. Doctson had an outstanding season at TCU in 2015 where he tallied 1,327 receiving yards on 79 catches and scored 14 touchdowns in 13 games. Doctson is expected to contribute immediately at least in wide receiver sets. View Josh Doctson as a player with some upside, capable of 700 yards receiving and 4 TDs on 50 receptions. He's a late round pick in fifteen round drafts. (IE)

59. Will Fuller, Texans - BYE: 9

The rookie speedster was taken by the Texans with the twenty-first overall pick in the 2016 draft and his role has yet to be unveiled as anything other than a player who can take the top off of the defense. **Will Fuller**'s hands were a major criticism coming out of the draft, but he was quick to jump into the **Brock Osweiler**-led offseason program where he impressed his teammates with his explosiveness. In college, Fuller went from a high volume receiver as a sophomore with 76 receptions and 1,094 yards to go with 15 touchdowns, to receiver an explosive big play receiver with 62 receptions and 1,258 yards to go with 14 touchdowns. Jumping in average yards per catch between 2014 and 2015 from 14.4 and 20.3 is why the Texans fell in love with Fuller's potential. He's battling with **Jaelen Strong** to be the Texans No. 2 wide receiver, and he should win that battle. Will Fuller should get 80 to 100 targets as the Texans look to push the pace. As long as he is the Texans No. 2 receiving option, Fuller should be good for 45 receptions for 675 yards and a hand full of touchdowns on the low side. Fuller is worth a late round pick in twelve team or bigger leagues. (SB)

60. Eddie Royal, Bears - BYE: 9

Royal is traditionally a slot receiver, and now that he need not play as the Bears' second wide receiver, a role never exactly suited for him, Royal's production should improve slightly. It felt as if he would go missing every other game (and indeed, he did not play in seven of the Bears 2015 games), which raises a major flag about durability. If Royal can stay on the field, he will likely draw some favorable cornerback matchups, as teams use their best corners on **Alshon Jeffery** and **Kevin White**. A conservative estimate is 600 yards and a handful of touchdowns. Eddie Royal is hardly worth a fantasy draft pick (late rounds if at all), but he should be a match-up based play or bye week option in favorable matchups. (GC)

61. Kenny Britt, Rams - BYE: 8

Kenny Britt does not have the same star power as his WR counterpart **Tavon Austin**, but he has the numbers. Britt went for 681 yards on 36 catches with 3 scores last season. He was top three in targets for the Rams and one of the other top three, **Jared Cook**, is no longer with the team. Kenny Britt has the talent. If the Rams could get him the ball, he could make a fantasy difference. Britt will start the season on fantasy waiver wires but monitor his performance. (JQ/JS)

62. Mohamed Sanu, Falcons - BYE: 11

Mohamed Sanu, formerly of the Bengals, was signed to be the Falcons No. 2 wide receiver. With the Bengals, Sanu failed to secure the Bengals No. 2 spot in 2015 after having been the No. 2 in 2014 when **Marvin Jones** missed the season due to injury. Regardless, Mohamed Sanu is in line for 50 receptions as **Julio Jones**' partner. Sanu is not a typical primary receiver, but a compliment to Julio Jones, which is what makes him so valuable. Defenses will double-team Julio Jones and Sanu will see more man-to-man coverage. If he can maintain his status as the team's number two, Sanu should be able to post 600 to 700 yards and 5 TDs or more. There's upside here as **Matt Ryan** tries to find the player who can be the team's productive No. 2 receiver. Sanu makes for a late round pick in leagues with 12 teams or more. (IE/JS)

63. Robert Woods, Bills - BYE: 10

Woods underwent groin surgery after the 2015 season but has made a full recovery and hopes to have a productive year. **Robert Woods** can put up solid numbers, hauling in 47 catches for 552 yards last season, but is the number two target in a Bills offense with a healthy **Sammy Watkins**. But even if Watkins misses time, Robert Woods has been little better without Watkins in the lineup. When he hauled in 65 receptions in 2014, he failed to top 699 yards receiving and 5 TDs. He isn't worth a draft pick except in deeper 14 or 16 team leagues. (JQ/JS)

64. Dorial Green-Beckham, Titans - BYE: 13

Dorial Green-Beckham is one of the most intriguing prospects of the 2016 wide receiver class for several reasons. At 6'5" tall, Green-Beckham is a true red zone weapon. At 237 pounds, he's also a bruiser who can make tough catches all over the field. In the last five weeks of the 2015 season, he came away with 16 of his 32 catches for 306 of his 549 yards and two of his four touchdowns while getting shutout against the Texans in Week 16. Despite this promise, the Titans signed **Rishard Mathews** to compete for one of the top receiving spots and drafted Tajae Sharpe, who is impressing in offseason workouts. The reports surrounding Dorial Green-Beckham this offseason have been largely negative. Green-Beckham is being over-drafted right now and is genuinely at risk of becoming a non-factor to start the season. Monitor the news coming out for Green-Beckham before you draft him in fantasy. The raw talent and upside is there. But, this won't do you any good if his team doesn't play him significant snaps. (SB/JS)

65. Davante Adams, Packers - BYE: 4

With **Jordy Nelson** falling to injury in the preseason in 2015, a lot was expected out of **Davante Adams** in his second season as a pro. Unfortunately, Adams didn't live up to his expectations and he was inured for part of the season. Adams finished the season with 50 receptions for 483 yards and only 1 touchdown. For Adams to be any threat in the Packers passing game, he will need to be stronger so he can get away from bump and run coverage. In addition, improved play from receivers like **Jeff Janis** have created a situation where it isn't guaranteed that Adams will be the team's number three option. **Aaron Rodgers** loves spreading the ball around to his receivers, which makes the number three wide receiver in their offense valuable in fantasy. But, there is no guarantee Adams will be the third wide receiver. So, when selecting a wide receiver late in your draft, steer clear of Davante Adams, at least until he proves he is the player the Packers are hoping he can become. (JW)

66. Jermaine Kearse, Seahawks - BYE: 5

Jermaine Kearse's role as the number two wide receiver on the Seahawks was challenged in 2015 by Tyler Lockett, but Kearse came away with some monster games against quality competition. He had six receptions or more in only four regular season games though, so there were plenty of weeks were he produced disappointing numbers. It can't be ignored that he showed up against the better teams in the league with touchdowns against the Steelers, Cardinals, Rams and Bengals, with a monster effort in the playoffs against the Panthers where he reeled in 11 of his 15 targets for 110 yards and two touchdowns. Jermaine Kearse has gotten better each year, but seeing the new additions to the offense keeps his value down to undraftable in standard sized leagues of ten or twelve teams, or a WR5/6 in deeper leagues. Topping over 600 yards and 4 TDs should prove difficult for him in an offense with so many playmakers. (SB)

67. Chris Hogan, Patriots - BYE: 9

The Patriots brought Chris Hogan over from the Bills on a 3-year, $12 million deal. He's earned the nickname "7-11" because he's always open. Hogan is a great fit in the Patriots scheme because he is silky smooth, runs great routes, and a heady player that will analyze the Patriots playbook. Chris Hogan was a lacrosse player in college before having to earn a spot on the Dolphins and Giants practice squads. Then, he had to work hard to carve out a niche and earn a spot on the Bills roster. Hogan is a self-made man and a diligent hard worker that the Patriots love. Chris Hogan could produce better numbers than his 36 catches, 450 yards, and 2 touchdowns in 2015. Monitor his offseason as the Patriots really like him. (DG)

68. Breshad Perriman, Ravens - BYE: 8

It's positive news that the Ravens' 2015 first round draft selection suffered no torn ACL this offseason, an injury which could have ended his second season as a pro just as quickly as his first. The dynamic speedster from Central Florida did not play last season after he hurt his knee in training camp. In his last year of college, **Breshad Perriman** produced 50 catches for 1,044 yards and 9 TDs as a mostly one-dimensional speed threat. The Ravens could use his big play ability in a similar role. The Ravens will bring Perriman along slowly given his early career injuries. Perriman will have to prove to the organization he is capable of extended playing time. He's worthy of a late round flier and remains a dynasty hold for now. Monitor his health in the preseason. (FG)

69. Seth Roberts, Raiders - BYE: 10

Seth Roberts proved to be an efficient third receiver for the Raiders this past season as he commanded the third most targets among *all* receivers on the team. This slot receiver compiled 480 yards on 32 catches and found the end zone 5 times. He found his niche in this Raiders offense. Roberts isn't worth a fantasy draft pick. But, if either Cooper or Crabtree go down, it seems almost certain Roberts would step up in the offense. (IE/JS)

70. Tajae Sharpe, Titans - BYE: 13

Rookie **Tajae Sharpe** is being over-looked by many in the fantasy community. But, this likely won't be the case much longer. Sharpe was drafted in the fifth round of the draft out of Massachusetts. He led the country in receptions with 111 which he transformed into 1,319 yards receiving and 5 TDs. The biggest criticism of Tajae Sharp has been his hand size and slender build at 6'2" tall, 194 pounds However, his drop rate was among the best at a lowly 3.0%. The reports on Sharp this summer have been positive. He's getting first team reps ahead of **Dorial Green-Beckham**. He's the sleeper on this team and is worth a late round draft pick in deeper leagues. Tajae Sharp is a later round pick in dynasty drafts. (JS)

71. Victor Cruz, Giants - BYE: 8

Victor Cruz is coming off two injuries (tendon and hamstring) in back-to-back seasons. The last time he played a full 16 game schedule was in 2012. Cruz also missed the entire 2015 season and only played six games in 2014. Before his injuries though, Cruz managed consecutive 1,000 yard seasons and was two yards shy of a third consecutive 1,000 yard season. Although he is familiar with new head coach **Ben McAdoo**'s offense, it's been difficult to view **Victor Cruz** returning to football playing at the same level as he did in earlier, healthier seasons. Cruz is expected to eventually take a back seat to **Sterling Shepard** in the offense. While some may draft Cruz ahead of Shepard, Cruz is better off left undrafted in most fantasy formats, except those with very large rosters in deeper leagues. (AG)

72. Michael Thomas, Saints - BYE: 5

Michael Thomas has the tools to be a phenomenally talented wide receiver. The big wide-out from Ohio State, the nephew of former All-Pro star, wide receiver **Keyshawn Johnson**, has the physical stature to be the Saints top wide receiver. However, there are small flaws in his game, plus he enters in to an offense in which his quarterback loves to spread the ball around. He is a lock to be one of the top three wide receivers in an offense that always runs three wide. Michael Thomas is in store for a good rookie season of 450 yards and a handful of touchdowns. He's only worth a draft pick in the later rounds of deeper 14 or 16 team leagues. Thomas is a solid dynasty draft pick and an obvious hold. (GC)

73. Phillip Dorsett, Colts - BYE: 10

Phillip Dorsett is coming off a hamstring injury but looks ready to go for the regular season. Despite the hamstring injury, Dorsett's role on the field should only expand in an offense which likes to feature three wide receiver sets. He is behind both **T.Y. Hilton** and **Donte Moncrief** on the depth chart, but this means favorable one-on-one matchups on Sundays. Phillip Dorsett could take a major step in his production this season. In terms of a projection, 40 receptions for 500 yards and 4 TDs is doable in an offense that will likely throw the football 600-plus times. Dorsett is worth a late round flier in deeper leagues. (IE/JS)

74. Nelson Agholor, Eagles - BYE: 4

The 2015 first-round pick will likely eclipse his disappointing rookie numbers. The speedster missed three games due to a high ankle sprain last season and never found his groove afterwards, finishing with 23 catches for 283 yards and a TD. While **Nelson Agholor** should improve on those numbers in his sophomore campaign, there's no indication he will. He's boom or bust. With so many better options out there, Nelson Agholor is a player to avoid in fantasy drafts. (JQ/JS)

75. Kenny Stills, Dolphins. BYE 8

Stills had a quiet season last year (27 rec., 440 yards, 3 TDs), but he remains a speedy deep threat. **DeVante Parker** can get the football, and **Kenny Stills** can run right past defenders. Tannehill's deep ball became much more prevalent at the end of last season, so Stills' fantasy significance could go up. However, he wasn't a startable fantasy receiver last season, and until he proves himself, he'll start the season on fantasy waiver wires. (TA)

76. Sammie Coates, Steelers - BYE: 8

Sammie Coates is the sleeper on this Steelers roster. With Bryant gone, **Ben Roethlisberger** will look for the big target. At 6'1" tall and 212 pounds, with good speed, Coates is the ticket. As the season progresses, Coates will become large in the offense. Conservatively, Coates should be in line for 40 catches for 550 yards and a few TDs but the upside is higher. (RB)

77. Marqise Lee, Jaguars - BYE: 5

Marqise Lee is fully healthy and some think he might have a breakout season. However, we've heard that before. Lee is a very talented receiver but he's clearly behind both Allen Hurns and Allen Robinson on the depth chart. Lee doesn't figure to be anything more than a late-round filler in deeper leagues. In standard leagues, he won't be worth a fantasy roster spot. (GC)

78. Andrew Hawkins, Browns - BYE: 13

Andrew Hawkins is one of the veteran wide receivers negatively affected by first round pick WR **Corey Coleman**. The 5'7" pass-catcher is not expected to be a very large contributor to the troubled Browns offense after finishing with only 276 yards and not a single TD last season. He has a concussion-filled injury history. (JQ)

79. Cecil Shorts III, Texans - BYE: 9

After an underwhelming 2015 campaign, the Texans made a move to get younger in the draft at receiver. **Cecil Shorts** was reportedly on the verge of getting cut until he agreed to reduce his salary to stay with the team. Health has always been a concern with Shorts and playing in 11 of 16 games last year was not good. At the slot position, his best weeks were in unpredictable garbage time as he racked up six receptions for 87 yards and a touchdown against the Falcons and six catches for 91 yards against the Bills. He still has above average quickness and speed, but waste no draft pick on Shorts. (SB)

80. Corey Brown, Panthers - BYE: 7

Corey Brown made big plays in the playoffs, especially the Super Bowl. But do not be fooled by that. **Cam Newton** has too many targets to get excited about Brown. He is young, he will grow, but this is not the season to draft Corey Brown in standard leagues. (GC)

81. Stevie Johnson, Chargers - BYE: 11

Johnson may well be a sleeper pick for the 2016 season, following a disappointing 2015 campaign in which he caught only 45 passes for 497 yards and three touchdowns before a groin injury ended his season. Stevie Johnson and **Travis Benjamin** will battle it out to see which receiver will be in the number two slot. While Johnson has a resume stronger than Benjamin, he is the weaker of the two in terms of an outside receiver. There isn't great value for the number three wide receiver in this offense. Let Stevie Johnson start the season on fantasy waiver wires. (GC)

82. Cole Beasley, Cowboys - BYE: 7

Cole Beasley, one of the smallest receivers in the league, doesn't play small. This 5' 8" slot receiver had a career year in all categories last season. Beasley caught 52 passes for 536 yards and 5 touchdowns. With **Dez Bryant** returning, Beasley should revert to a more normal 400 yards receiving on 40 interceptions for 4 TDs. (IE)

83. Rashad Greene, Jaguars - BYE: 5

Let's be clear: Rashad Greene was not drafted to replace the void Cecil Shorts left. That would be a tall order for a fifth round pick. However, Greene can move around as a receiver and has a good set of hands. Greene joins a young, solid core of receivers trying to find a collective identity. He's not on the top of anyone's list, but watch him during training camp. Rashad Greene could well become a reliable target for Blake Bortles, which (as we know) means lots of targets, and especially if Marquise Lee continues to underperform. The Jags have a pass-heavy offense in the red zone, which makes us more optimistic on Jaguars wide receivers. (GC)

84. Justin Hardy, Falcons - BYE: 11

Justin Hardy did not have a great rookie season. He caught 21 passes for 194 receiving yards with no scores. His strong offseason development should help. Nothing is for certain with Hardy even if he is the team's No. 3 wide receiver. Justin Hardy should largely go undrafted. (IE/JS)

85. Brian Quick, Rams - BYE: 8

After putting up a miniscule 935 total receiving yards over four seasons, **Brian Quick** has failed to put up consistent numbers for a second round draft pick. Quick has shown promise as his 25 receptions for 375 yards (15.0 YPR) and 3 TDs in 2014 suggests. The deep threat receiver is a player to monitor in the offseason. But if recent history holds fast, he'll go undrafted in fantasy leagues. (JQ/JS)

86. Albert Wilson, Chiefs - BYE: 5

Albert Wilson has made great strides to increase his role in the offense since being drafted in 2014. Despite missing two games last season, Wilson was the third most targeted player on the team. Wilson compiled 35 catches for 461 yards and two touchdowns, which were all nearly doubled from the year before. Despite entering his third season as a pro, there are no indicators to suggest Albert Wilson will morph into a fantasy super star, especially in a conservative Chiefs offense. However, if the injury bug should strike the receiving group, Wilson might be the first to benefit. (IE/JS)

87. Kolby Listenbee, Bills - BYE: 10

Drafted in the sixth round of the April draft, the 6'0" tall **Kolby Listenbee** could become a deep threat for Tyrod Taylor and the Bills offense with his 4.39-forty speed, that earned him honorable mention Big 12 honors two years in a row at TCU. Listenbee has many of the same problems as most rookie wide receivers, like a limited route tree for example. He could make an impact in the offense but it will likely be uneven game to game. Listenbee is a dynasty hold. (JQ/JS)

88. Rueben Randle, Eagles - BYE: 4

Rueben Randle is one of the more seasoned WRs on the Eagles roster. The former Giants wide-out still can put up good numbers, finishing 2015 with 797 yards and 8 TDs. Although the Eagles are not expected to be as reliant on their passing game, Randle is proven and should show he can still produce. Still, his role on the offense is not set. Regardless, due to his uneven fantasy production, Randle will likely go undrafted in many fantasy drafts. (JQ)

89. T.J. Jones, Lions - BYE: 10

Entering his third season as a pro, **T.J. Jones** is finally healthy after missing his entire rookie season and playing less than 100% last season. Drafted by the Lions, Jones is expected to compete for the number three wide receiver spot with newcomer **Jeremy Kerley**. Jones appeared in only 10 games last season, hauling in 10 of 18 targets and scoring 1 TD. Though he is competing with Kerley, T.J. Jones looks like the favorite to win the battle. He'll get ample opportunity to showcase his skill with the retirement of superstar receiver **Calvin Johnson**. Jones won't put up enough numbers to be fantasy worthy, but keep his name in the back of your head if injury strikes the Lions wide receiver group. (JQ/JS)

90. Jarius Wright, Vikings - BYE: 6

Jarius Wright was originally drafted as a slot receiver. Entering his fifth year as a pro, Wright has yet to reach his potential despite flashing, occasionally, the talent of an all-pro wide receiver. Wright's best season came in 2014, when he caught 42 passes for 588 yards and 2 touchdowns. When Teddy Bridgewater took over as the starting quarterback that season, he and Wright forged a bond, a bond that the Vikings were hoping would grow even more in 2015. However, that never materialized. Wright's numbers dropped in 2015, catching 34 balls for 442 yard. He caught no single touchdown pass. Wright doesn't have enough value to be selected in fantasy drafts. Besides his lack of development, Wright must fight off wide receiver **Charles Johnson**, who limped through 2015 with injury issues, as the number three wide receiver. (JW)

91. Danny Amendola, Patriots - BYE: 9

The oft-injured Danny Amendola is coming back from knee and ankle injuries suffered in 2015. Amendola had his best year since joining the Pats, snagging 65 receptions for 648 yards and 3 TDs. Not only will Amendola be battling the big TEs and **Julian Edelman** for targets, but will battle new-comer, former Bills wide receiver Chris Hogan for targets too. Amendola is an injury risk. He should start the season on fantasy waiver wires. (DG)

92. Jamison Crowder, Redskins - BYE: 9

Jamison Crowder showed up when his number was called in 2015. Crowder caught 59 receptions for 604 yards and had two scores in his rookie season. With a whole offseason learning the offense and having more of an opportunity to work with **Kirk Cousins**, the arrow is pointing up for Crowder. However, the negative is he'll be battling first round draft pick **Josh Doctson** for touches. (IE)

93. Tyler Boyd, Bengals - BYE: 9

Second round draft picks often carry high expectations, and **Tyler Boyd** is no exception, especially on a team notorious for its solid draft picks. Boyd is versatile, something the Bengals will miss after **Mohammed Sanu** departed. Both Boyd and Sanu were virtual Swiss army knives, something the Bengals hope he can carry into the pros. At Pitt, Tyler Boyd ran the ball both from the backfield and on jet sweeps as a wide receiver, caught passes in the slot and as an outside receiver, and was even known to throw the ball occasionally. He could have a great year. Tyler Boyd will likely start the fantasy season on waiver wires in standard sized leagues. He's a solid pick in dynasty leagues and a must hold. (GC)

94. Jaelen Strong, Texans - BYE: 9

Strong is the wild card in this group. **Jaelen Strong** came in as a rookie overweight and struggled with the playbook. However, he showed his potential as a big physical red zone threat. Strong really progressed as the season went along and against the Colts, he caught all four of his targets and three were touchdowns, with on being a 'Hail Mary' where he showed his great leaping ability. When he play in garbage time against the Titans to end the season he came away with six catches and 56 yards which was a welcomed surprise. The offseason has been a rocky one for Jalen Strong but supposedly, he's adjusted for the better. His potential might be realized this season, but the pick of Will Fuller has him fighting for a spot from Day 1. Both he and **Will Fuller** will see plenty of game action. Whoever comes out on top, there are only so many opportunities with **Lamar Miller** and **DeAndre Hopkins** on the field. (SB)

95. Kamar Aiken, Ravens - BYE: 8

After **Steve Smith, Sr.**, and three other receivers went down to injury last season, **Kamar Aiken** emerged as the top passing threat for the Ravens and responded with 56 catches for 673 yards and three TDs over the last nine games of the season. **Kamar Aiken** averaged almost ten targets per game. When Smith was in the starting lineup, Aiken's role was reduced (25 receptions, 333 yards, 2 TDs). Adding **Mike Wallace** should reduce it further. Aiken's prospects of making an impact in fantasy and reality are further affected by the health of **Breshad Perriman**. Aiken will likely not be a significant factor in the offense. 300 yards receiving and a few TDs is the likely end result. Unless injuries linger or new ones develop, Kamar Aiken will start the season on fantasy waiver wires. (FG)

96. Marquess Wilson, Bears - BYE: 9

This is a big year for Wilson's future. The Bears seem contented with their receiving corps as **Alshon Jeffrey, Kevin White, Eddie Royal** and Wilson. If Wilson can show some continued growth, he has the potential to factor in to the Bears' *long-term* plans. He improved vastly in 2015, improving from 140 yards to 464 and making several highlight plays. Unfortunately, he re-broke his earlier injured left foot in mini-camp. So, his pro future is up in the air. (GC)

97. Qunicy Enunwa, Jets - BYE: 11

Qunicy Enunwa was third in targets among the Jets wide receivers in 2015. It's hardly much, however, when it translates to 22 receptions for 322 yards and 0 TDs. In Enunwa's favor is he is entering his third year as a pro. Should **Eric Decker** or **Brandon Marshall** miss time due to injury, Enunwa's role could grow. (JS)

98. Josh Huff, Eagles - BYE: 4

With the new staff and front office, the versatile former third-rounder hopes to finally live up to his potential. **Josh Huff** has the speed to play outside and the strength to be effective in the slot. However, nothing indicates he's ready to make the jump as a 25 reception wide receiver to someone special. Like **Nelson Agholor**, with so many better options out there, Josh Huff is a player to avoid in fantasy drafts. (JQ/JS)

99. Quinton Patton, 49ers - BYE: 8

Many 49ers fans have written off Patton as a bust up since he's disappointed in each of his first three seasons since being selected in the fourth round of the 2012 draft. To Patton's credit, former coach Jim Harbaugh didn't give rookies ample opportunities to shine. Still only twenty-five years old, Patton's in a make-or-break season. In his first two seasons, he could only play in six games, largely due to injuries. Last year, he hauled in 30 receptions for 394 yards and 1 TD. If Patton doesn't succeed this season, he never will find himself in a new jersey next fall. (DG)

100. Leonte Carroo, Dolphins. BYE 8

Rookie **Leonte Carroo** has a lot of potential. Carroo found the end zone 29 times in three college seasons, and he has great hands. His size and speed give him a chance to excel in the league, especially in the slot, but there is talent in front of him on the depth chart. Carroo could beat out Stills for the Dolphins' third wide receiver spot. Monitor how he does both in the preseason and after the season commences. (TA)

101. Chris Givens, Eagles - BYE: 4

Givens, who put up minimal numbers with the Ravens last season, is trying to revamp his career after posting solid stats his first couple years in the league. The deep threat WR is reuniting with QB **Sam Bradford**, with whom he put up his best numbers, at the beginning of his career. Givens will compete for playing time with a young group of unproven Eagles wide receivers, but given his previous history with Bradford, he has as good of a chance as anyone to make the team and be the No. 2 or No. 3 wide receiver option. (JQ/JS)

102. Ted Ginn, Panthers - BYE: 7

Ted Ginn's 2015 campaign was by far the best of his nine-year career as he finished with 739 yards and 10 touchdowns, which was much more than could ever have been expected from Ginn, who had never snagged over five touchdowns in a season. However, don't expect Ginn to repeat. The return of **Kelvin Benjamin** will substantially diminish the number of targets Ginn will see, so much so Ted Ginn is undraftable in fantasy. His role last season was one of desperation, and this season, he'll return to being more of a return specialist. Add to this his age and he is a likely candidate for regression. (GC)

103. Devin Smith, Jets - BYE: 11

Devin Smith just adds to the good list of wide receivers the Jets have on their roster. Smith is athletic and fast, which makes for a great deep threat. The only downfall with Smith is that he tore his ACL late in his rookie year in December. There is no date for his return. If he can play come the start of the season, he will most likely be limited since this injury typically takes about 8 to 9 months to recover. Besides, there's a huge production drop-off from the number one and two wide receivers on the Jets, to the number three and four wide receivers. (IE)

104. Braxton Miller, Texans - BYE: 9

Braxton Miller has impressed as a sure-handed player on the field and as a speedster in field work. The Texans will experiment with Miller in a multitude of ways as he had an unorthodox career at Ohio State, both as a quarterback and as a wide receiver. Comparisons to former college quarterbacks like **Julian Edelman, Josh Cribbs** and **Antwan Randle-El** will come, but it's important to remember none made a significant impact as fantasy players in their first season. Despite the athleticism, Braxton Miller won't beat out a veteran like **Cecil Shorts III** as a slot receiver early on, and that really hinders his chances of getting on the field early which he needs badly. Miller is a project player as it stands and isn't worth a fantasy draft pick this season. Hopefully Braxton Miller progresses, but he will be a distant fifth option behind the likes of **DeAndre Hopkins, Cecil Shorts, Jalen Strong** and **Will Fuller**. (SB)

105. Rashard Higgins, Browns - BYE: 13

It is still a question mark whether rookie **Rashard Higgins** can produce at the same level he did in college, hauling in an impressive 238 passes for 3,648 yards and 31 touchdowns over three seasons at Colorado State. These numbers made him the all-time receiving leader in each category at State. Ion 2015, Higgins posted a 75-1062-8 stat line. He boasted the second lowest drop rate for wide receivers. **Rashard Higgins** is flying under the radar right now and has deep, super sleeper appeal. Someone must be the Browns No. 2 or No. 3 wide receiver. At 6'1" tall and 196 pounds, Higgins can make an impact. Monitor Higgins in the offseason and let's see how he does this season. (JQ/JS)

106. Malcom Mitchell, Patriots - BYE: 9

Only four rookie wide receivers have caught over twenty balls while on Patriots: Deion Branch (43 in 2002); Julian Edelman (37 in 2009); Aaron Dobson (37 in 2013); and, Kenbrell Thompkins (32 in 2013). Clearly, it takes time for receivers to earn the trust needed to get the attention it takes and to learn the playbook to do well in the offense. Mitchell brings that outside, downfield receiver with home-run speed and youth at the position they desperately needed. Mitchell will be a fantasy-relevant player in time, but likely not this season. (DG)

107. Kenny Bell, Buccaneers - BYE: 6

After missing his rookie season with a hamstring injury, the buzz around mini-camp is Kenny Bell looks explosive. Last year, the slot receiver was carouseled between **Louis Murphy, Donteea Dye**, and **Adam Humphries**. Humphries led the group with 260 yards. The Buccaneers will need much more production from their third wide receiver. By now, it sounds like Bell is expected to emerge from the group as that option. From a fantasy prospective, Bell carries little value and will not be drafted in fantasy drafts. Bell should be monitored on the waiver wire, however. He'll be a fantasy consideration if injuries strike the group. (EG)

108. Jaron Brown, Cardinals - BYE: 9

Every good team needs depth, and **Jaron Brown** provides just that for the Cardinals. The third year man out of Clemson has good size at 6'2" tall and 205 pounds, to pair with slightly above-average speed and route-running. But Brown excels on special teams more than he does on offense, and was relegated to just 11 catches in 2015. Jaron Brown is someone to consider in deep leagues, or in smaller leagues if there's an injury to another Cardinal WR during the season. He's out of the discussion in most leagues to start the year. (CB)

109. JJ Nelson, Cardinals - BYE: 9

Rookie **JJ Nelson** contributed as a slot receiver and on special teams, and ended up with 299 yards and 2 TDs. The slight-of-build burner can make an impact in the Arians' offensive scheme, and will figure to contribute even more in 2016. Nelson is still off the radar for most leagues. But, he is an interesting dynasty play, and a potential flier in the late rounds of deeper redraft leagues. Watch the waiver wire if the Cardinals' WR corps falls victim to injury. (CB)

110. Cody Core, Bengals - BYE: 9

Core had the misfortune of sharing a field with **Laquon Treadwell,** who went twenty-third overall in the draft, while at Ole Miss. Treadwell was an easy target for a young quarterback, which led to 1,153 yards for the talented Treadwell. **Cody Core's** numbers suffered and he doesn't jump off the page as a fantasy target. However, Core has a lot of potential, as he has impressed coaches in camp. One particular notable moment came when he torched first round pick, defensive back **William Jackson III** for a deep touchdown. Cody Core does have value as a deep threat, looming at 6' 3" tall, but he will have to prove himself on special teams before he sees any real action. (GC)

111. Brandon Coleman, Saints - BYE: 5

If you are in a deeper 14 or 16 team league, or carry a roster of twenty or more players, **Brandon Coleman** is worth a sleeper pick. However, he struggled mightily to find any consistent targets in 2015. While the departure of **Marques Colston** will help some with that, Coleman will likely never replace Colston. Coleman has been plagued with inconsistency during his pro career. He is in a contract year, though. (GC)

112. Rod Streater, Chiefs - BYE: 5

Rod Streater spent his first four seasons in the league with the Raiders. In his first two seasons, he combined for over 1,472 yards and 99 catches, while in his last two seasons, he caught a combined 10 catches for 92 yards. His decline in performance was partly due to a small foot injury and the growth of athleticism among the Raider's receiving corps this past season. Rod Streater signed this offseason with the Chiefs. Streater is an intriguing prospect on a team which has no real second option at the wide receiver position. (IE)

113. DeAndre Smelter, 49ers - BYE: 8

The Georgia Tech product is basically a rookie after missing all of last season with a torn ACL suffered his senior season at Georgia Tech. The 49ers picked Smelter in the fourth round of the 2015 draft with the 132nd overall selection. Smelter's main NFL comparison is soon-to-be-ex-49ers wide receiver Anquan Boldin. Smelter is a big target for whoever is throwing him the rock this season at 6-foot-2-inches, 226 pounds with 32 5/8-inch inch arms and 11 inch hands. Smelter is also a tenacious blocker after playing in Tech's triple-option offense. Keep an eye on Smelter's production as he could be a solid waiver wire pickup at some point this season. (DG)

114. Charone Peake, Jets - BYE: 11

Charone Peake was a late round draft pick for the Jets this year, who some had tagged as a potential second round pick. Peake had a solid final season at Clemson (50 rec., 716 yards, 5 TDs), in which he helped them go all the way to the National Championship. He joins a select group of former Clemson players now playing pro football including **Sammy Watkins, Martavis Bryant** and **DeAndre Hopkins**. All three have done well in the league. The good news for Peake is that history will be on his side. The bad news is there are a lot of good players ahead of him on the depth chart. (IE)

115. Aaron Burbridge, 49ers - BYE: 8

A sixth-round rookie from Michigan State, Burbridge can have success in the slot for the 49ers. He is not going to "wow" you with his measurables, but is a gifted athlete that make plays in traffic. Burbridge only had one season for the Spartans to showcase his potential and produce at a high level. He is a grinder with the work ethic to compete and carve out a place in this offense drawing consistent targets. Don't forget about Burbridge as he may surprise. (DG)

116. Eric Rodgers, 49ers - BYE: 8

The little-known Canadian Football League (CFL) product signed a two-year deal with the 49ers this offseason after tearing up the Canadian Football League for the last two seasons. Rodgers was a sought after talent this off season receiving 13 offers after visiting 16 clubs. He ultimately opted for San Francisco due to the massive opportunity at the wide-open wide receiver position. Rodgers went undrafted after playing his college football at Division III California Lutheran. But, he was a top 10 player in the CFL in 2015 hauling in 87 catches for a league-high 1,448 yards and 10 touchdowns. Rodgers is still young at 25 years old and presents a lottery ticket of sorts for the 49ers. Rodgers could have a swift transition into Chip Kelly's offense putting up weekly fantasy points a-plenty, or fading into the background and not even be an active player on game day. Rodgers is a player to monitor this offseason. (DG)

117. Chris Conley, Chiefs - BYE: 5

Second year wide receiver **Chris Conley** is still developing a role in the Chiefs offense. Conley has fantastic athleticism and is a physical specimen. The trouble he faces is the Chiefs have an abundance of players just like him, best characterized as "untapped talent." Now that young receiver Chris Conley has a year of experience under his belt, he could be in line for a larger role in the Chiefs offense, but nothing to consider for upcoming fantasy drafts. (IE)

118. Andre Holmes, Raiders - BYE: 10

Andre Holmes has spent all four of his pro seasons with the Raiders. In 2014, Holmes looked promising with 47 receptions for 693 receiving yards. Holmes did not come near these numbers in 2015, totaling 14 catches for 201 yards. He went from third on the depth chart to fifth with adding **Amari Cooper** and **Seth Roberts**. Andre Holmes will be off fantasy radars to start the season. (IE)

119. Greg Salas, Bills - BYE: 10

Greg Salas, who suffered a knee injury in the preseason in 2015, was signed by the Bills last December as a free agent but saw limited action. The journeyman WR fills the void left by **Chris Hogan's** departure as a reliable target on the Bills offense. The No. 3 wide receiver in the Bills offense makes little impact in the Bills offense. Salas will begin the season on fantasy waiver wires. (JQ)

120. Ricardo Louis, Browns - BYE: 13

The fourth round pick out of Auburn was underused in college, with just 47 receptions for 715 yards and 3 TDs in his final season. **Ricardo Louis** has decent size (6'1", 215 pounds) and speed (4.43-forty) and has made the big play before. Louis will need time to develop at the pro level. (JQ/JS)

121. Jeremy Kerley, Lions - BYE: 10

Kerley has flashed potential with the Jets but is coming off the worst season of his career statistically. Although the five year veteran may have potential, Jeremy Kerley is primarily a slot receiver. **Golden Tate** plays his best when he is inside at the slot position so it could prove difficult for Kerley to see much action. He'll be off fantasy radars to start the season. (JQ)

122. Pharoh Cooper, Rams - BYE: 8

Pharoh Cooper is one of many young skill players that will be with the Rams this season. If he gets a chance, the former Gamecock could take some of the defensive focus off of **Tavon Austin**, while proving that his quickness and athleticism can help him be a playmaker in the league. He's the No. 4 among the wide receivers. Cooper will be undrafted in redraft fantasy leagues. (JQ)

123. KeShawn Martin, Patriots - BYE: 9

Martin signed a two-year extension with the Patriots practically guaranteeing him a roster spot for 2016. He is more of a lower-end role player in this offense, so don't expect fantasy fireworks. Martin posted 24 grabs for 269 yards and 2 TDs for the nine games he was active last year. Martin is only worth a roster spot if some players in front of him go down. Otherwise, Martin will start the season on fantasy waiver wires. (DG)

124. Nate Washington, Patriots - BYE: 9

Going on 33 years of age, the Patriots are Nate Washington's fourth team in his 11 NFL seasons. Washington is more of a role player at this point in his career. But, the Patriots badly need his outside receiver playmaking ability with their surplus of slot wide-outs. Nate Washington hauled in 47 balls for 658 yards and four TDs last year for the Texans. Monitor his offseason as he still must earn a roster spot. (DG)

125. Harry Douglas, Titans - BYE: 13

Harry Douglas had flashes of brilliance during his career with the Falcons, but failed to seize his opportunity as the Titans No. 2 wide receiver last season. With just 36 catches for 411 yards over 14 games, Douglas isn't worth drafting this season. At 31 years of age, he's more than likely a veteran presence for this young receiving group to look up to. (SB)

126. Justin Hunter, Titans - BYE: 13

A lot of people had high hopes for the 6'4" tall, 203 pound speedster. However, injuries and a lack of explosive plays has **Justin Hunter** plummeting down the Titans' depth chart. He'll have a week or two where he might provide fireworks, but then struggle to see the field as **Kendall Wright, Rishard Matthews, Tajae Sharpe,** and **Dorial Green-Beckham** all seem like locks to play ahead of him. (SB)

127. Bennie Fowler, Broncos - BYE: 11

Last season, **Bennie Fowler** caught only 18 passes, yet each had a huge impact (i.e., his 31-yard reception against the Steelers in the Divisional playoff game and the two-point conversion that put icing on the Broncos Super Bowl victory cake). Fowler's route running and hands catapulted him to third on the depth chart ahead of the uber-disappointing **Cody Latimer**. Do not be surprised to see him take the third spot yet again, and his fantasy value will probably increase if the injury bug bites either Thomas or Sanders. (DK)

128. Cody Latimer, Broncos - BYE: 11

2016 is a make-or-break year for the 2014 second-round pick from Indiana. Latimer climbed up draft boards in 2014 due to his freakish measureables and his ability to make Odell Beckham-esque catches in traffic. So far, Cody Latimer has demonstrated those traits on the practice field, but not on the playing field. In addition, Peyton Manning's practice buddy from last winter, *Jordan "Sunshine" Taylor*, could make a push for his roster spot. Although Latimer's special teams play might preserve his roster spot, Latimer is only worth an investment if injury strikes Thomas or Sanders and if he's able to show he's ready to contribute on offense on Sundays. (DK)

129. Jordan Norwood, Broncos - BYE: 11

Norwood is the leading candidate for punt returns, which makes sense since he just set the Super Bowl record for longest punt return. He may also see time in the slot, but not enough to warrant even the slightest fantasy consideration, since Gary Kubiak will use more "12" personnel sets than "11" personnel sets. Norwood should start the season on fantasy waiver wires. (DK)

130. Darrius Heyward-Bey, Steelers - BYE: 8

The suspension of **Martavis Bryant** makes several of the Steelers' wide receivers interesting options heading into 2016. However, don't look for DHB to hold a large enough role in the offense to justify space on your roster. Heyward-Bey will likely continue to only see the field in four and five wide receiver sets. (RB)

TIGHT END RANKINGS (PPR)

	Player	Team	Value	BYE
1.	Rob Gronkowski (IRSK)	Patriots	294.3	9
2.	Jordan Reed (IRSK)	Redskins	231.6	9
3.	Gary Barnidge (NO)	Browns	228.4	13
4.	Greg Olsen	Panthers	218.2	7
5.	Tyler Eiffert (INJ)	Bengals	207.6	9
6.	Coby Fleener (NO)	Saints	201.7	5
7.	Antonio Gates (NO)	Chargers	199.7	11
8.	Jimmy Graham	Seahawks	194.2	5
9.	Travis Kelce (3)	Chiefs	185.4	5
10.	Zach Ertz	Eagles	185.4	4
11.	Delanie Walker	Titans	184.8	13
12.	Julius Thomas	Jaguars	182.0	5
13.	Jason Witten	Cowboys	177.0	7
14.	Zach Miller (UPS)	Bears	176.8	9
15.	Martellus Bennett (NO)	Patriots	176.0	9
16.	Lardarius Green (NO) (UPS)	Steelers	175.2	8
17.	Will Tye (2)	Giants	173.4	8
18.	Dwayne Allen	Colts	166.0	10
19.	Jordan Cameron (NO)	Dolphins	162.0	8
20.	Vance McDonald (UPS)	49ers	161.4	8
21.	Eric Ebron (3)	Lions	148.7	10
22.	Jacob Tamme	Falcons	148.0	11
23.	Jared Cook (NO) (UPS)	Packers	147.0	4
24.	Crockett Gillmore (INJ)	Ravens	146.0	8
25.	Charles Clay	Bills	140.4	10
26.	Clive Walford (2)	Raiders	139.0	10
27.	Jeff Heuerman (2)	Broncos	132.3	11
28.	Austin Seferian-Jenkins (3) (DNS)	Buccaneers	130.9	6
29.	Kyle Rudolph	Vikings	130.0	6
30.	Lance Kendricks	Rams	88.0	8

Ranks reflect value based on 16 weeks of play. Past performance was considered as were issues relating to each team's offense including the offense run by the team's offensive coordinator, any coaching changes and personnel changes, and which players are listed as starters and back-ups on the most recent depth charts.

KEY: (NO) = New Offense; (UPS) = Upside; (IRSK) = Injury Risk; (INJ) = Injured; (DNS) = Downside; (R) = Rookie; (2) = 2nd Year TE; (3) = 3rd Year TE

TIGHT END RANKINGS (Non-PPR)

	Player	Team	Value	Bye
1.	Rob Gronkowski (IRSK)	Patriots	204.3	9
2.	Gary Barnidge (NO)	Browns	148.4	13
3.	Tyler Eiffert (INJ)	Bengals	147.6	9
4.	Jordan Reed (IRSK)	Redskins	146.6	9
5.	Greg Olsen	Panthers	143.2	7
6.	Coby Fleener (NO)	Saints	131.7	5
7.	Jimmy Graham	Seahawks	124.2	5
8.	Antonio Gates	Chargers	124.7	11
9.	Delanie Walker	Titans	119.8	13
10.	Julius Thomas	Jaguars	117.0	5
11.	Dwayne Allen	Colts	116.0	10
12.	Zach Miller (UPS)	Bears	116.8	9
13.	Zach Ertz	Eagles	115.4	4
14.	Travis Kelce (3)	Chiefs	115.2	5
15.	Will Tye (2)	Giants	113.4	8
16.	Lardarius Green (NO) (UPS)	Steelers	109.2	8
17.	Jason Witten	Cowboys	107.0	7
18.	Martellus Bennett (NO) (UPS)	Patriots	106.0	9
19.	Jordan Cameron	Dolphins	102.0	8
20.	Vance McDonald (UPS)	49ers	101.4	8
21.	Eric Ebron (3)	Lions	98.7	10
22.	Jared Cook (UPS)	Packers	97.0	4
23.	Crockett Gillmore (INJ)	Ravens	96.0	8
24.	Clive Walford (2)	Raiders	89.0	10
25.	Jacob Tamme	Falcons	88.0	11
26.	Austin Seferian-Jenkins (3) (DNS)	Buccaneers	85.9	6
27.	Charles Clay	Bills	80.4	10
28.	Kyle Rudolph	Vikings	80.0	6
29.	Jeff Heuerman (2)	Broncos	77.3	11
30.	Lance Kendricks	Rams	48.0	8

Ranks reflect value based on 16 weeks of play. Past performance was considered as were issues relating to each team's offense including the offense run by the team's offensive coordinator, any coaching changes and personnel changes, and which players are listed as starters and back-ups on the most recent depth charts.

KEY: (NO) = New Offense; (UPS) = Upside; (IRSK) = Injury Risk; (INJ) = Injured; (DNS) = Downside; (R) = Rookie; (2) = 2nd Year TE; (3) = 3rd Year TE

TIGHT END PROFILES

1. Rob Gronkowski, Patriots - BYE: 9

Rob Gronkowski did his typical All-World tight end 'thing' last season, throwing down 1,176 yards receiving, 11 TDs on 72 catches. Gronkowski stayed healthy, playing in 15 games. Even though he is the undeniable best tight end today, Gronkowski has battled his fair share of injuries in the past. As long as he can stay on the field, expect Rob Gronkowski to go late in the first round and put up 1,200-plus yards, 10-plus TDs, and 75-plus receptions, even with new TE **Martellus Bennett** now in the fold. (DG)

2. Jordan Reed, Redskins - BYE: 9

Jordan Reed finished the 2015 season as one of the best tight ends in the game. Reed complied 952 yards on 87 receptions and scored 11 touchdowns. **Kirk Cousins** and Reed developed solid chemistry on the field last season. Both Cousins and Reed are in their prime. Reed will most likely be one of the first tight ends taken in most fantasy leagues. However, he hasn't played a full season as a pro the past two seasons, missing two and five games, respectively. Reed should pace 900 plus yards on 85 receptions for 9 TDs. View him as a top TWE1 who you can draft Rounds 4 or 5. (IE)

3. Gary Barnidge, Browns - BYE: 13

Barnidge broke out in 2015 to lead the lowly Browns in receptions (79), yards (1,043), and TDs (9). As the veteran among a cast of rookie wide receivers, Barnidge will likely lead the Browns in receiving again. Double-digit TDs are a real possibility. Barnidge makes for a Top 5 tight end option in all formats. However, because he plays for the Browns you can likely select Barnidge in the middle of most standard fifteen round drafts. (JS)

4. Greg Olsen, Panthers - BYE: 7

Greg Olsen is the paragon of reliability of tight ends. His improvement as a player has been linear. Olsen has increased his production by an average of 150 yards over the last four years and improved by roughly a touchdown every other year over that same period. He has appeared in every game aside from his rookie season, immune to injury in a league dominated by it. Greg Olsen is hands down the most dependable tight end in the league. Draft him by Round 5 of fantasy drafts. Another 1,000 yards receiving and 6 to 7 TDs should be expected. (GC)

5. Tyler Eifert, Bengals - BYE: 9

The tight end position has been a tight one as of late. Aside from the top five, which includes **Tyler Eifert**, there isn't a ton of production to be found. Eifert was a monster in 2015, catching 52 passes for 615 yards and 13 touchdowns despite missing time. Due to an untimely injury in the Pro Bowl, Eifert was forced to undergo ankle surgery. It's unclear whether he'll be ready for Week 1 and in football shape. There will be an impulse to draft him early, rightly so. But monitor him in the preseason and see if he'll be ready for the start of the season. If there's any question on his health or readiness, err on the side of caution and wait until later rounds to draft Eifert. When healthy, he's a late fifth round, early sixth round draft pick. (GC)

6. Coby Fleener, Saints - BYE: 5

The Saints *love* their tight ends. They typically recruit and develop solid big men, and use them often. **Jimmy Graham** put up monster numbers over his Saints tenure, and even forgotten veteran tight end **Benjamin Watson** rejuvenated his career last season with the Saints and became a fantasy asset. With **Marques Colston** gone, there will be plenty of opportunities for **Coby Fleener** to get his hands on the ball. For Fleener to haul in 70 receptions for 750 yards and five or more TDs would be no surprise. He'll be a great value pick in the middle rounds of fantasy drafts. (GC)

7. Antonio Gates, Chargers - BYE: 11

Every single year, someone new tries to tell the fantasy community this is the season **Antonio Gates** will crumble. It hasn't happened yet. Despite sitting out the first four games of last season, Gates caught 56 passes for 630 yards and five touchdowns. If you project those 11 games to a full season, he would have seen the most targets of his Hall of Fame career. His opportunities were surely bolstered by injuries to key wide-outs, but even if he regresses, there isn't a ton of risk to Gates. He won't be the flashiest, he won't be a league leader, but he will be solid. A 75-850-6 stat line isn't too much to ask for. (GC)

8. Jimmy Graham, Seahawks - BYE: 5

Jimmy Graham was a huge disappointment for fantasy team managers who spent a high draft pick on him in 2015, even before he was injured. While his yardage may have ended up similar to the 2014 season when he was with the Saints, his TD total for the season was set to be down by roughly 8 scores. In Week 12, Graham sustained a patellar tear which is a difficult injury to rehab from, especially for athletes. It's genuinely unclear whether Graham will be ready for Week 1 even though the Seahawks seem to indicate he will be ready. For argument, if Graham is ready for Week 1, the area of his game he will likely improve on is his TD receptions. He projects as a low-end TE1 in standard leagues. However, if the uncertainty involving the injury continues into the preseason, the better approach is to avoid Jimmy Graham altogether or draft him as a TE2 in the latter rounds. Graham is not expected to be the focal point of the offense even if he is 100% come Week 1.

9. Travis Kelce, Chiefs - BYE: 5

Travis Kelce's season last year fell short of many expectations. Yet, Kelce totaled a still impressive 875 receiving yards with 5 touchdowns, numbers which nearly matched his 2014 totals (67 rec., 862 yards, 5 TDs). His consistency makes him one of the more reliable tight ends in the league. Kelce is a Top 10 tight end in PPR formats and Top 14 in non-PPR leagues. (IE)

10. Zach Ertz, Eagles - BYE: 4

Zach Ertz has improved his numbers in each of his first three seasons in the league. **Doug Pederson** has featured a tight end in his offense the past two seasons as offensive coordinator of the Chiefs. Brent Celek could be better than **Travis Kelce** as Ertz's numbers (75 rec., 853 yards, 2 TDs) were almost identical to Kelce's except for TD catches (72 rec., 875 yards, 5 TDs). Even with veteran **Brent Celek** returning, Ertz will continue getting most of the TE targets. Ertz is a low-end TE1 (with upside) in 10 and 12 team leagues who you can likely draft in the latter rounds of fantasy drafts. (JQ/JS)

11. Delanie Walker, Titans - BYE: 13

Delanie Walker was one of the top tight ends last season but will likely be over-drafted this season. Walker had a monster 2015 campaign in which he caught 94 passes on 133 targets for 1,088 yards and six touchdowns. This season, however, it appears two things could get in his way: the Titans re-emphasizing the running game and the Titans developing more weapons in the passing game. The smash-mouthed style offense the Titans are developing will likely require Delanie Walker to block more and restrict his game to the shorter and intermediate parts of the field in play-action passing situations. As several snaps go to new additions **Demarco Murray** and **Derick Henry**, all logic and reasoning suggests there will be fewer targets for Walker and the other receivers. Walker remains a nightmare for linebackers because of his quickness, and his reach and stature make him near impossible for safeties to out muscle. He'll remain a red-zone threat and a likely top three option in the passing game. A more realistic projection for Delanie Walker is 60 to 65 catches and 775 to 850 yards with a handful or more number of touchdowns. Walker is being over-drafted right now. He's a good later round pick as a low TE1 in Round 9 or Round 10. (SB/JS)

12. Julius Thomas, Jaguars - BYE: 5

Julius Thomas is ear-marked for a rebound season. Thomas is being drafted in the ninth round, which is low given his upside. Yes, he had a subpar season last year, but was hampered by injury. Looking at his statistics, he's caught 29 TDs over the last three seasons (despite missing 9 games), more than Jimmy Graham and even

Robert Gronkowski, both of whom have missed game-time too. By all reports, Julius Thomas had great OTAs. In the red-zone especially, tight ends are impossible to cover in the passing game. Given how much the Jaguars like to throw the ball in the red zone, look for Thomas' TD total to improve after last season's dip. If he can stay healthy, he is an excellent value for a tight end. You can snag him later in your fantasy draft after padding the rest of your roster. (GC)

13. Jason Witten, Cowboys - BYE: 7

Jason Witten has been the Cowboy's primary tight end for 12 of 13 seasons. The veteran has compiled career statistics that only few tight ends in league history can even compare to. Witten caught 77 balls for 713 yards and 3 scores in 2015. While reliable, Witten's best years could be behind him as some tight ends have leap-frogged him in the rankings. Witten's projected 770 yards for 5 TDs on 70 receptions make him a borderline TE1 in PPR leagues only. (IE)

14. Zach Miller, Bears - BYE: 9

Miller absolutely excelled despite limited time last season, the first legitimate season he's logged in some time for him. **Zach Miller** caught 34 of 42 targets, earning himself 439 yards and five touchdowns. Miller outperformed starter **Martellus Bennett,** who caught 19 more passes for the same yards and two fewer touchdowns. Miller likely won't be one of the best tight ends in the league. But if he can stay healthy, and is used in the offense as much as Martellus Bennett was used, Zach Miller can produce at least like a low-end TE1, capable of posting 800 yards, 6 TDs, on 60 receptions. (GC)

15. Martellus Bennett, Patriots - BYE: 9

Bennett came over via trade from the Bears, giving the Patriots the great one-two tight end combination they've been looking for since 2013. Like **Rob Gronkowski,** "Marty B" is a mammoth target at 6-foot-6-inches, 273 pounds. Bennett has never won a title, so he's on a mission with the Patriots to achieve it in his ninth season as a pro. Plus, this is a contract year for Bennett. In 2015, he put up a modest 439 yards and 3 TDs for the Bears. Expect a bump in those numbers around the 650-750 range and 5 TDs. **Martellus Bennett** should dance with TE1 status at some point this season. (DG)

16. Ladarius Green, Steelers - BYE: 8

Signed as an insurance policy due to the retirement of **Heath Miller, Ladarius Green** is listed as the starting tight end by this writing. Green was drafted to be the next big thing for the Chargers, to replace the aging **Antonio Gates**. Gates is still there. Green has struggled to show the talent of an elite tight end. He has never been the big play tight end and has never caught over 37 balls. Ladarius Green was signed as a free agent this offseason on a four-year deal. He also had offseason ankle surgery. There are plenty of reasons to think Ladarius Green could falter this season. Until he proves himself, he's more of a TE2, who will be over drafted in some leagues. Monitor the situation between Green and second year tight end **Jesse James** this offseason. Jesse James could push to be the starter. (RB)

17. Will Tye, Giants - BYE: 8

In his 2015 rookie season, Will Tye started in 7 of the 13 games he played in, totaling 42 receptions for 464 yards and 3TDs. His late season production surge, in which he scored 3 touchdowns in the last 4 games of the season, makes Tye an interesting option in fantasy. Should he start in Week 1, he'll make for a high TE2 in a pass-heavy offense in line for 700-plus yards and 6 TDs. (AG)

18. Dwayne Allen, Colts - BYE: 10

In 2014, **Dwayne Allen** had a career year with eight touchdown reception on 29 receptions. However, 2015 was different with a banged up Andrew Luck. Last season, Allen saw his touchdown total plummet to one and his reception total fall to 16. Aside from Andrew Luck getting hurt, the Colts also struggled with their offensive line and injuries. This season, things should be different especially because **Coby Fleener** is no longer in the picture. Dwayne Allen should see a jump in production to Fleener-like numbers in the area of 50 receptions for 700 yards and 8 TDs. If all goes as expected, Allen should knock on low TE1 status in non-PPR leagues in 12 team or deeper leagues. (IE/JS)

19. Jordan Cameron, Dolphins - BYE 8

Jordan Cameron was unreliable last season. Outside of four or five players, tight end is a tough position to find a consistent fantasy starter. Cameron stayed healthy last season, something he's had trouble with in the past. Still, he finished with just 35 receptions for 386 yards and 3 touchdowns. This was less than what was expected from him in the Dolphins offense. His chemistry with Ryan Tannehill seemed better towards the end of last year, but look elsewhere for a fantasy tight end. His projected 660 yards and 6 TDs makes him a TE2 to start the season. (TA)

20. Vance McDonald, 49ers - BYE: 8

Entering his fourth season, Vance McDonald has yet to live up to his second-round draft value having yet to amass a 100-yard game or 350+ yard season. But, with Vernon Davis gone, the door opens for McDonald to be the clear #1 TE option. Coaches and players on the offense have voiced their opinions on needing to utilize McDonald more in the passing game and all the skills he brings to the table. The 6-foot-4-inch, 267-pound mighty man should be an option throwing across the middle of the field and on third downs. He just needs to decrease his number of drops. In a rather deep tight end class, McDonald is a decent option as TE2 given the number of targets he's likely to see. (DG)

21. Eric Ebron, Lions - BYE: 10

Eric Ebron has not been as productive as many thought he would be out of college as the 10th overall pick. However, he doubled his rookie numbers last season (47 rec., 537 yards, 5 TDs) which indicates he's made the jump to the pro level. With **Calvin Johnson** retired and the Lions continuing to lean on the pass, Ebron could easily have a breakout year as one of the Lions top targets. View Eric Ebron as a quality TE2 in line for increased receptions and yards. (JQ)

22. Jacob Tamme, Falcons - BYE: 11

Jacob Tamme was **Matt Ryan's** second favorite target last season. Tamme caught 59 catches for 657 yards (a career high) and 1 TD. Tamme started 12 games, the most he has started since 2012. This will be his ninth year in the league. It is unlikely Tamme does better in 2016. He's a low end TE2 who you can use in a bye week. (IE)

23. Jared Cook, Packers - BYE: 4

The Packers offense hasn't had a field-stretching tight end since **Jermichael Finley**. With the Packers offseason signing of **Jared Cook**, they are hoping he fills that void. Cook has a similar build to Finley at 6'5" tall, 254 pounds, but appears to be faster. Last season, while with the then St. Louis Rams, Cook caught a meager 39 passes for just 481 yards and no touchdowns. But, this was due to below average quarterback play from various quarterbacks. Jared Cook hasn't played with a quarterback with the passing ability of **Aaron Rodgers**. Cook is expected to be an asset in the Packers' offense in 2016. Whether he can quickly gain the confidence of Rodgers remains to be seen. Cook had a procedure done on his foot early this summer. The Packers have said that he should be at full strength when the season starts, but still, it is something to keep an eye on. If Cook is healthy, he might be quite a find when the premiere tight ends come off the board. (JW)

24. Crockett Gillmore, Ravens - BYE: 8

Over ten games in his second season, **Crockett Gillmore** caught 33 passes for 412 yards and 4 TDs on a meager 47 targets. Gillmore missed two games earlier in the year due a calf issue, and his season ended in December with a back and shoulder injury. In 2015, the Ravens completed 84 passes to the TE position for 875 yards and five TDs on 121 targets. Gillmore has more competition for playing time with the team acquiring **Ben Watson** and the expected return of **Dennis Pitta**. He's also rehabbing from offseason shoulder surgery. Crockett Gillmore will likely get the chance to be the team's No.1 tight end. Gillmore is a low-end TE2. (FG)

25. Charles Clay, Bills - BYE: 10

After a hot start to the 2015 season, Clay struggled after Week 4 to make a significant impact. **Charles Clay** finished the season with 51 catches for 3 TDs. With the questionable health of Bills top pass catcher, **Sammy Watkins**, Clay will have success again right away. However, he's not worth a fantasy roster spot unless he can prove he can sustain his role for more than a few weeks. Clay is a borderline TE2. (JQ)

26. Clive Walford, Raiders - BYE: 10

As a rookie, Clive Wolford had a good first season in 2015 with 329 receiving yards and 3 touchdowns. Most tight ends make the jump to relevancy in their second season as a pro. The Raiders have talked Walford up this offseason and have indicated he will have a bigger role in the offense. Walford hasn't done enough to endear himself to fantasy owners in standard leagues. In deeper leagues, he's a late round flier. In dynasty leagues, he's a "hold." (IE/JS)

27. Jeff Heureman, Broncos - BYE: 11

The Broncos are expecting big things from second year player Jeff Heureman, who missed his entire rookie campaign after suffering a torn ACL in minicamp. The Broncos might wish too much on a player with scarce collegiate production at Ohio State and who showed no "wow" traits on film. Even though this is his second NFL season, Heureman is a de facto rookie, and since the tight end position has one of the steepest learning curves from college to pro, it would be wise to avoid to start the season. (DK)

28. TE Austin Seferian-Jenkins, Buccaneers - BYE: 6

By far one of the biggest disappointments of the 2015 season, Seferian-Jenkins struggled after he caught 110 yards and two touchdowns in the season opener. In part, this was because of injury as he missed 9 games. The 6-foot 5-inch talent cannot be consistent enough for anyone to rely on. Austin Seferian-Jenkins' offseason has been shaky too. Earlier in mini-camp, Jenkins was removed from practice. This will be a situation to monitor, with Cameron Brate tight end in the wings. Seferian-Jenkins' fantasy numbers (if he gets significant playing time) should hover around 500 yards with 3 to 5 touchdowns. He's not worth having on your roster. (EG)

29. Kyle Rudolph, Vikings - BYE: 6

Rudolph has everything you want in a tight end: speed, size, and good hands. But, **Kyle Rudolph** has struggled with staying healthy. Until last season, Rudolph hadn't played a full 16 game schedule since 2012. Coincidentally, last season, Rudolph finally stayed healthy for the whole season and put up the second best numbers of his career: 49 receptions for 495 yards and 5 touchdowns. He became **Teddy Bridgewater**'s security blanket, when things broke down. While Rudolph should at least post similar numbers to last season, he's not worth a draft pick just yet except maybe as a low-end TE2 in deeper leagues. (JW)

30. Lance Kendricks, Rams - BYE: 8

Lance Kendricks has done little in the passing game hauling in 25 receptions for 245 yards and 2 TDs last season. With **Jared Cook** gone, Kendricks could step up in the passing game. He's a player to monitor who will likely not put up the numbers to make him valuable enough to be in any fantasy lineups. (JQ)

31. Ryan Griffin, Texans - BYE: 9

Griffin will likely be the number one tight end in the Texans offense and he's coming off a 2015 campaign in which he caught 20 passes for 251 yards and two touchdowns. This seems impressive when you realize he was only targeted 34 times. But, you're still taking a plethora of tight ends before him in the draft. (SB)

32. Jermaine Gresham, Cardinals - BYE: 9

The tight end position has been a position of relative obscurity for the Cardinals in recent years. Though not prominently featured in the offensive scheme, a talented pass-catching TE has an opportunity to make an impact. **Jermaine Gresham** never fully clicked with the offense in 2015, overcoming injury to register just 18 catches and a lone TD on the season. But Gresham was a valuable blocker, and could figure to recapture some of the talent he showed with the Bengals. Gresham is only worth a flier at the end of drafts in deep leagues if two tight ends are started. (CB)

33. Cameron Brate, Buccaneers - BYE: 6

With **Austin Seferian-Jenkins** struggling to produce last season and injured, Cameron Brate came out of nowhere to step up in Jenkins' absence. Statistically speaking, Brate's season was nothing to mention. But, it was significant for his red-zone targets and as a safety blanket for Winston. The Buccaneers will look to see if Brate can escalate his game to a much higher level this season while they monitor Austin Seferian-Jenkins. (EG)

34. Virgil Green, Broncos - BYE: 11

Another annual offseason hype piece yet to gain traction, this could be Virgil Green's best last chance to carve out a niche in the Broncos passing attack. With only unproven and raw **Jeff Heureman** as a legit threat and **Garrett Graham** nothing more than a veteran body, Green might persuade the Broncos to finally put his severely underutilized receiving skills to work. However, he was limited during most of OTA's with a finger injury, and the Broncos have preferred his blocking to his pass catching for the last few years. There is no indication that will change. (DK)

35. Larry Donnell, Giants - BYE: 8

Larry Donnell took a step back statistically last season. Plus, because of a neck injury, he played just eight games, making it halfway through the season. Even before the injury however, Donnell under-performed with 29 receptions for 223 yards and 2 TDs through eight games. He never topped over forty yards in one game. It is tough to say what Larry Donnell's future is with the Giants especially with second year man Will Tye, who played well in Donnell's absence, in the fold. Larry Donnell was signed to a one-year deal this past offseason. Avoid Donnell in fantasy leagues for now. (AG)

36. Tyler Kroft, Bengals - BYE: 9

Kroft will be the primary tight end for the Bengals if **Tyler Eifert** isn't ready for Week 1. The timetable of Eifert's return means Kroft could see more reps in training camp, an invaluable asset for the second-year tight end. Injuries to Eifert at the end of last season afforded **Tyler Kroft** the chance to get a taste of being the primary tight end, which he turned into 11 receptions for 129 yards and a touchdown. He is someone to monitor over the summer. Tyler Kroft is unlikely to start once Eifert returns, but he could be a productive stop gap for the first couple weeks of the season. (GC)

38. Hunter Henry, Chargers - BYE: 11

There will be a season in which Chargers veteran tight end **Antonio Gates** won't be able to function at a high level. This is not that season, and **Hunter Henry** will greatly benefit from Gates' tutelage, as Henry will likely become the eventual replacement to the Hall of Famer. He has potential to be a solid secondary target as Henry was viewed as the top tight end in the draft. He was first team All-SEC at Arkansas, finishing with 51 catches for 739 yards and three touchdowns, all without a drop. Hunter Henry is a solid blocker. After losing pass catching tight end **Ladarius Green** in free agency, the Chargers needed someone to fill that gap. Henry will do just fine, and may play a large role in the second half of the season. (GC)

39. Jesse James, Steelers - BYE: 8

Jesse James is listed third behind free agent acquisition, **Ladarius Green** and **Matt Spaeth** on the Steelers depth chart for tight end. Make no mistake, Spaeth is a blocker. With Heath Miller retired, Jesse James looks to have quite the expanded role. Ladarius Green was supposed to take over for **Antonio Gates** for about three years, but never had the talent to push out the aging star. James is primed to receive lots of looks from Ben Roethlisberger if Ladarius Green doesn't carve out a role for himself in the offense. The 6'7" tall, 260 pound tight end can run and catch. James could easily see 45 to 50 catches and 500 yards this season if he's made the starter. Monitor the situation this offseason because this job could eventually go to James. Until James is made the starter, he'll go undrafted in fantasy. (RB)

40. Austin Hooper, Falcons - BYE: 11

The Falcons drafted **Austin Hooper** of Stanford in this year's draft. Hooper played in a similar pro-style offense at Stanford and finished last season with 34 receptions for 438 yards and 6 TDs. The Falcons see him as a potential red zone weapon. It's rare that rookie tight ends make a fantasy impact. Austin Hooper is a hold in dynasty leagues. (IE)

41. Garrett Celek, 49ers - BYE: 8

Celek signed a four-year, $14 million extension this offseason, so he isn't going anywhere. Primarily used as an in-line blocking tight end, Celek' stats don't blow you away: 19 receptions for 186 yards and three touchdowns in 2015 and 27 career catches overall. He could get as many career catches this year alone, but doesn't stand out as a viable tight end fantasy option with the likes of McDonald and Bell in front of him taking third-down and red-zone snaps away from him. (DG)

42. Richard Rodgers, Packers - BYE: 4

With signing **Jared Cook**, **Richard Rodgers** finds himself as the Packers No. 2 tight end in their offense for this coming season. Although players don't like to be demoted, Rodgers could thrive in his new role. Rodgers doesn't have the athletic ability that Cook has, but he gets open. The overall numbers from last season --- 58 catches for 510 yards with 8 touchdowns --- aren't anything to be ashamed of. Richard Rodgers lack of speed is why the Packers picked up Cook this offseason. Rodgers doesn't have the speed to open up the middle of the field, but Rodgers has a knack for getting open, especially in the red zone. Rodgers shouldn't be looked at as a starting tight end for your fantasy team, but he might be a number two at some point, especially if Jared Cook goes down to injury. (JW)

43. Brent Celek, Eagles - BYE: 4

Celek is coming off of one of his least productive seasons since coming into the league ten years ago. There are still expectations for Celek after signing a three year extension with the Eagles this offseason, but he seems firmly behind tight end **Zach Ertz** as the team's pass catching tight end. Celek hasn't eclipsed 400 yards or 3 TDs in the past two seasons despite playing every game. Celek should go undrafted in fantasy. (JQ)

44. Ben Watson, Ravens - BYE: 8

Say what you will about the twelve year veteran, but **Ben Watson** had his best season as a pro last season playing for the Saints, where he caught 74 balls for 825 yards and 6 TDs. But with the youth of the Ravens' recently drafted tight ends, and the return of **Dennis Pitta** after missing two years from two separate hip surgeries, Ben Watson, while likely insurance, has a solid chance to be **Joe Flacco**'s go-to at the TE position if the team's young tight ends struggle or fail to take the next step in their maturation. Ben Watson will likely go undrafted but could be a solid waiver wire add like he was last season if he emerges as Joe Flacco's No. 1 tight end in the passing game. Watson is likely the best blocker in the bunch. So, the opportunity is there. (FG)

45. Blake Bell, 49ers - BYE: 8

A fourth-round rookie out of Oklahoma last year, Bell saw limited playing time behind Vernon Davis, Vance McDonald and Garrett Celek. The "Belldozer," as the Sooners faithful nicknamed him, is still learning the tight end position since he was a quarterback for three college seasons before turning to TE for his senior year. His 6-foot-6-inch, 251-pound size makes him an ideal red-zone target. Bell has gobs of potential as he continues to get more comfortable in his tight end skin. (DG)

46. Devon Cajuste, 49ers - BYE: 8

The undrafted free agent TE/WR hybrid from Stanford is a fascinating prospect. He has stands 6-foot-4-inches tall, and is 234 pounds, posting a 36 inch vertical and 4.62 40-yard dash. He has the athleticism fitting into today's "move" tight end of H-back position. Cajuste should make the 53-man roster and compete for receiving targets in the pre-season. He is tall, lean and built with strong, capable hands. Cajuste could fit in nicely with coach Kelly's offense carving out a fantasy productive niche for himself in the process after this season. Don't expect big numbers from him year one, but keep a look out on the Cardinal product. Cajuste is a dynasty add. (DG)

47. Vernon Davis, Redskins - BYE: 9

Vernon Davis signed a one year deal with the Redskins this past offseason. Despite getting a Super Bowl ring while playing for the Broncos in 2015, Davis is 32 years old and has some talented tight ends ahead of him on the depth chart. While he has a reputation for dropping passes, he can still catch the football as his 38 receptions for 395 yards last season indicates. For Davis to play this season, he'll need an injury to **Jordan Reed** and probably one other tight end to get a chance. Fantasy owners should avoid Vernon Davis in fantasy drafts. (IE/JS)

48. Maxx Williams, Ravens - BYE: 8

In his first season in the league, **Maxx Williams** caught 32 passes for 268 yards and 1 TD on 48 targets. The Ravens will use him as a moveable TE with limited value in blocking. Williams has good hands and can test defenses deep down the middle. While many tight ends make a jump in their statistical production as second year pros, Maxx Williams is battling for playing time against some awfully good tight ends. Avoid Maxx Williams in fantasy drafts. (FG)

49. Tyler Higbee, Rams - BYE: 8

Tyler Higbee, the 110th overall pick out of Western Kentucky, is viewed as a player with the ability to give the Rams some desperately needed production out of the tight end position. While Higbee will likely see the field, rookie tight ends have a tougher time breaking through in fantasy because not only must they learn the passing routes, but they must also learn all the blocking combinations. In college, he was a red zone threat with 8 TDs in 2015. Tyler Higbee is a solid dynasty draft pick but will be off fantasy radars in redraft leagues. (JQ/JS)

50. Thomas Duarte, Dolphins. BYE 8

Thomas Duarte is a wide receiver converted to tight end the Dolphins drafted in the seventh round of this year. Duarte has a ton of play making ability as he hauled in 53 receptions for 872 yards and 10 TDs for UCLA. The Dolphins already have Jordan Cameron, Dion Sims, and Jake Stoneburner on the roster. His playing style has been compared to Jordan Reed, who has had large success so far in his short career. With Cameron being so unreliable, keep an eye on Duarte if he makes the team. He's a later round grab in dynasty drafts. (TA)

51. Luke Willson, Seahawks - BYE: 5

Despite great size at 6'5" tall and 252 pounds, **Luke Willson** struggled last season to replace **Jimmy Graham** when Graham went down to injury. It's important to remember the Seahawks traded for Graham because they had limited production already from the tight end position in an offense that needed a presence in the middle of the field for play action passing and check downs. Luke Willson hasn't had over 400 yards yet in a single season and as the n umber one tight end for the Seahawks in 2014, he came away with just 22 receptions in 15 games. Willson shouldn't be drafted in fantasy regardless of Jimmy Graham's status and regardless of format. (SB)

52. Darren Fells, Cardinals - BYE: 9

Fells emerged as the Cardinals' most consistent threat at TE in 2015, meager as that was. Fells grabbed 28 balls and scored 3 TDs but was a popular check-down target on many key plays down the stretch. The TE will never tear it up in an Arians' system, and Fells figures to split targets with **Jermaine Gresham**. In most leagues, his name won't come up all year unless the Cardinals suffer injuries to other receivers. (CB)

53. Nick Vannett, Seahawks - BYE: 5

Nick Vannett is entering a unique situation with a dynamic cast of offensive players at every position besides TE. However, the pedigree at Ohio State suggests he's best viewed as a blocking tight end since he only caught 19 passes in each of his last two seasons. At 6'5" tall and 265 pounds, Vannett will have a tougher time in match-ups against much more athletic and larger players than he was accustomed to seeing in college. Rookie tight ends hardly ever make an impact. (SB)

54. Stephen Anderson, Texans - BYE: 9

Undrafted free agent **Stephen Anderson** was coveted by the Texans for the pass-catching ability he showed at California. Anderson ran a 4.62-forty and registered a 38 inch vertical, which are both great numbers for a tight end. However, at 6'2" tall and 230 pounds, he will not be used in blocking situations which hurts his role. It can't be ignored, however, that he caught 87 passes for 1,135 and seven touchdowns in the two years he converted from receiver. Texans tight ends **Ryan Griffin** and **C.J. Fiedorowicz** will start the season ahead of him. But, Anderson can't be ignored for next season if he progresses as a receiving tight end during this season.

Defense / Special Teams (DSTs)
Rankings and Profiles

By Sammy Bissett
Featured Contributor, TheFantasyGreek.com

1. **Cardinals**
2. **Broncos**
3. **Texans**
4. **Seahawks**
5. **Panthers**
6. **Bengals**
7. **Vikings**
8. **Chiefs**
9. **Patriots**
10. **Rams**
11. **Steelers**
12. **Jets**
13. **Raiders**
14. **Jaguars**
15. **Packers**
16. **Bills**

1. Cardinals. The Cardinals added the incredible talent, Defensive End **Robert Nckemdiche** and the Patriots former pass rushing stud, **Chandler Jones. Patrick Peterson** patrols an uber talented secondary with the talented **Justin Bethel** opposite him. The player to watch in this group is **Tyrann Mathieu**. His season was cut short last year, but his coverage against slot receivers was among the best, and the Cardinals' 19 interceptions backed up the hype. It doesn't hurt that the Cardinals replaced **Rashad Johnson** with speedy **Tyvon Branch** formerly of the Chiefs.

By the numbers, this unit finished tied for first with the Broncos with 22 forced fumbles. The six touchdowns the Cardinals produced gave fantasy owners an added boost to their weekly totals.

It's a dangerous front seven. With adding Nkemdiche and Jones, the Cardinals should raise their sack total of 36 which tied tem for twentieth last season. With an offense that should produce near its 2015 level, the Cardinals should be top three all year long.

2. Broncos. By this writing, **Von Miller** hasn't been signed to an extension. Though it isn't an issue yet, elite players should be compensated to motivate young players working towards earning their big contracts. The Broncos still boast one of the best secondary groups, as **Chris Harris Jr.** and **Aquib Talib** are among the most talented corners in the league. **TJ Ward** is no slouch either at the safety position.

The twenty-seven turnovers the Broncos defensive unit had last season was good enough for seventh overall, but their thirty-one giveaways hurt with 23 in interceptions. While the takeaways might dip just a little bit, the run first approach the Broncos are looking to instill should significantly drop their turnovers and help give their defense more rest.

Defensive Coordinator **Wade Phillips** picked up **Jared Crick** through free agency and **Adam Gotsis** through the draft to fill the void left on the defensive line by the departed **Malik Jackson**. However, the void left by **Danny Travathan,** now with the Bears, remains. The front seven must remain dominant for the secondary ranking to remain one of the league's best. Unless the injury bug hits or the offense falls off of a cliff (which could happen), the Broncos should remain a top five defensive unit in 2016.

3. Texans. After an abysmal start to the 2015 season, the Texans defense went on a tear, finishing the season leading the league in passes defended (90), tied for eleventh in fumble recoveries (11), tied for thirteenth in interceptions (14), and registering the fifth most sacks (45) in the league. From Week 8 to Week 17, the Texans defense was the No. 1 DST in fantasy football because they also allowed 10 or fewer points in six of their last nine games.

The Texans are looking to replace **Jared Crick** along the defensive line, but they have several defensive end and tackle hybrids that can fill the void. **J.J. Watt**, **Jonathon Joseph**, **Brian Cushing**, and **Whitney Mercilus** all can make the Pro Bowl this season. Talented second year corner **Kevin Johnson** and second year linebacker **Bernardrick McKinney** proved they can start.

4. Seahawks. This tried and true number one defense in previous seasons stepped back in 2015 despite consistently producing good defensive numbers. Consistency is nice, but roster turnover hurts their ranking going into 2016. Losing linebacker **Bruce Irvin** and defensive lineman **Brandon Mebane** hurts a team whose sack total and sack percentage has fallen over the past three seasons. This is still a good defense which ranked first in points allowed and second in yards per game allowed.

The Seahawks brought in veteran defensive end **Chris Clemons** and youthful outside linebacker **Tavaris Barnes** to add depth. The Seahawks took a flier on **Brandon Browner** to nearly complete the reunion of the legion of boom. This season, **Kam Chancellor** will be with the group from day one, so the Seahawks should rely a little less on **Jeremy Lane** and **DeShawn Shead** to produce even though they are promising players. It remains to be seen if the Seahawks can improve on their 22 takeaways. Keys for this defense is they have good depth, a good offense, and reasonable schedule to start, with their first five games offering an opportunity for them to figure things out if they need to.

5. Panthers. It's safe to say the loss of 2015 shut-down corner **Josh Norman** will hurt. However, the Panthers still have the best linebacker combination with **Luke Kuechly** and **Thomas Davis**. The defensive line received a much needed boost with adding **Vernon Butler** in the draft. The front seven makes the Panthers a Top 10 option, but the secondary went from above average to one of the most questionable groups in the league. This alone leads to the conclusion that their league leading 24 interceptions from last season falls to between 15 to 18 for 2016.

Although rookies **Daryl Worley** and **James Bradbury** have potential, it's far too early to view them as dominant options. However, they are behind unproven corner **Bene Benwikere** and undersized journeyman **Robert McClain** waived by the Panthers in 2011 and spent time with the Jaguars, Falcons and Patriots before returning to the Panthers. The offense is dominant enough to take pressure off of the defense. The front seven will disguise the weaknesses of the secondary, something the unit did *before* Josh Norman broke out last season.

6. Bengals. The Bengals finished with the sixth most takeaways with 28 and they resigned their best secondary players retaining **Adam Jones** and **George Iloka**. The likes of **A.J. Hawk, Leon Hall** and **Reggie Nelson** were replaced with young, promising players including talented cornerback **William Jackson III**, linebacker **Nick Vigil**, and beefy nose tackle **Andrew Billings**. Linebacker **Karlos Dansby** is a solid addition and should help a defensive unit whose pass rush greatly improved from their 2014 league-worst sack total of 20.0 to the their tenth best total of 42.0 sacks in 2015.

The Bengals must likely rely on at least one rookie or one young defensive back to go with **Dre Kirkpatrick** and **Daquez Denard** at corner. What helps though is the Bengals potent offense. With a rested defense, the Bengals defense's rate of three-and-out drives in 2015 should remain high in 2016. The Bengals also finished second in points allowed per game, so they're arguably one of the most reliable groups in fantasy football.

7. Vikings. A TFG sleeper in 2015, there is no reason for the Vikings DST to be rated as low as twelve or lower this off-season. Undrafted in 2015, the Vikings DST isn't very sexy at any position group but still finished seventh in sacks (43), seventeenth in interceptions (13), and thirteenth in yards allowed per game (344 yards). What should be attractive to you as a fantasy owner is that they allowed a fifth best 18.9 points per game allowed. Coupled with a plus-five turnover margin with 22 takeaways, it says the offense doesn't put the defense in terrible positions.

The additions the team made through the draft give this team more depth at key positions.

They'll go from having a terrible wide receiving group to a good one with **Laquon Treadwell**. This will only help the run first offense stay on the field and the defense off the field. Defensive back **Mackensie Alexander** is a day one starter for the Vikings, most likely at the slot CB position. Stars like **Davin Joseph, Anthony Barr** and **Harrison Smith** help this defense stay tough. The Vikings defensive unit is one which can only improve.

8. Chiefs. Coming off of a stellar 2016, defensive campaign the 2016 Chiefs were left trying to find someone to replace starting CB **Sean Smith** who they could couple with stud rookie **Marcus Peters** (8 interceptions). At least on paper, **Phillip Gaines** is expected to replace Smith but he saw little playing time in 2015 as his seasons ended early due to an ACL injury. The Chiefs drafted CB **Keivarae Russell** in the third round and CB **Eric Murray** in the fourth round, just in case. Rookie DT **Chris Jones** joins a front seven which totaled 47 sacks (fourth most) in 2015.

In other areas of the defense, the Chiefs still boast plenty of studs.

Two issues could hold the Chiefs DST back. The unit must likely rely on multiple rookies in the secondary and the offensive line looks to have gone from average to poor. The latter matters as this ball control offense has been key to the defense staying fresh. There's still a lot of talent on this defense even with outside linebacker **Justin Houston** (knee) likely missing the first part of the season. The Chiefs DST should remain one of the more reliable options in 2016 but a Top 5 finish may be difficult to attain.

9. Patriots. There were skeptics of the Patriots, particularly their secondary, before the 2015 season began. However, the trio of **Malcolm Butler, Logan Ryan**, and **Devin McCourty** turned out to be an impressive group. Adding second round pick **Cyrus Jones** to the mix provides depth to this group that must play well with what has happened to the front seven this off-season.

The Patriots traded young pass rusher **Chandler Jones** for one year of **Chris Long.** Along with young studs **Jaime Collins** and **Don't'a Hightower**, this group makes for a very capable linebacker core.

The issue for the Patriots this year is whether 2015 first round pick DT **Malcolm Brown** can take the next step as a starter while older defensive linemen **Terrance Knighton, Alan Branch,** and **Rob Ninkovich** maintain their level of play. This unit is a mystery. But, the depth and veteran makeup should make for a potent pass rushing attack.

The Patriots gave up 19.7 points per game last year and forced the fourth most fumbles with 28, but only recovered nine. Fantasy managers must be patient with Patriots, particularly through the first few weeks of the season, with **Tom Brady** suspended. This unit will likely be up and down all season.

10. Rams. It's surprising that you can go from an assumed elite DST option one year, and then an underrated option the next year. The Rams finished the 2012 season ranked as the twelfth best defense, which given their 7-9 record might surprise people. The truth is the Rams came away with a turnover in all but two of their games last season.

The Rams dedicated the meat of their draft to their offense as their first four picks were on that side of the ball. Losing **Janoris Jenkins, Chris Long, Nick Fairley** and **Rodney McLeod** this off-season might be too much to overcome, but their defensive line will cause a ton of havoc one again, making them relevant in all fantasy football formats.

11. Steelers. The Steelers DST surprised last season, finishing third in sacks with 48. But, the 31 takeaways the Steelers created were even more surprising as this unit had several question marks on defense before last season. Unfortunately, there were as many bust weeks as there were boom weeks as the Steelers defense scored four or fewer fantasy points six times while posting double digit points in six weeks.

The Steelers invested in their secondary early by drafting CB **Artie Burns** in the first round and safety **Sean Davis** in the second round. These two add to a secondary which came away with 17 interceptions last season, good for a sixth place tie.

The Steelers found gems in defensive end **Stephon Tuitt** who posted 6.5 sacks his rookie season and outside linebacker **Bud Dupree** who posted 4.0 sacks his rookie season. It was once a joke to make fun of the age of the Steelers defense, but now all but two players are in their twenties. Veterans like **Cameron Heyward, Lawrence Timmons** and **William Gay** will lead the way, but fantasy owners won't have to worry about this defense depending on any one player. What's great, the Steelers DST should be available in the latter rounds of fantasy drafts.

12. Jets. The Jets DST cooled off significantly in the second half of the 2015 season after a very hot start, allowing 20-plus points in 11 of their 16 games. This made this unit appear to under achieve despite the defensive talent on their roster. From a statistical perspective, outside of points allowed, the Jets were fifth in interceptions (18), twelfth in sacks (39.0), and eighth in fumbled recovered (12).

The Jets still haven't resigned Ryan Fitzpatrick makes it difficult to have confidence with the performance of this team, including the defense. In a time where the Jets need stability, there is instability. This monkeying around is just no good. If Ryan Fitzpatrick does not return as the starting quarterback for 2016, this would be a big blow to the defense. The Jets still boast a talented core of players and deserve consideration despite a rather brutal schedule early on.

13. Raiders. Many are touting the Raiders defense this off-season but it's hard to make the jump from a below average defense to a top tier defense in one season, after allowing 24.9 points per game. However, the Raiders made monster additions this off-season which provide them fantasy upside. The Raiders signed **ILB Malcolm Smith, CB Sean Smith** and **S Reggie Nelson.** All three players were starters on playoff teams and will play a significant role along with developing star in **Khalil Mack.** They Raiders reached selecting S **Karl Joseph** with their first round pick, but the gamble could pay off immediately if he returns to form coming off his knee injury.

The Raiders finished the 2015 season with a respectable 25 takeaways which was a monumental improvement from their 14 takeaways in 2014. As **Derek Carr** develops and the defense gels, it will be less likely that the defense is put in the tough positions their offense put them in for so many years. The Raiders are worth a late round grab in twelve team leagues or larger.

14. Jaguars. There wasn't a better infusion of young talent on the defensive side of the ball than what the Jaguars did this off-season. Their revamped secondary is comprise of the most versatile defensive back in the draft, elite prospect **Jalen Ramsey.** Then, the Jaguars took a chance on elite passer rusher **Myles Jack,** who due to concerns over his knee, fell into the second round of the draft. Well, the risk paid off as his knee appears to be healthy.

In addition, the Jaguars brought in key veterans like defensive end **Malik Jackson** and cornerback **Prince Amukamara** to provide leadership along the defensive line and secondary. It's also easy to forget that the Jaguars third overall pick from last year, **Dante Fowler Jr.,** is returning from a torn ACL. Part of having a good defense is having a capable offense. The Jaguars offense is not just capable, it's potent. It will force teams to take more chances against this defensive unit. The Jaguars are the sleeper defensive unit of the 2016 fantasy season.

15. Packers. An injury to Jordy Nelson and the down season **Eddie Lacy** had seemed to impact both sides of the ball for the Packers in 2015. The Packers defensive units went from one of the best preseason units to one of the worst in-season units.

This off-season the Packers let **Casey Hayward** walk in free agency which hurt their secondary. However, the Packers still have **Damarious Randall, Quinten Rollins,** and **Sam Shields.** The Packers did a great job of loading up on their front seven talent in the draft with defensive tackle **Kenny Clark** expected to replace **B.J. Raji** while linebackers **Kyle Fackrell** and **Blake Martinez** work their way from back-ups/special teams to eventual starters, possibly sooner rather than later.

The Packer defense produced a takeaway in all but one game in 2015. However, they had several bad weeks in which their turnover differential was negative. Much of the blame falls on the offense as they went from an upper-tier time of possession unit to more of an average one. Their rush defense also took a small but material step back in 2015. This year their offense should play better. A solid secondary and a deeper front seven should help the Packers flirt with Top 10 status.

16. Bills. On paper, the defensive unit of the Bills was supposed to be a monster unit. Ironically, it was the secondary, the most questionable of their positions groups, which may have played best. The Bills played like one of the best defensive units and like one of the worst. The unit finished with a +6 turnover differential, but with just 21 totals sacks for the entire season. What's more shocking is that free safety **Corey Graham** finished as their leading tackler with 127 tackles. It shows how terrible the pass rush was and the Bills' top draft pick, **Shaq Lawson,** is already having surgery. Lawson is likely to produce more than **Mario Williams** did last year, and fellow draftees, linebacker **Reggie Ragland** and defensive tackle **Adolphus Washington,** will present offenses with several problems. The Bills have the makings of a great defense on paper, but the questionable pass rush keeps them out of the Top 10 for now.

Kicker Rankings & Profiles

By Alexander George
Contributor, TheFantasyGreek.com

A fantasy football manager's selection of a FG kicker in fantasy drafts can be significant in acquiring loads of points during a season. Despite some turnover in the rankings from year-to-year, listed below are the top-half of the notable field goal kickers around the league you should draft in fantasy football.

1. **Stephen Gostkowski, Patriots**
2. **Steven Hauschka, Seahawks**
3. **Justin Tucker, Ravens**
4. **Graham Gano, Panthers**
5. **Mason Crosby, Packers**
6. **Blair Walsh, Vikings**
7. **John Brown, Giants**
8. **Chris Boswell, Steelers**
9. **Dan Bailey, Cowboys**
10. **Chandler Catanzaro, Cardinals**
11. **Adam Vinatieri, Colts**
12. **Brandon McManus, Broncos**
13. **Robbie Gould, Bears**
14. **Cairo Santos, Chiefs**
15. **Mike Nugent, Bengals**
16. **Robert Aguayo, Buccaneers**

XP - Extra Point; XPA - Extra point Attempts; FG - Field Goals; FGA - Field Goal Attempts

1. Stephen Gostkowski, Patriots

2015 FG/FGA: 33/36 (91.7%)
2015 Long: 57 yards
XP/XPA: 52/ 52 (100%)

Last season was another career year for Stephen Gostkowski with his third consecutive Pro-Bowl appearance. Gostkowski led in scoring while making four field goals in five attempts from 50-plus yards out. His current record of 463 XP's has been intact for almost ten seasons. Stephen Gostkowski is the only kicker worth drafting early, in the eleventh or twelfth round in twelve team fantasy leagues.

2. Stephen Hauschka, Seahawks

2015 FG/FGA: 29/31 (93.5%)
2015 Long: 54 yards
XP/XPA: 29/29 (91%)

Stephen Hauschka got back on track with his FG percentage increasing from 83.8 % (2014) to 93.5% (2015). Hauschka has not missed a FG for the second consecutive year, kicking a perfect 16 for 16 in the 20-39 yard range last season. Hauschka converted a perfect 6-for-6 in FGs from over 50 yards away last season. With the Seahawks wanting to get back to running the football, look for Hauschka to stay on top.

3. Justin Tucker, Ravens

2015 FG/FGA: 33/40 (83.3%)
2015 Long: 52 yards
XP/XPA: 29/29 (100%)

Tucker turned in a terrible season in missed field goals. His field goals made percentage fell to 83.3% However, six attempts were from 50-plus yards. Otherwise, Tucker was a perfect 33-for-33 from 49 yards in. So, despite the misses, his accuracy has been spotless. He's perfect in extra points the past four seasons as a pro and has only missed three field goals from 49 yards in the past three seasons. The Ravens offense is expected to be improved from last season.

4. Graham Gano, Panthers

2015 FG/FGA: 30/36 (83.3%)
2015 Long: 52 yards
XP/XPA: 56/59 (95%)

One of the most notable, basic stats, which is very important in the fantasy football world pertaining to kickers, is the ability to convert on the XP. Although Graham Gano missed three XPs last season, it was on 59 attempts, most in the league! For field goals, Gano has been almost automatic from the 0 to 29 yard range, 55 for 58 since joining the league. Behind a potent Panthers offense, Gano is an elite kicker.

5. Mason Crosby, Packers

2015 FG/FGA: 24/28, (85.7%)
2015 Long: 56 yards
XP/XPA: 36/36 (100%)

Mason Crosby's numbers were down in 2015 because he had his lowest number of field goal attempts since 2008, and he had the fewest extra point attempts of his career. Crosby made all twelve FGA from the 0 to 39 yard range. He also converted 80% of his 50-plus yard FGA (four of five). Last season, Mason Crosby's attempts were limited as the Packers offense struggled to move the football without Jordy Nelson and without a real running game to speak of. Nelson is expected to be 100% this season and the rushing game much improved. Except for one season, Crosby has been reliable, steady, and consistent.

6. Blair Walsh, Vikings

2015 FG/FGA: 34/39 (87.2%)
2015 Long: 54 yards
XP/XPA: 33/37 (89.2%)

This one time Pro-Bowler, improved his FG percentage and accuracy from 2014 by almost thirteen percentage points. Walsh kicked eight more FGs on just four more attempts than 2014, and was a perfect 9-for-9 from the 0-29 yard range. Where he came through for fantasy managers was his 6-for-8 from 50-plus yards! His best game last season came in Week 16 against the Giants, where he was a perfect 5-for-5 in FGs and 4-for-5 in XPs. His most notable statistic to remember when drafting a kicker is his 71.8% career percentage converting field goals from fifty-plus yards.

7. Josh Brown, Giants

2015 FG/FGA: 30/32 (93.8%)
2015 Long: 53 yards
XP/XPA: 44/ 45 (97.8%)

In 2015, Josh Brown had his most field goal attempts since 2010 and posted his highest field goal kicking percentage of his thirteen year career. In addition, for a second season in a row, he kicked at least 44 extra points, the most since 2005. He has had back-to-back years of converting over 90% of his FGA. He was a perfect 3-for-3 in FGA from 50-plus yards out last season. As long as the Giants maintain one of the top offenses in the league, there will be plenty of opportunities for Josh Brown to score more points.

8. Chris Boswell, Steelers

2015 FG/FGA: 29/32 (90.6%)
2015 Long: 51 yards
XP/XPA: 26/27 (96.3%)

Among the several second year kickers this season, Chris Boswell is the best. Boswell replaced kicker Shaun Suisham, who was injured in last season's Hall of Fame game, and has since retired. Boswell, who went undrafted in 2014, played no regular season game that year. He kicks for one of the best offenses in the league and will continue getting opportunities in both extra points and field goal attempts. His ninety-plus percentage accuracy rate is another reason he makes for a top ten fantasy prospect.

9. Dan Bailey, Cowboys

2015 FG/FGA: 30/32 (93.8%)
2015 Long: 54 yards
XP/XPA: 25/ 25 (100%)

This Pro-Bowl player was the NFL leader in FG percentage last season at over 93%, a percentage he has topped three of his five seasons as a pro. Dan Bailey kicks indoors in eight games a year minimum and is on a team whose offense gives him opportunities. He has missed field goals from 0 to 39 yards just three times in his career on 85 attempts. Dan Bailey has never missed an XP in his career in 204 attempts. Last year, he posted a career low 25 extra point attempts due to the injury to Tony Romo and an offense which was anemic most of last season. This won't happen in 2016 as Romo returns and the rushing game should be much better with Ezekiel Elliott. Forty-five extra point attempts is doable.

10. Chandler Catanzaro, Cardinals

2015 FG/FGA: 28/31 (90.3%)
2015 Long: 47 yards
XP/XPA: 53/58 (91.4%)

Chandler Catanzaro would have been higher on this list had he been able to convert either of his two 50-plus yard three point attempts, which makes him 2-for-5 in his career. In two seasons, he is near perfect in field goal attempts from 0-39 yards out (39/41). Most of Catanzaro's value last season was due to the 53 extra points he hit on 58 attempts. The Cardinals are expected to again have a good offense.

11. Adam Vinatieri, Colts

2015 FG/FGA: 25/27 (92.6%)
2015 Long: 55 yards
XP/XPA: 32/35 (91.4%)

Adam Vinatieri continues to be one of the best kickers in the league after twenty seasons despite his first extra point misses in six seasons. In back-to-back seasons, his field goal percentage has bettered 90%. Vinatieri remains on fantasy radars because of Andrew Luck. Just two seasons ago, playing behind a healthy Luck, he was a perfect 50-for-50 in extra points. With Andrew Luck 100% healthy this season, Adam Viniateri should once again be in line for 30 field goal attempts and 40 extra point attempts.

12. Brandon McManus, Broncos

2015 FG/FGA: 30/35 (85.7%)
2015 Long: 57 yards
XP/XPA: 35/36 (97.2%)

Brandon McManus was 20 for 20 in the 0 to 39 yard range in 2016. Despite some misses, McManus was given plenty opportunity to kick long, going 5-for-8 from 40 to 49 yards out and 5-for-7 from 50-plus yards out. Because of their quarterback issues, the Broncos are expected to run the football much more. With the offense expected to stall often, and the defense again one of the best in the league, McManus should see his field goals remain high in 2016. McManus is a borderline fantasy starter in 10 or 12 team leagues.

13. Robbie Gould, Bears

2015 FG/FGA: 33/39 (84.6%)
2015 Long: 55 yards
XP/XPA: 28/29 (96.6%)

Robbie Gould is one of the more consistent kickers in the league but a spate of injuries two of the last three seasons made him miss seven games. While perfect from 0-29 yards out last season (86-for-86 over his career), he missed two kicks in each subsequent distance (30-39, 40-49, 50-plus) to finish the season 84.6%. On extra points, he's almost been perfect over his eleven year career with four misses. Gould's 39 field goal attempts last season was a career high. Robbie Gould is back in the discussion as a top twelve option because the Bears offense is expected to be improved as is the defense.

14. Cairo Santos, Chiefs

2015 FG/FGA: 30/37 (81.1%)
2015 Long: 53 yards
XP/XPA: 39/41 (95.1%)

This below-the-radar kicker has become one of the most reliable kickers in fantasy. Cairo Santos quickly established himself as the Chiefs kicker in his rookie year in 2014, where he was 25/30 on field goal attempts and 38/38 for extra point attempts. Last season, Santos kicked the most field goals in a game in Chiefs history with seven, tied for second in the league for most field goals in a game. Although Santos' field goal percentage is not as high as one would like, Andy Reid lets him take deep shot field goals. Last season, Cairo Santos made eight field goal attempts of 50-plus yards and converted on four.

15. Mike Nugent, Bengals

2015 FG/FGA: 23/28 (82.1%)
2015 Long: 56 yards
XP/XPA: 48/49 (98.0%)

A kicker who has improved from last season, Mike Nugent has been a perfect 40-for-40 from the 0 to 29 yard range since he joined the Bengals in 2010. Nugent struggles, more than others, in distances beyond this. From 2010 to 2015, Nugent was 94-for-123, or 76.4%, on longer distances of 30-plus yards, having missed 14 from 40 to 49 yards during that stretch. Nugent gets most of his value kicking in an Andy Dalton led offense which thrived last season, and where he converted 48 of 49 extra point attempts, second most in his career. If Dalton stays healthy, Mike Nugent should top fifty extra points in 2016.

16. Robert Aguyo, Buccaneers

2015 FG/FGA: 21/26 (80.8%)
2015 Long: 53 yards
XP/XPA: 49/49 (100.0%)

Robert Aguyo was this off-season's top kicking draft prospect. His overall college record is impressive with an 88.5% field goal accuracy (69-for-78) and a perfect 100% extra point accuracy (198-for-198) over three seasons. Aguyo was a perfect 49 for 49 on FGA inside 40 yards. His longest FG was 53 yards. The Buccaneers offense should give Aguyo plenty of opportunity to show off his big leg. Consider Aguyo a sleeper this season.

Top IDP Ranks

By Andrew Miley
Dynasty Football Factory

The game of fantasy football is exciting, full of twists and turns. While I love the excitement created by the quarterback and whomever he gives the ball, there is more to this wonderful sport than just offense.

Perhaps it's because I played offensive line I like my fantasy football to be based on what happens on *both sides of the ball*. **Richard Sherman** getting into the head of a receiver or **Bill Belichick** designing a new offensive or defensive wrinkle that changes the course of a playoff run. This is why I play with individual defensive players, simply known as IDPs for short.

To some of you, this might seem intimidating. There are already plenty of offensive players one must learn, and this writer is asking for more work to be done. But, I play fantasy football for my love of the game, not just the offensive players.

Even when watching the offense, most of us notice the better defensive players trying to thwart their every move. So why not incorporate their importance into fantasy football games as well?

There are three basic positions to set in all IDP lineups in fantasy football.

The first group are the **linebackers** who play usually two yards off the line of scrimmage and always seem to lead their defensive squads in tackles. These need to be some of the best students of the game, see the field well, and can shed blockers on their way to the ball carrier. Inside linebackers get more tackles and outside linebackers get more sacks.

The **top twenty** linebackers I would want on my squad in 2016 are:

1. Luke Kuechly, Panthers
2. Navorro Bowman, 49ers
3. Jamie Collins, Patriots
4. Alec Ogletree, Rams
5. Lavonte David, Buccaneers
6. D'Qwell Jackson, Colts
7. Brandon Marshall, Broncos
8. Malcolm Smith, Raiders
9. Jordan Hicks, Eagles
10. Sean Lee, Cowboys
11. DeAndre Levy, Lions
12. CJ Mosley, Ravens
13. Derrick Johnson, Chiefs
14. Deone Bucannon, Cardinals
15. Ryan Shazier, Steelers
16. Bobby Wagner, Seahawks
17. Karlos Dansby, Bengals
18. Telvin Smith, Jaguars
19. Deon Jones, Falcons
20. Darron Lee, Jets

The next group of players to discuss are the **defensive linemen**. These are the ends, tackles, and nose guards that line up against the other team's offensive linemen along the line of scrimmage. **Defensive** linemen are more valuable when they play on a four defensive linemen front (4-3 defense) versus a three defensive linemen front (3-4 defense). The 4-3 defense makes it more difficult to double team any player. The exception to the rule is all-star **JJ Watt** who plays in a 3-4 defensive scheme.

Nose guards (or nose tackles as they are more commonly known) are usually worthless in all formats as their job is to plug a hole and take on multiple blockers on every down. They don't tackle or sack as much.

These are my **top twenty** defensive linemen for 2016:

1. JJ Watt, Houston Texans
2. Ezekiel Ansah, Lions
3. Robert Quinn, Rams
4. Carlos Dunlap, Bengals
5. Cameron Jordan, Saints
6. Everson Griffith, Vikings
7. Muhammad Wilkerson, Jets
8. Aaron Donald, Rams
9. Rob Ninkovich, Patriots
10. Robert Ayers, Buccaneers
11. Jason Pierre-Paul, Giants
12. Jabaal Sheard, Patriots
13. Michael Bennett, Seahawks
14. Mario Williams, Miami Dolphins
15. Vinny Curry, Eagles
16. Olivier Vernon, Giants
17. Calais Campbell, Cardinals
18. Malik Jackson, Jaguars
19. Sheldon Richardson, Jets
20. Danielle Hunter, Vikings

The final group to include in your IDP leagues are **defensive backs**. These will be cornerbacks and safeties (both free and strong). **Strong safeties** can be very valuable when they play on teams with weaker linebackers as they hover close to the line of scrimmage and get more tackle chances or opportunities.

Most veteran quarterbacks like to pick on younger, less experienced cornerbacks; this is called the "rookie cornerback rule." The **slot cornerbacks** are also valuable because they get more targets than their counterparts playing on the line. **Free safeties** play like a baseball center fielder would, flowing to where the ball is going, but always making sure it doesn't get behind them.

Here are my top twenty defensive backs:

1. Reshad Jones, Dolphins
2. Malcolm Jenkins, Eagles
3. Ha-Ha Clinton-Dix, Packers
4. Landon Collins, Giants
5. Eric Berry, Chiefs
6. Harrison Smith, Vikings
7. Barry Church, Cowboys
8. Karl Joseph, Raiders
9. Keanu Neal, Falcons
10. Morgan Burnett, Packers
11. Eric Weddle, Ravens
12. Corey Graham, Bills
13. Trumaine Johnson, Rams
14. Rashad Johnson, Titans
15. Kurt Coleman, Panthers
16. Kenny Vaccaro, Saints
17. Clayton Geathers, Colts
18. Ron Parker, Chiefs
19. Earl Thomas, Seahawks
20. Tyrann Mathieu, Cardinals

It's difficult making the choice to go to a full blown IDP league without trying it first. Perhaps start with eliminating the team defense position and then incorporate starting one linebacker, one defensive lineman, and one defensive back with a defensive flex spot that could be any of those positions to get every owner comfortable with the concept.

Top 10 Comeback Players

By Derek Guilford
Featured Contributor, TheFantasyGreek.com

Every season, a group of players stands ready to have a better season than they did the season before. Some players are coming off injury, some players are coming off a season of disappointing, poor play. This list of ten players have comeback written all over them and figure to make you fist pump with joy instead of face plant with agony.

1. WR Jordy Nelson, Packers. Nelson holds a fantasy stud reputation after being a reliable producer posting an average of 1,210 yards and 10.8 TDs over the 2011 to 2014 seasons. Last year, Nelson tore his ACL in training camp, missing the entire 2015 season. He is still Aaron Rodgers' #1 target.

2. RB Jamaal Charles, Chiefs. Coming off his second ACL surgery in the last five years, Charles is out to prove he's not ready to limp into fantasy obscurity just yet. The latest reports on Charles has him rehabbing nicely from the knee injury. He was jumping rope and catching footballs on a balancing board in mid-February. He was participating in individual drills in mid-June. The Chiefs will no doubt take it easy on him until the season starts in early September. Andy Reid likes to prioritize his running backs, and Charles should remain at the top. Outside of the pair of ACL tears of '11 and '15, Charles has put up 1,746 total yards along with 9.75 TDs per season. His touches should go down, but his per game productivity should remain high.

3. WR Dez Bryant, Cowboys. Tony Romo and Dez Bryant are one of the elite QB/WR duos today. In 2015, they and the Cowboys faltered to a 4-12 record largely due to injury. Romo missed 12 games with a broken collarbone, while Bryant missed seven games with a broken foot. This adversely affected Bryant who previously posted three consecutive seasons of 80-plus receptions, 1,200-plus yards receiving, and double digit touchdowns. With the return of Romo, Dez Bryant should once again post solid fantasy numbers like a top ten option as he had in seasons past. The risk in selecting Dez Bryant with an early round pick in Romo will need to stay healthy.

4. Andrew Luck, Colts. Last season was supposed to be the season Andrew Luck rose into the super-elite of the league, leaving the Mannings, Brady and Big Ben behind. It was hyped as an MVP season. Instead, it was a lost season for the Colts' signal caller who injured his shoulder, forcing him to miss 11 games as the resultant Colts tailspin led to a mediocre 8-8 record. Now, with a retooled offensive line, a plethora of weapons at his disposal including a healthy T.Y. Hilton, Luck is back and ready to fulfill all of his potential and the massive expectations that follow.

5. WR Kelvin Benjamin, Panthers. "KB" is another victim of the training camp ACL injury putting him on IR all last season. In his rookie season of 2014, Kelvin Benjamin quickly ascended to be Cam Newton's #1 target hauling in 73 catches for 1,008 yards and 8 TDs while playing in all 16 games. Benjamin is a great beat to hit 150 targets. Benjamin should bounce back strong in 2016.

6. RB LeSean McCoy, Bills. McCoy put together a lackluster campaign his first year for the Bills, logging 895 yards on 203 rushes. However, he battled injuries all season. Despite Karlos Williams, McCoy dominated the running back touches. He should be just fine behind a great offensive line. LeSean McCoy is still in a position to have a 'big' 2016 season at twenty-years of age to start the season.

7. RB Eddie Lacy, Packers. Two words: CONTRACT YEAR! Lacy was a frequent member of Head Coach Mike McCarthy's doghouse last year. After averaging 1,500 total yards and 12 TDs his first pair of seasons as a pro, Lacy backslid to a disappointing 946 total yards and five TDs in 2015. The main concern for Lacy has always been his weight. He was reportedly playing at a tight-end like 260 pounds last year. To shed the excess weight, Lacy teamed up with fitness guru Tony Horton this off-season, shaving off 20 pounds to get back to the more acceptable, but still beefy, 240 lbs. range. With Lacy entering a make-or-break contract season, he will be motivated more than ever. Most will shy away from Lacy so he should fall in most drafts.

8. RB Carlos Hyde, 49ers. "El Guapo" began 2015 on an absolute tear, shredding the Vikings for 168 yards on 26 carries scoring a pair of TDs. Then, he struggled compiling a pedestrian 302 yards over his next six games. An ankle injury ended his season in Week 8. From reports, Hyde has slimmed down to 225 pounds. Hyde is a perfect fit for new Head Coach Chip Kelly's power running scheme. Add to this the uninspiring collection of talent outside of Hyde on the 49ers offense and it's easy to get excited about Hyde's 2016 season where he should become a fantasy football star.

9. WR Mike Wallace, Ravens. The wheels came off for Wallace in 2015 after an unexceptional season playing for the Vikings. Wallace hauled in a paltry 39 receptions for an uninspiring 473 yards and a pair of touchdowns. This offseason, Wallace found a home in Baltimore where Joe Flacco's big arm should be good for another 600-plus pass attempts in Marc Trestman's offense. Mike Wallace's choice to play for the Ravens should be very wise as only sophomore WR Breshad Perriman (injured) and veteran Steve Smith are serious competition vying for targets. Despite burning fantasy team owners in the past, Wallace should fall in drafts so the risk-reward should be favorable.

10. TE Jordan Cameron, Dolphins. Finding an effective tight end late in fantasy drafts is pure gold. Cameron was overvalued in 2015. Cameron struggled mightily in Joe Philbin's offense catching only 50% of his targets and never charting over 35 yards in any game after Week 2. New Head Coach Adam Gase has a documented history of making the tight end position a featured position in his offenses. So, Cameron should bounce back to fantasy relevancy this season.

Top 10 Undervalued Players

By Rick Briggs
Fireside Sports

1. RB Melvin Gordon, Chargers. With all the injuries the Chargers suffered last year, look for the team to bounce back competitively in 2016. **Melvin Gordon** ran hard last season behind a banged up offensive line and had little to show for it. Current ADPs have Gordon going in the sixth round behind unproven **Jay Ajayi**, and right with **Frank Gore**. Do yourself a favor and take Gordon ahead of these guys. The Chargers will be an improved team. The offensive line will be healthier and the receiving corps better.

2. WR Travis Benjamin, Chargers. Except for **Gary Barnidge**, **Travis Benjamin** was the bright spot on the Brown offense in 2015. Amassing 68 catches for 966 yards, Benjamin is a fast slot receiver with good hands. He will be the No. 2 wide receiver for the Chargers behind **Keenan Allen**. This will undoubtedly mean more opportunities for Benjamin, as the dangerous Keenan Allen draws the top coverage. Travis Benjamin will now be with a quarterback who is a 4,500 to 5,000 yard passer. Benjamin can do things **Malcom Floyd** couldn't, and **Stevie Johnson** is a health risk. Everything points to Benjamin's stock rising. Going midway through the ninth round of mock drafts, he's a steal.

3. TE Martellus Bennett, Patriots. Remember when the Patriots offense featured two tight end sets from 2010 to 2012? The second tight end caught up to 79 passes. With **Martellus Bennett** now in the fold, the Patriots should feature more two tight end sets again. Bennett is big, has attitude, and can catch a football. Despite missing five games last season, Bennett hauled in 208 receptions in three years with the Bears. Bennett should be perfect for the Patriots offense and could be one of those players that *lifts* a fantasy team to victory. One cautionary note, however. Bennett must study and grasp the Patriot offense. Remember **Chad Ochocinco** in New England? **Bill Belichick** has no patience for those who don't get with the program.

4. WR Randall Cobb, Packers. How many fantasy owners were burned by **Randall Cobb** in 2015, thinking he would be an instant treasure trove of statistics with **Jordy Nelson** out? We now know Cobb needs a healthy Jordy Nelson to thrive. Without Nelson, Cobb still hauled in 79 catches last season despite drawing top coverage. However, his yards per catch were down almost four yards and his touchdowns were cut in half. Things will be different in 2016. Cobb is available at the beginning of the third round in PPR leagues and at the end of the third round in non-PPR leagues. Remember in 2014, when Cobb caught 91 passes for almost 1,300 yards and 12 touchdowns? He was a top five wide receiver in PPR. Believe in Randall Cobb again. **Aaron Rodgers** will give him plenty of chances.

5. WR Devin Funchess, Panthers. Rookie Devin Funchess was thrown into the fire head first last season after **Kelvin Benjamin** tore up his knee, ending his season. It's true, veteran **Ted Ginn** got all the fantasy accolades in 2015, but Funchess got something more important for a rookie --- experience. Even Coach **Ron Rivera** has said how impressed he is with **Devin Funchess** in OTAs. At 6'4" tall and 225 pounds, and boasting sub 4.6-forty speed, Funchess is primed to explode. The Panthers went to the Super Bowl without Benjamin in 2015. Adding him back into the mix not only gives **Cam Newton** another weapon, but gives Funchess more leeway in the passing game. He is a steal as his current ADP is the middle to the end of the thirteenth round.

6. RB Isaiah Crowell, Browns. As the Browns continue rebuilding, there are a few bright spots team. **Isaiah Crowell** got in gear toward the end of last season. While Crowell will share running back duties with **Duke Johnson**, the lion's share of carries should still be Crowell's. He is a third year man, and new coach **Hugh Jackson** is excited about Crowell. The Browns are one of those teams that aren't as bad as they are expected to be. Duke Johnson is going three rounds ahead of Crowell right now. Crowell should fill in your roster as a nice RB3 this season.

7. RB Jeremy Hill, Bengals. Hill did little to impress fantasy owners last season except for scoring 11 touchdowns. His yards per carry dropped from 5.1 to 3.6, his rushing yards dropped 330 yards on one more rushing attempt, and his receiving numbers were down sixty-three percent. This is precisely why you should target the third year running back. At 6'1" tall and 235 pounds, **Jeremy Hill** can kill a defense. Although Hill will continue to split work with **Gio Bernard**, Hill is the Bengals' touchdown running back. Look for Jeremy Hill to bounce back strong this year. Hill is being drafted in the fifth round of mock drafts.

8. WR Larry Fitzgerald, Cardinals. It's unimaginable that one of the most gifted receivers playing who is coming off a 109/1,215/9 season, and is heading into the final year of his contract can be cast aside and available in the sixth round of mock drafts. Yes, **Larry Fitzgerald** will be 33 years old come Week 1. However, other veteran talents continued to produce at age thirty-three and beyond like the Ravens **Steve Smith**. The Cardinals will continue to have a good offense this season and Larry Fitzgerald will play a big part. Will he duplicate his 2015 numbers? Maybe not. But, he should still pop fantasy numbers like a low end WR1 to high end WR2 in 2016. That's a bargain when drafted in the sixth or later rounds.

9. RB TJ Yeldon, Jaguars. Just as **Chris Ivory** is overvalued, **TJ Yeldon** is undervalued. All offseason, Yeldon has been working on strength and quickness with his old college conditioning coach. This shows dedication and discipline. Ivory replaces inadequate backups who couldn't run the football. Yeldon is the Jaguars more dynamic running back, on a team boasting a potent offense in 2016.

10. WR Kamar Aiken, Ravens. Aiken came alive in 2015 after the injuries piled up for the Ravens. In the back half of the season, **Kamar Aiken** amassed 50 receptions for 611 yards and 3 TDs, on his way to his best season as a pro (75 rec., 944 yards, 5 TDs). This is Aiken's third year in the Ravens offense. He's a big receiver at 6'2" tall, 215 pounds, and has good hands. With **Breshad Perriman** already injured, Aiken should lock down a role in the Ravens offense and put up decent numbers. The Ravens will not be as bad as last year, and Aiken's stats should provide WR3 numbers with **Joe Flacco** back at the helm.

Top 10 Sleepers

By Chad Bellin
Featured Contributor, TheFantasyGreek.com

One of the most enjoyable aspects of fantasy football is having the inside scoop on a player who is underrated or off the radar. Depending on the size and sophistication of your league, 'sleepers' --- players poised to break out, overachieve, or surprise --- can be extremely valuable in building a championship roster.

This list of sleepers is for most standard leagues where there's 12-plus teams, mainstream scoring rules, and common roster sizes. Always beware of drafting risky players too early. Also, be wary of drafting too many risky players all on one roster.

Here are a few players to consider later in your fantasy drafts who could be fantasy gold in 2016.

1. RB Melvin Gordon III, Chargers. Few players had a more disappointing 2015 season than the highly touted rookie. With only 600 yards rushing and zero TDs, the 2015 first round pick disappointed fantasy team owners who spent a draft pick on him. Many factors contributed to **Melvin Gordon**'s plight including an offensive line, one of the worst at run blocking. Gordon was also never healthy. This season, the offensive line has improved and Gordon should be at full strength heading into camp. Plus, the offensive scheme will be orchestrated by Offensive Coordinator **Ken Wisenhunt**. When Wisenhunt last held the position with the Chargers in 2013, **Ryan Mathews** rushed the football 285 times for 1,255 yards and 6 TDs. Gordon has many pundits already giving up on him. At twenty-three years old, it's way too early to give up on Gordon based on one poor season with the upside he has in this offense.

2. WR Marvin Jones, Lions. With **Calvin Johnson**'s premature retirement, an enormous hole opened on the Lions offense. Enter free agent acquisition **Marvin Jones** formerly of the Bengals. Jones started opposite **AJ Green**, even posting solid numbers for 2015 (65-816-4). Marvin Jones won't replace Calvin Johnson's productivity. But, Jones could definitely emerge as one of **Matthew Stafford**'s favorite targets with only **TJ Jones** and **Golden Tate** in the mix. On the high side, 1,200 yards receiving is within reach but the number of TDs he scores will dictate whether Jones is a better bench player or starter in fantasy football.

3. WR Steve Smith Sr., Ravens. Dynasty players, nothing to see here. In redraft leagues, **Steve Smith** remains a sneaky pick in the latter rounds. Through seven games last season, Smith posted 670 yards receiving and 3 TDs and looked as capable a receiver at age 36 as he did at age 26. Smith has excellent chemistry with and the full trust of **Joe Flacco**. Plus, **Breshad Perriman** has already sustained another knee injury which has put a substantial portion of his season at risk. While this may be the end of the line for this fantasy football stud, Smith will aim to go out on top. The top end is roughly 1,000 yards and 6 TDs which is tremendous value for a player drafted as a reserve or even landing on waiver wires in smaller redraft leagues.

4. WR Kevin White, Bears. With **Alshon Jeffery** back for 2016, White should be able to get experience as the #2 option in the passing game while he prepares to become an elite talent in the years to come. Sidelined by a preseason injury in 2015 which caused him to miss his rookie year, the former West Virginia star adds instant star-power to the Bears aerial attack. Many have compared **Kevin White** to **DeAndre Hopkins**. While he may not put up Hopkins-like numbers in 2016, Kevin White should build towards 1,000 yards and multiple TDs. If White can remain focused and minimize drops, dynasty owners will be delighted to carry him on their roster for the next decade.

5. WR Mohamed Sanu, Falcons. Part of a crowded group vying for the same numbers in Cincinnati, Sanu had an off year in 2015. While he racked up a few rushing TDs, his numbers were nowhere near the 800 yards and 5 TDs he posted as a part-time starter in 2014. Now on the Falcons, **Mohamed Sanu** has the inside track on a starting spot in 2016 with **Roddy White** out of the picture. Sanu is a capable complement to all-pro wide receiver **Julio Jones**, and will benefit from the defensive schemes designed to shut down Jones. With his combination of size and speed, Sanu could see near 100 targets. He has a shot at 800 yards and 5 to 6 TDs in the Falcons offense.

6. WR Bruce Ellington, 49ers. Some think **DeAndre Smelter** will be the receiver to emerge for the 49ers this season in Chip Kelly's offense. However, chances of success are better for Andre Ellington. **Torrey Smith** and **Quinton Patton** are the veterans ahead of Ellington on the depth chart and only Smith's role is fairly assured. Patton is coming off injury and Smelter missed the 2014 season. The diminutive Ellington has the inside track on the slot position which leads to impressive opportunities in the Chip Kelly system. Comparisons to the Rams' Tavon Austin aren't out of line.

7. TE Ladarius Green, Steelers. If you miss out on one of the top tight ends early in your fantasy draft, there will be several secondary options to consider. One is **Ladarius Green** who has been on fantasy football sleeper lists before. Unfortunately, Green has roundly underachieved. Now, free from the shadow of **Antonio Gates**, Ladarius Green is in an offense which uses the tight end position part of its offense. The retired **Heath Miller** put up as much as 800 yards and 8 TDs playing tight end for the Steelers. Green has better size, is a better athlete, and has reliable enough hands to achieve this reasonable projection. As an added bonus, **Martavis Bryant** has been suspended for the year. This puts Ladarius Green in line to be one of **Ben Roethlisberger**'s red zone TD targets.

8. TE Jared Cook, Packers. Not too far in the past, **Jared Cook** was a 'sexy pick' to have a monster fantasy season, only to fall far short of expectations. Cook has amazing size and agility for a tight end, and more than "looks" the part of an elite pass-catching TE. And while he has been the victim, in part, of poor quarterback play while playing for the Titans and Rams, Cook is prone to making drops. The excuse for his underachievement disappears playing for the Packers. Jared Cook's career highs of 52 catches, 759 yards, and 5 TDs are all within reach with **Aaron Rodgers** throwing him the football. If there was ever a year where Jared Cook could surprise, this is it.

9. RB C.J. Prosise, Seahawks. Fantasy star **Marshawn Lynch** is retired, and despite **Thomas Rawls**' successful 2015 season, the Seahawks selected **C.J. Prosise** in the third round of the draft. Prosise is a prototypical 6'1, 220 lbs. running back. His biggest impact, however, might be in the passing game. A converted receiver, Prosise has a skill set similar to **David Johnson** of the Cardinals with a rare combination of size and speed, and the ability to catch anything and anywhere out of the backfield or in the slot. Prosise may get his share of carries. Prosise is a no brainer handcuff to Rawls, but is also a good late-round selection in standard leagues, commanding a premium in PPR formats. He's difficult to pass up in dynasty leagues.

10. QB Jay Cutler, Bears. Quarterback **Jay Cutler** has had an up-and-down career. This season, Cutler is a 'Renaissance Man' with the talent the Bears have assembled around him. Long characterized as having a big arm and a gunslinger mentality, the veteran quarterback will have an opportunity to showcase his skills in 2016. The backfield has moved on from **Matt Forte**, so there are questions about the ground game. The Bears feature what should be one of the best wide receiver duos in the league in **Alshon Jeffrey** and **Kevin White**, and a capable pass-catching tight end in **Zach Miller**. If Cutler gets the protection he needs, he could finally top 4,000 yards of offense, a fete he accomplished in 2008, and 30-plus TDs, something he has never done. With these type of numbers, Cutler is in the conversation as a low-end QB1, especially in deeper fourteen or sixteen team leagues.

Top 10 Deep Sleepers

By Chad Bellin
Featured Contributor, TheFantasyGreek.com

In larger fourteen or sixteen team leagues and dynasty formats, identifying 'Deep Sleepers' is a valuable, if not essential skill. In smaller redraft leagues, these are players to remember as the season unfolds and you play the waiver wire. 'Deep sleepers' are players who may have played well at one time but fell off the fantasy radar due to injury or poor performance. 'Deep Sleepers' may be young or obscure rookies or practice squad players who get an opportunity to make an impact. Each of these players particular circumstances invite an opportunity to play and play well in the pros.

1. WR Jeff Janis, Packers. Reality bit the Packers hard last season when stud WR Jordy Nelson was lost to an ACL tear for the year. **James Jones** stepped in to keep things moving, but **Randall Cobb** could not replicate his 2014 production when Nelson missed time. Along the way, **Davante Adams** was exposed and **Ty Montgomery** could not distinguish himself. Jeff Janis became an interesting option because of his steady hands and above-average deep speed. With Jones no longer in the picture, Janis will jockey with Adams, Montgomery, **Jared Abbrederis**, and rookie **Trevor Davis** to see who can man the WR3 position in the Packers offense. The position should yield 600-800 yards and a few TDs, with the chance at more given game situations and injuries.

2. WR Tyler Boyd, Bengals. A lot of rookie receivers in this year's draft class could end up making an immediate impact in the league. **Tyler Boyd** was selected No. 55 overall in the second round of the draft. Boyd has an immediate opportunity to step into a very good offense and provide instant production with the void left by the departures of **Mohamed Sanu** and **Marvin Jones.** The Bengals are looking for their next playmaker behind veteran **A.J. Green**. Boyd's quickness, sure hands, and route-running ability make him an ideal fit for the Bengals aerial attack. With limited options ahead of him on the depth chart (**Brandon LaFell, Brandon Tate,** and **James Wright**), Boyd is near an opportunity to be an outright starter this season.

3. WR Sammie Coates, Steelers. Third year wide receiver **Martavis Bryant** is suspended for 2016. **Markus Wheaton** and **Darrius Heyward-Bey** filled in during a similar stretch in 2015 when Bryant was suspended, but did not overly impress. This makes for a tremendous opportunity for **Sammie Coates** to assert himself. Coates struggled last season to make any impact, catching one ball for 11 yards. However, the talent is there as a deep threat to post 500 or more yards receiving and 5 or more TDs.

4. RB Kenneth Dixon, Ravens. Aging **Justin Forsett** had a tremendous season in 2014, but could not replicate that success in 2015. He finished the season on IR with a broken arm. **Buck Allen** stepped in to head the Ravens running back by committee, but was fairly unimpressive averaging 3.8 yards per carry. **Kenneth Dixon** should push for playing time. Dixon has a stocky frame well suited to the Ravens power running game. He also has tremendous quickness, and set school records for career rushing yards and TDs at Louisiana Tech. More importantly, Kenneth Dixon can catch the football out of the backfield (88 receptions, 972 yards, 15 TDs), an essential quality for a running back in Marc Trestman's offense.

5. RB DeAndre Washington, Raiders. Third year pro **Latavius Murray** delivered for the Raiders last season with over 300 total touches for 1,298 all-purpose yards and 6 rushing TDs. QB **Derek Carr** was second on the team in rushing, and Murray has never scored a receiving TD in his career. Short on other options out of the backfield, the Raiders selected **DeAndre Washington** in the fifth round of this year's draft. Washington should step right in as a backup to Murray and as a third down specialist. Despite missing a season in college due to a knee injury, the diminutive Washington was quite the rusher for Texas Tech averaging 6.4 yards per carry for 1,492 yards. He also tacked on 41 receptions for 385 yards, finishing out the season with 16 total TDs. Washington is a solid late round grab in points-per-reception leagues.

6. QB Trevor Siemian, Broncos. Unless you're a die-hard Broncos fan (or a Northwestern alum), you've probably never heard of **Trevor Siemian**. Siemian was a 7th round selection in 2015 who served as Brock

Osweiler's backup in the second half of the 2015 season when **Peyton Manning** was injured. With a year of study under Gary Kubiak, Siemian holds a unique edge of the presumptive starter, **Mark Sanchez,** who was only acquired this offseason. Sanchez is obviously not in the Broncos long-term plans. With **Paxton Lynch** not ready to play yet, Siemian has an opportunity to not only start, but to win the Broncos some games with the likes of **Demaryus Thomas** and **Emmanuel Sanders** to throw to. If he makes it that far, there could be real upside.

7. RB Terrell Watson, Browns. Rookie **Terrell Watson** was a standout running back at Azusa Pacific who went undrafted in 2015. Watson saw preseason reps with the Bengals, spending the rest of the season on the practice squad. Upon **Hue Jackson**'s departure from the Bengals, and subsequent hire by the Browns, Watson was released and immediately signed with Cleveland. There's no doubt **Duke Johnson** will be a force in the Browns' backfield. **Isaiah Crowell**, underwhelming as he has been, figures to be the lead running back on opening day. But Jackson saw something in Watson while with the Bengals to resign him. Watson has a similar skillset to Crowell but is about 15 lbs. heavier.

8. RB Jordan Howard, Bears. The Bears have moved on from long time bell cow **Matt Forte**, and many expect the backfield will be handed over to second year man **Jeremy Langford**. Not so fast. **John Fox** has a history of utilizing multiple backs in a rotation. Howard was a very productive running back at Indiana who averaged 6.2 yards per carry and rushed for 1,213 yards. He slid to the middle rounds of the 2016 draft. More of a power running back, **Jordan Howard** is ideal to pair with Langford in the Bears backfield. In that scenario, Howard would likely see goal line carries. If he can break through, 600 yards from scrimmage and 6 to 7 TDs on the ground would be doable.

9. RB/WR DJ Foster, Patriots. Everyone who has watched the Patriots knows there are two roles for running backs in the Belichick system. The first is the RB who gets carries on first and second down. Sometimes this role is split among a bigger back and a smaller back, but it's effectively the same role. The second is the RB who is the pass-catcher, a role Shane Vereen filled ably for several seasons and a role **Dion Lewis** and **James White** filled last season. Undrafted rookie **DJ Foster** can stick on the roster and potentially push for time in a pass-catching capacity. A running back turned wide receiver at Arizona State, Foster returns to the backfield to display his reliable hands and playmaking ability. At 5'10" tall, 193 lbs. (sound familiar), keep an eye on Foster if he gets momentum in the preseason, as he could emerge from obscurity to put up numbers right away as either a running back or a wide receiver.

10. QB Colin Kaepernick, 49ers. Veteran **Colin Kaepernick** is the biggest boom-or-bust name on this list. One season he's leading the 49ers to an NFC Championship and a Super Bowl berth, and within the next few seasons, he's sitting on the bench watching **Blaine Gabbert** play. The knocks on Kaepernick are many. But, the biggest factor in his regression may be the loss of his mentor, **Jim Harbaugh**. Enter **Chip Kelly** and his dynamic offense which made a fantasy star of the improbable **Nick Foles**. While Blaine Gabbert has the line on the starting QB job, Kaepernick still has a chance given his incredible athletic ability. He also has more upside potential than Gabbert who caps out sort of like a poor man's Alex Smith. Under Chip Kelly's guidance, if Kaepernick gets to play, he could thrive in the new up-tempo attack.

Top 10 Second Year Wide Receivers

By Rick Fleeger
Asylum Fantasy Sports

We keep hearing, "40 is the new 30," and "50 is the new 40," but really? For some of us, these words are a distinction without real meaning. In fantasy football, however, these words make sense: the second year wide receiver is the new third year wide receiver.

More and more in the new high-flying NFL, wide receivers are breaking into fantasy stardom in their second season. The 2015 class of sophomore wide outs included fantasy stars **Odell Beckham, Jr., Allen Robinson, Jarvis Landry,** and **Mike Evans**. Below are the members of the 2015 draft class primed for a breakout in the upcoming fantasy season, year two of their pro careers.

1. Amari Cooper, Raiders. The name "**Amari Cooper**" is by far, the biggest 'no-brainer' on this list. Cooper burst onto the 2015 scene in a big way his rookie season, and was the best rookie wide receiver in the league. In his freshman campaign, Cooper put up 72 catches for 1,070 yards and 6 touchdowns. Cooper is big, quick, and playing with an emerging star in quarterback **Derek Carr**. Things can only get better for the Raiders top wide receiver in 2016.

2. DeVante Parker, Dolphins. After an injury-riddled rookie season, **DeVante Parker** is primed for a breakout. While he missed half of the Dolphins games last season, Parker still put up just shy of 500 yards and added to that three touchdowns. What is most intriguing is Parker's 20 yard per reception average. Playing opposite rising star **Jarvis Landry** should help open up opportunities for the sophomore wide receiver. If Parker can stay on the field, he is in line for a jump in statistical production in 2016.

3. Willie Snead, Saints. Trivia question: who was the second leading rookie wide receiver of 2015? Believe it or not, it was **Willie Snead** who signed with the Saints as an undrafted free agent. Posting 984 yards and three touchdowns on 69 catches, Snead far outperformed the likes of **Tyler Lockett, Stephon Diggs,** and **Dorial Green-Beckham**. Snead is a steady performer with only 27 targets fewer than teammate **Brandin Cooks**. His lack of red zone production is the only factor keeping him from being higher on this list. Look for Snead to fill a similar role in the upcoming season.

4. Tyler Lockett, Seahawks. **Tyler Lockett** electrified fans in Seattle throughout his rookie season. The 2015 third round pick out of Kansas State ended his freshman campaign with 684 yards and 6 touchdowns and added 2 more touchdowns on special teams. His versatility, speed, and nose for the end zone makes him a prime candidate for a big breakout in 2016. The Seahawks offense appears to be opening up and Lockett is a perfect complement to **Russell Wilson**, **Doug Baldwin**, and **Thomas Rawls**.

5. Kevin White, Bears. Having missed his entire rookie season due to injury, it's tough to call **Kevin White** a second year receiver. But, the West Virginia wide receiver is an exciting prospect whose college play blew scouts and analysts away. White should have an immediate impact with the Bears offense. Kevin White is the perfect size and speed combination and should get plenty of targets from Jay Cutler, especially playing opposite a healthy **Alshon Jeffrey**. White is definitely worth a selection in the later-middle rounds of your draft.

6. Devin Funchess, Panthers. The Panthers offense is intriguing. With weapons like **Cam Newton, Kelvin Benjamin,** and **Greg Olsen**, the Panthers are in position to build on their 2015 success. **Devin Funchess** has been receiving high praise this spring and appears primed and ready to build on his 473 yard, 5 touchdown rookie season. The return of Kelvin Benjamin should provide Devin Funchess with the favorable matchups he needs to be a legitimate fantasy option in 2016.

7. Stefon Diggs, Vikings. After a slow start to his rookie season, **Stefon Diggs** burst onto the scene as one of the most exciting, young wide receiver of the 2016 season. While his production dropped as the season progressed, his speed and quickness coming out of the slot makes him a true weapon for a still improving **Teddy Bridgewater**. Adding **Laquon Treadwell** should open up the field and give Diggs plenty of room to operate in space. This could lead to big yards after the catch type numbers for Diggs in 2016.

8. Dorial Green-Beckham, Titans. What's better than a 6'5" receiver? How about a 6'5" receiver who can run a 4.49 forty yard dash. This makes **Dorial Green-Beckham** a true candidate for fantasy stardom. Green-Beckham managed only 32 catches and 4 touchdowns in his rookie season but the best should be yet to come for this young receiver. The additions of **DeMarco Murray** and **Derek Henry** point to a run first offense for the Titans. This bodes well for DGB as his red zone opportunities should see an increase. Monitor his offseason progress because despite his struggles, it's a real possibility this second year pass catcher could be in line for double digit touchdowns in 2016.

9. Nelson Agholor, Eagles. Nelson Agholor had a tough rookie season. The Eagles offense suffered under Chip Kelly's leadership and Agholor never lived up to his offseason hype. The quarterback position in Philadelphia continues to be a question mark. But, **Jordan Matthews** has emerged as a true number one which should provide Agholor with some favorable matchups in Doug Pederson's run and shoot offense. Provided he misses no time, Agholor should improve in 2016.

10. Sammie Coates, Steelers. With only one catch in 2015, it won't be hard for **Sammie Coates** to improve on his rookie season. But, with the one year suspension of **Martavis Bryant**, Coates will have every opportunity to thrive in the high powered Steelers offense. He will compete with **Markus Wheaton** for the second wide receiver spot but with his size and athleticism, Coates could be the perfect replacement for Bryant as a red zone threat. And, that could equal big numbers in 2016.

Top 10 Third Year Wide Receivers

By Rick Fleeger
Asylum Fantasy Sports

In fantasy football circles, the third year as a player for a wide receiver is his breakout season. This is the case for a great percentage of some of the great pass catchers. However, the pass happy offenses have made stars out of many rookie and second year wide receivers already. The list below is a "Who's Who" of emerging and, often, already established fantasy studs.

1. Odell Beckham, Jr., Giants. What is there to say about **Odell Beckham**? Beckham followed up an outstanding rookie season with a better 96 catch, 13 touchdown 2015 sophomore season. More importantly, OBJ stayed healthy. Odell Beckham is already a bona fide star and should be the second receiver off the board in nearly all fantasy football league formats.

2. Allen Robinson, Jaguars. Allen Robinson burst onto the scene in 2015 as one of the most consistent receivers in the league. His season leading 14 touchdowns with 80 receptions made Robinson a fantasy-points gold mine. Look for the good times to continue rolling as Allen Robinson enters his third season. With emerging stars **Blake Bortles** and **Allen Hurns**, Robinson, Bortles, and Hurns form one of the best offensive trios in the NFL.

3. Mike Evans, Buccaneers. Entering his third season, **Mike Evans** is already in the upper echelon of fantasy wide receivers. In two seasons, Evans has racked up over 2,200 yards and been a true target hawk. While his 2015 touchdown production dropped significantly in his second season, Evans continued to be the top option in the Buccaneers offense. Look for Mike Evans to continue to see the top targets while approving on his 4 touchdown 2015 campaign.

4. Jarvis Landry, Dolphins. Jarvis Landry is the player on this list with the largest breakout potential in 2016. Already a solid fantasy option coming off of a 110 catch 2015 campaign, Landry has the potential to enter elite status this season. Look for him to greatly increase his 4 touchdown performance while continuing to see double digit targets each week. Couple that with the threat Landry poses in the running game, and Jarvis Landry has Top 12 wide receiver potential in his third season.

5. Brandin Cooks, Saints. In the **Drew Brees** era, it has always been tough to rely on any Saints receiver. Brees has always spread the ball around and attacked the best matchup. In 2015, however, **Brandin Cooks** emerged as a true number one target in a still potent offense. Coming off of a season with 84 receptions and 9 touchdowns, it appears there is finally a true number one in New Orleans. His inconsistent target numbers are the only reason Cooks is not higher on this list.

6. Sammy Watkins, Bills. Coming out of Clemson, there was tremendous anticipation for **Sammy Watkins**. In 2015, fantasy owners saw his potential realized. His 9 touchdowns with 1,047 yards were a welcome surprise. There is still concern with his relatively small reception total of 60, and some injury issues still loom. However, the emergence of **Tyrod Taylor** should increase Watkins' opportunities in 2016.

7. Kelvin Benjamin, Panthers. Kelvin Benjamin missed his entire sophomore season due to a preseason knee injury. However, his strong rookie campaign is still fresh on the minds of many fantasy owners. Benjamin rejoins the suddenly high flying Panthers offense and he should be an intriguing option to all fantasy owners.

8. Jordan Matthews, Eagles. Matthews is a mystery wrapped in an enigma. In his two seasons with the Eagles, he has shown flashes of being a true superstar. However, he has also been nearly invisible for long stretches. Look for 2016 to be the season **Jordan Matthews** puts it all together. After a slow start to the 2015 season, Matthews finished the season with 8 touchdowns and was three yards shy of 1,000 yards receiving. Matthews is the top target in what should be a much improved Eagles offense and should be in line for a strong 2016 campaign. He'll likely be one of the Eagles top offensive players.

9. John Brown, Cardinals. Brown is one of the most electrifying talents in the NFL today. Speed kills, and **John Brown** used that speed to average over 15 yards per catch in 2015. Add the fact Brown hauled in a solid 7 touchdowns, and you have true star potential. The only concern for Brown is he shares the field with two solid receivers in **Larry Fitzgerald** and **Michael Floyd**. There has already proven to be plenty of balls to go around and rest assured, Brown has and will continue to earn an even larger share of the targets.

10. Donte Moncrief, Colts. Donte Moncrief showed strong signs of being an emerging star in 2015. While his production gradually slipped throughout the season, Moncrief showed the ability to put up solid numbers, especially at the beginning of the year. All indications are **Andrew Luck** is finally healthy. That should bode well for Donte Moncrief as he builds on his solid 2016 sophomore campaign.

Top 10 Rookies

By Jim Weidner
Featured Contributor, TheFantasyGreek.com

Doing research on top rookies is simple. Except for a few of them, avoid rookies in your redraft leagues. In dynasty leagues, expect little from them until next season when many make the "jump" to respectable pro levels of production.

This season there is one no-brainer top draft pick rookie running back, and at least five other latter round rookie running backs, who could contribute if not outright start if injury strikes.

Unlike running backs, the learning curve for wide receivers is steeper than for running backs jumping from college football play to the pro game. So, finding a top rookie wide receiver in your fantasy football draft to help you is harder than choosing a rookie running back.

But, as last year's crop of rookie wide receivers proved, a rookie wide receiver can be a contributor for a fantasy football team. Rookies **Amari Cooper, Willie Snead,** and **Tyler Lockett** were solid providers for their respective teams, in reality and in fantasy.

As for rookie tight ends, it's a general rule you should avoid them in redraft leagues. It is very rare that they contribute materially in fantasy football. However, we mention one tight end in a unique situation who could get a chance.

1. RB Ezekiel Elliott, Cowboys. When Jerry Jones and the Cowboys selected **Ezekiel Elliott** with the fourth overall pick, it was a match made in heaven. Not only was Elliott the best running back in this year's draft class, he is going to a team that thrives running the football. The Cowboys have one of the best run blocking offensive lines in the league. Back in 2014, former Cowboys and current Titans running back **DeMarco Murray** rushed for 1,845 yards and 13 touchdowns. When Murray left for the Eagles and played behind their offensive line, he rushed for just 702 yards and 6 touchdowns. Ezekiel Elliott has been compared to former Hall of Fame running back Marshall Faulk, and playing behind the current Cowboys' offensive line, Elliott could put up similar numbers to Faulk when he played with the "Greatest Show on Turf," assuming he stays healthy.

2. WR Corey Coleman, Browns. Rookie **Corey Coleman** is going to a team needing a wide receiver, especially a wide receiver with speed, which Coleman has a lot of. His production will come down to how well Browns' quarterback **Robert Griffin III** (or whoever else might start) plays. It will take time for Coleman to get used to a pro-style offense, but you can't teach speed and Coleman has it. Coleman is in line for 60 to 70 receptions as one of the Browns top receiving options.

3. Laquon Treadwell, Vikings. Treadwell was the fourth wide receiver selected in the first round of this year's draft. The major reason for this was his "slow" forty time (4.64). **Laquon Treadwell** is arguably the most pro-ready wide receiver from this year's draft. This past season, playing in the always tough SEC, Treadwell led the conference in receiving. Although not blessed with blazing speed, he understands the nuances of playing the wide receiver position. Laquon Treadwell has great size at 6'2" tall, and runs precise routes. His game is a perfect match to his new quarterback, **Teddy Bridgewater**. Bridgewater struggles with the deep passes, but is precise with his short to intermediate passes, something that fits right into Treadwell's game.

4. Sterling Shepard, Giants. The Giants used a second round pick on wide receiver **Sterling Shepard** from Oklahoma. Shepard had a stellar career at Oklahoma and with **Victor Cruz** coming back from an injury, he might see more action, especially early in the season with Cruz making his way back. In addition, Shepard could supplant Victor Cruz in the offense if Cruz is slowed or is injured again.

5. Devontae Booker, Broncos. The selection of **Devontae Booker** in this year's draft might be the most underrated pick in this year's draft. Booker is a perfect match for what Head Coach **Gary Kubiak** wants to do in Denver. Kubiak loves to run the football and he has a track record of making unknown running backs into stars like **Arian Foster**. The Broncos matched the contract offer the Dolphins made to **CJ Anderson** this offseason, but the reality is Anderson struggled in Kubiak's offense last season. Devontae Booker has the skill set to unseat CJ Anderson and thrive in Kubiak's offense.

6. Josh Doctson, Redskins. Doctson has the size and more than enough speed to play in the pros. Redskins quarterback **Kirk Cousins** is coming off a career year and is entrenched as the Redskins starting quarterback, which should help **Josh Doctson** be productive. At a minimum, he should be the third wide receiver option in the Redskins offense. Next season, Doctson should have a bigger role.

7. Will Fuller, Texans. I am not as high on Fuller as some people might be. Will Fuller has good size and speed, but struggled with drops while at Notre Dame. He also will play with a quarterback, **Brock Osweiller**, who is relatively unproven and is learning a new system. While Will Fuller should start opposite **DeAndre Hopkins,** his impact in fantasy football is not expected to be great.

8. Michael Thomas, Saints. Michael Thomas is joining a great team as a rookie wide receiver and **Drew Brees** is his quarterback. Thomas isn't a blazer, but he can run great routes and separate from coverage. He has an uncanny ability catching a football. Saints Head Coach **Sean Payton** has utilized big receivers without speed in the past and will do so with Thomas. He'll have to beat out **Willie Snead** for more snaps but that could happen given Thomas' abilities. Michael Thomas could move up this list quickly if everything falls into place for him.

9. Jared Goff, Rams. Goff might not be as pro-ready as **Carson Wentz**, but Goff is going to a team that will give him the best chance to survive his rookie season. The Rams have the best young running back in the pro football in **Todd Gurley**. This should help **Jared Goff** immensely. At least initially, the offense will go through Todd Gurley in similar fashion to the way the Vikings run their offense with **Adrian Peterson**. Goff won't be asked to win games with his arm, at least not during his rookie season. If he is given an opportunity to throw the football, it will be due to an injury to Gurley or a Rams defense which uncharacteristically tanks. Otherwise, Goff will be asked to make timely passes and protect the ball.

10. Hunter Henry, Chargers. Hunter Henry takes over back-up duties for Ladarius Green who signed as a free agent with the Steelers this offseason. Henry will back up future Hall of Fame tight end **Antonio Gates**, which will take pressure off the former Razorback. Gates has battled injuries, however, so maybe he will see playing time at some point this season. Henry will be helped along by playing with one of the most underrated passers in the league, **Phillip Rivers**.

Top 10 Overrated Players

By Rick Briggs
Fireside Sports

These are players whose current average draft position (ADP) in mock drafts appears high. These players present an injury risk or a production risk.

1. WR Demaryius Thomas, Broncos. For four straight years, **Demaryius Thomas** has surpassed 1,300 yards receiving and has been a stalwart fantasy performer. Coming off a 105/1,304/6 campaign in 2015, things are very different in Denver in 2016. **Peyton Manning** has retired, and even **Brock Osweiller** has left town. **Mark Sanchez** is Denver's apparent answer to the quarterback dilemma. With Manning gone, look for **Gary Kubiak** to go back to what he utilized in Houston for so long: running the football. With two good running backs in Denver, the offense will run much of the passing game through them. Demaryius Thomas is still a viable fantasy option, but not the top five wide receiver he has been in years past. **Emmanuel Sanders** will be scooping up catches, so Thomas' production will drop off dramatically. Avoid him if you can altogether.

2. RB Jonathan Stewart, Panthers. Stewart makes this list for a second year in a row. Some will say we were wrong about him last season. But, remember the 'great' season **Jonathan Stewart** had in 2015 was for less than 1,000 yards rushing, with a paltry 16 receptions. He will disappoint your team's chances for success in 2016 if you take him at his current ADP of the early fifth round. Twenty-two missed games in the last four seasons is a significant statistic. Jonathan Stewart is 29 years old and has been banged up annually.

3. TE Tyler Eifert, Bengals. Fourth year tight end **Tyler Eifert** is a big, sure handed tight end. What people are doing is anointing him the next **Rob Gronkowski**. You have to love the 13 touchdowns Eifert scored in 2015, but he had over 200 receiving yards less than **Benjamin Watson**. I want more than his 52 catches and 615 receiving yards to select him in the middle of the fifth round in my fantasy draft. Current ADPs have Eifert a full round ahead of **Gary Barnidge**. Barnidge and stalwart **Greg Olsen** had at least 20 more catches than Eifert and more receiving yards.

4. RB Chris Ivory, Jaguars. While adding **Chris Ivory** to the Jacksonville running back stable was a brilliant move for the Jags, let's not get ahead of ourselves thinking he is moving into a No. 1 running back position. The $32 million contract for Ivory only has $10 million guaranteed with $5 million a signing bonus. Ivory is injury prone due largely to his bruising running style. Current ADPs have Ivory being selected a round and a half ahead of the likes of **Danny Woodhead** and **Gio Bernard**. In PPR formats, that is not sound judgement.

5. RB Dion Lewis, Patriots. For a brief time last year, **Dion Lewis** set the fantasy football world on fire. Then, he got hurt. Current ADPs have him going in the fourth round. I like this kid, but know depending on a Patriots running back for fantasy supremacy will bring about a collapse of your team. Lewis is small and has only played in 16 games the last four seasons. He will give you a little flash and dash, but when you can have **Gio Bernard** and **Demarco Murray** around the same time, pass on Lewis.

6. RB Frank Gore, Colts. Frank Gore is 33 years old, and he has a lot of running back mileage on his legs. Gore has been an amazing athlete, but it is time to realize he can no longer carry the load. With **Andrew Luck** coming back, the Colts will do much more passing. Gore will not be relied on to keep the Colts competitive in games.

7. WR Dez Bryant, Cowboys. It was difficult listing **Dez Bryant** because he is a comeback player, but Bryant will be overvalued in 2016. It's not that Bryant isn't recovered from his foot injury, nor that Bryant is not as talented as before. The concern is his 36 year old quarterback Tony Romo who has had 3 collar bone injuries (two that were major). We all saw the debacle that was the Dallas Cowboys when **Tony Romo** went down in 2015. Dez Bryant had one 100 yard game and no other game over 62 yards. The backup quarterbacks could not even find the huge target in the red zone as Bryant ended with 3 touchdowns. Bryant was and would continue to be a wasted pick if that happens again. Will we buy into Bryant stock this year? Yes, but not ahead of guys like **Allen Robinson** and **Brandon Marshall**.

8. RB Jamaal Charles, Chiefs. It is hard to overvalue a talent like **Jamaal Charles**. But Charles is coming off his second major knee injury. Charles is a slight of build back that relies on quickness and elusiveness. This could be the beginning of the end to a spectacular running back. He is the sixth running back being taken in the early second round. Don't avoid Jamaal Charles altogether. Rather, if you are picking a running back then, consider **Ezekiel Elliott, Lamar Miller** or **Eddie Lacy** instead. Despite being a physical specimen, Charles will turn 30 in December.

9. RB Jeremy Langford, Bears. Jeremy Langford is the heir apparent to the throne of **Matt Forte**. But many reports coming out of Chicago indicate the Bears may look at a Running Back by Committee approach. While it's true Langford posted 537 rushing yards and 6 touchdowns in his rookie campaign, it is also true he posted 3.6 YPC. It's a concern because Langford wasn't good after contact suggesting he was not breaking tackles. Be careful to assume Jeremy Langford will be the Bears bell cow running back. As long as he's healthy, he should be effective. It's just **John Fox** confounded fantasy owners for years with the way he used running backs while the Panthers Head Coach. Fox could do it again.

10. TE Gary Barnidge, Browns. Barnidge was nothing short of spectacular in 2015. **Gary Barnidge** boasted a wonderful 79/1,043/9 campaign that put him on the fantasy map. Gary Barnidge is 30 years old and has never had over 13 receptions in a year before last season. Barnidge is likeable, but the Browns have done little to improve at the quarterback position.

Top 10 Injury Risks

By Derek Guilford
　　Featured Contributor, TheFantasyGreek.com

1. TE Rob Gronkowski, Patriots. Gronkowski's injury history is well-documented. From **TJ Ward** taking out his knee in 2013 tearing his ACL/MCL, to his broken forearm which required four surgeries, **Robert Gronkowski** has missed some serious time due to various injuries and ailments. Gronkowski is still a first round pick. However, this high pick still bears a modicum of risk.

2. RB Jonathan, Stewart, Panthers. Stewart is a seasoned veteran who is entering his ninth year as a pro, all with the Panthers. Over that time, he's developed an injury history despite combination usage with former Panthers running back **DeAngelo Williams** before the 2015 season. **Jonathan Stewart** missed most of 2013 and seven games in 2012 due to foot and other injuries. Last year was the first year Jonathan Stewart was designated the Panthers feature running back. Now, factor in he's 29 years old, has nearly 1,300 career attempts, and will continue as the featured back, and questions arise as to whether Stewart can maintain his health all season long, or at least for enough of it, to make him a worthwhile fantasy draft pick. Certainly, he's going to carry some risk.

3. RB Ryan Mathews, Eagles. Since breaking in with the Chargers in 2010, **Ryan Mathews** has been much maligned in the fantasy community for not fulfilling expectations or potential. He seems always banged up whether it was a fractured collarbone in 2012 that put him on injured reserve, a broken hand in 2011, a 2014 MCL injury, or last year's sports hernia surgery. You can confidently say Mathews has had serious issues shaking the injury bug. He's also had over 1,000 carries during his six-year career which is nothing to ignore either. While he was competing for touches last season with **DeMarco Murray**, this season, he should get the lion's share of the touches among the running backs with rookie **Wendell Smallwood** his main competition. Given the history and circumstances, it's difficult to view Mathews as a player who will play a full sixteen game slate.

4. Demarco Murray, Titans. Murray was dealt from the Eagles to the Titans after a disastrous 2015 season. He lands with the Titans who have the makings of a solid offensive line along with a rising star in signal caller in **Marcus Mariota**. **DeMarco Murray** will be called on to carry the football as much as possible to take the pressure off Mariota and open up the passing game. Murray has a myriad of past injuries. He's missed time with a broken ankle, sprained MCL, broken finger, and multiple hamstring injuries.

5. Dion Lewis, Patriots. Lewis tore his ACL against the Redskins last November, prematurely ending his season. Lewis has dealt with various injuries dating back to his time with the Eagles and Browns, as well as when he played his college ball for Pitt. His five foot, eight inch, 195-pound frame makes him prone to injuries in the physical game of football. Lewis has been seen making cuts during team drills and is fully expected to be 100% by training camp. Nonetheless, the injury red flags still exist.

6. Chris Ivory, Jaguars. Ivory is the running back who, "Man, if he could only shake off the injury bug, he'd be an elite running back." Over the last few seasons, **Chris Ivory** has dealt with quadriceps, groin, and sprained MCL injuries. Nothing overly serious, but nagging injuries nonetheless that have slowed him down from being the force he could be with the football in his hands, rushing 25 times per game. The Jets allowed him to leave in free agency, where Ivory has signed with the Jaguars on a five-year $32.5 million deal where he'll start ahead of second year running back **T.J. Yeldon**. Ivory is now out to prove the doubters wrong about his large contract at 28 years old and about his ability to stay healthy this season. If you have him in as your fantasy running back, there is always the likelihood he'll be injured regardless of his ultimate role because Ivory runs hard and many times, with reckless abandon.

7. Adrlan Peterson, Vikings. The 31-year old Peterson is still the workhorse for the Vikings even with third-year quarterback Teddy Bridgewater developing into a solid franchise QB. Adrian Peterson has been in the league since 2007 racking up 11,675 yards on a whopping 2,381 attempts and 4.5 yards per carry. Peterson has been coined a 'freak of nature' that came back to rush for 2,000 yards following an ACL knee surgery. But, at some point, 'Father Time' catches up to all. In addition to the ACL surgery, Peterson has also dealt with groin, foot, ankle, leg and shoulder injuries over his career. These have caused him to miss some games too. All of these nicks add up at some point. Package this with his age and workhorse usage and you have some legitimate injury concerns when clicking the "Draft This Player" button by the 'Adrian Peterson' name.

8. Jamaal Charles, Chiefs. Fantasy hero **Jamaal Charles** went down with the second ACL injury of his career last season. While Charles came back strong after his first ACL injury, posting 1,000-plus rushing seasons, can he come back again without further injury? Indications are he will. However, Charles turns 30 in December. And, with Andy Reid favoring having a featured back in the offense, Charles will likely be given a heavy workload. This will again expose him to a higher risk of not just injury but re-injury. While Charles will still command a high draft pick in redraft leagues because of his expected high level of productivity, a late first or early second round pick, the pick comes with obvious risk.

9. Jay Ajayi, Dolphins. In 2015, **Jay Ajayi** was considered by most draft analysts a lock to be selected on Day 2 (Rounds 2 and 3) of the draft. But, rumors of a supposed bone-on-bone knee condition caused him to slide to the Dolphins in the fifth round. Jay Ajayi did have a serious knee injury while at Boise State but this was back in 2011. With **Lamar Miller** now with the Texans, Jay Ajayi is expected to get the lion's share of carries. This is Ajayi's chance to show his knee can hold up over the course of an entire season as lead running back. For fantasy team managers who select him in the mid-rounds, they'll hope it holds up too.

10. Lamar Miller, Texans. Lamar Miller bolted the Dolphins for the Texans for a four-year, $26 million deal this offseason. There, he'll combine with **Brock Osweiler** to form the Texans newly minted backfield. Miller's flashed in his play and looked like a fantasy stud at times. But, he's never had the season where he's put it all together. This season, Miller will be the Texans workhorse running back, replacing **Arian Foster** in the offense. He'll be in line for 300-plus touches. The running back position is already fraught with injury risk, and the amount of touches Miller gets will increase the risk Miller misses time due to injury.

FREE TFG Access

"Thank you!" for purchasing The Fantasy Greek's 2016 Fantasy Football Draft Guide! As a way to show our gratitude, TFG is offering you the following FREE access at TheFantasyGreek.com:

- **<u>Fantasy Draft Guide Updates</u>**: Top 200s and Player Rankings as necessary to help you with your fantasy football drafts.
- **Favorable/Unfavorable Fantasy Football Playoffs Schedules:** Learn your players' strength of schedule for the playoffs to help evaluate trades or waiver transactions.
- **Ask The Fantasy Greek:** Send TFG your lineup, and TFG will tell you who to play!

"Your Second Opinion for Your Fantasy Football Instinct."

To get your FREE TFG Access, send an e-mail to support@thefantasygreek.com. In the subject line write, "Hey Greek, give me my FREE TFG Access!" In the body of the e-mail indicate your full name and the user name you desire. That's it. We'll do the rest. Also, read the terms and conditions of the site. By signing up, you agree to those terms and conditions, and you agree to be registered to the site using your name and e-mail address to receive post notifications of public and private articles.

DRAFT GRID

Round	1	2	3	4	5	6
1						
2						
3						
4						
5						
6						
7						
8						
9						

DRAFT GRID

Round	7	8	9	10	11	12
1						
2						
3						
4						
5						
6						
7						
8						
9						

DRAFT GRID

Rd	1	2	3	4	5	6
10						
11						
12						
13						
14						
15						
16						
17						
18						

DRAFT GRID

Rd	7	8	9	10	11	12
10						
11						
12						
13						
14						
15						
16						
17						
18						

Where do you get your draft info?

Not sure?

Visit The NFL Draft Oracle at ourlads.com

Over 34 years of NFL Scouting Experience

THREE CONVENIENT WAYS TO ORDER — PHONE US AT		1-800-776-3723
ORDER ONLINE AT	www.ourlads.com	
SEND CHECK OR MONEY ORDER TO	OURLADS, BOX 235, HIAWATHA, IA 52233	

CPSIA information can be obtained
at www.ICGtesting.com
Printed in the USA
LVOW02s0210110816

499846LV00025B/199/P